"*Writing Politics* builds on Mike Shapiro's scholarship to carefully de-reify and refig thinking. Examining aesthetic explorations of historically situated forms of violent mentalities, this essential book broadens the methodological capacity of political analysis and sharpens our ability to critique violence in our contemporary circumstances."

Matt Davies, *Newcastle University and Pontifícia Universidade Católica do Rio de Janeiro*

"Michael J. Shapiro's novel method of bringing fiction to bear upon the question of the political is sure to explode the limits of traditional social-scientific discourses, modes of aesthetic inquiry, and the uncertain relation between them. With impressive interdisciplinary scope and the author's characteristic exactitude, *Writing Politics* incisively renders literature's potential for resistance or radical subversion in the face of the worst instances of mass violence. This is a welcome and refreshing addition to the long-standing and ever-renewing problem of the politics of form."

Nathan Gorelick, *Associate Professor, Utah Valley University*

"Mike Shapiro exemplifies the master's sensitivity needed to approach novels as sites for political experimentation, to interrogate political being, and to explore opportunities for the re-textualisation of history. *Writing Politics* sensitises us through the Barthes-inspired approach of writerly-reading, so that as readers we become the producers of text (thought). True to his erudite and pedagogical style, Shapiro prioritises the imagination of the reader as the vehicle for thought. Highly recommended as fundamental methodology for Political Scientists and students of power."

Luis Lobo-Guerrero, *Professor of History and Theory of International Relations, University of Groningen*

"*Writing Politics*, a timely meditation on authoritarian and fascist rhetoric conducted via an examination of the under-recognized genre of historiographic metafiction, is at the same time what has traditionally been called a defense of poetry – an argument that the devices of literary fiction often get to the heart of political matters in a way that social and psychological theory cannot. It is provocative, deeply thoughtful, and brilliantly executed."

John Rieder, *University of Hawaii*

"In *Writing Politics* Shapiro discusses the power of writing focusing on 'mentalities' and the production of intimate violence in the examples spanning from the Balkan war and the Holocaust to assassinations. Combining literary works – concerned with how events are experienced – and political theory, Shapiro showcases the power of his method. Here philosophical ideas turn from dry concepts to rich reservoirs of emotions, complexities and layers of character enriching social and political analysis. *Writing Politics* is an outstanding book written in Shapiro's unique style."

Andreja Zevnik, *Senior Lecturer in International Politics, University of Manchester*

WRITING POLITICS

Writing Politics is a methods book designed to instruct on politically focused literary inquiry.

Exploring the political sensibilities that arise from the way literary fiction re-textualizes historical periods and events, the book features a series of violence-themed inquiries that emphasize forms of writing as the vehicles for politically attuned historiography. Each investigation treats the way the literary genre, within historiographic metafiction, enables political inquiry. It's a form of writing that inter-articulates history and fiction to rework a textual past and unsettle dominant understandings of events and situations. Central to the diverse chapters are fictional treatments of authoritarian, fascist, or zealous mentalities. Featured, for example, are Radovan Karadzic (the architect of the Bosnian genocide), Reinhard Heydrich (the architect of the Holocaust's "final solution"), and the Trotsky assassin Ramon Mercader.

Michael J. Shapiro has produced another original and sophisticated bookshelf staple; the only contemporary investigation in Political Studies that instructs on method in this way.

Michael J. Shapiro is Professor of Political Science at the University of Hawai'i at Manoa. His research and teaching interests are in the areas of political theory and philosophy, critical social theory, global politics, politics of media, politics of aesthetics, politics of culture, and indigenous politics. Among his recent publications are *The Cinematic Political: Film Composition as Political Theory* (2020); *Punctuations: How the Arts Think the Political* (2020); *The Political Sublime* (2018); *Politics and Time: Documenting the Event* (2017); and *Deforming American Political Thought: Challenging the Jeffersonian Legacy, 2nd edition* (2016).

WRITING POLITICS

Studies in Compositional Method

Michael J. Shapiro

Routledge
Taylor & Francis Group

NEW YORK AND LONDON

First published 2021
by Routledge
52 Vanderbilt Avenue, New York, NY 10017

and by Routledge
2 Park Square, Milton Park, Abingdon, Oxon OX14 4RN

Routledge is an imprint of the Taylor & Francis Group, an informa business

Library of Congress Cataloging-in-Publication Data
Names: Shapiro, Michael J., author.
Title: Writing politics : studies in compositional method / Michael J. Shapiro.
Description: New York, NY : Routledge, [2021] |
Includes bibliographical references and index. |
Identifiers: LCCN 2021002059 (print) | LCCN 2021002060 (ebook) |
ISBN 9780367701628 (hardback) | ISBN 9780367707286 (paperback) |
ISBN 9781003147701 (ebook) | ISBN 9781000394283 (adobe pdf) |
ISBN 9781000394313 (epub)
Subjects: LCSH: Political science–Authorship.
Classification: LCC JA86 .S525 2021 (print) |
LCC JA86 (ebook) | DDC 808.06/632–dc23
LC record available at https://lccn.loc.gov/2021002059
LC ebook record available at https://lccn.loc.gov/2021002060

ISBN: 978-0-367-70162-8 (hbk)
ISBN: 978-0-367-70728-6 (pbk)
ISBN: 978-1-003-14770-1 (ebk)

Typeset in Bembo
by Newgen Publishing UK

CONTENTS

ACKNOWLEDGMENTS

I am deeply indebted to the students in my Spring 2020 Writing Politics Seminar: Ari Eisenstat, Ryan Ferguson, Hildre Herrera, Robert Hopper, Anastasia Kriachko Roeren, Mathew Markman, Kalikoaloha Martin, Morsaline Mojid, Eliaquim (Ken) Reyes, and Varun Sanadhya. The ideas in this book were initially inspired by our conversations, based on the reading and writing we shared. Thanks are due as well to Katie Brennan whose invitation to a potential anthology encouraged my "War of Words" chapter and to my Czech colleague Petr Kouba for his contribution to my "Czech Connections" chapter. I have had the pleasure once again of working with my Routledge editor, Natalja Mortensen, whose advice about including an epilogue helped me to consummate the book's perspective and to Taylor and Francis's Charley Baker for skillfully leading me through the production process. I am grateful as well to Joyce Faust a research associated at the Guggenheim Museum who helped me secure the Franz Marc image for my cover. Finally, my greatest debt is to my wife, Hannah Tavares, who shares my passion for ideas and daily enriches my intellectual and emotional life.

INTRODUCTION

Epistemology and Style

> Humans are political animals because they are literary animals.
>
> *Jacques Rancière*

With a series of investigations that are philosophically informed and literature-attuned, this book explores the political sensibilities that derive from the way literary fiction re-textualizes historical periods and events. Featuring critical readings of historically oriented novels, each chapter addresses compositional strategies for interrogating relationships between mentalities and violence. I advance the conceptual argument that literature often offers more compelling insights into mentality than can be provided by psychological and social psychological studies. Félix Guattari suggests as much: "[A]re not the best cartographies of the psyche ... those of Goethe, Proust Joyce, Artaud and Beckett, rather than Freud, Jung and Lacan?"[1] The book's instructional focus on writing follows from a graduate political science seminar I often teach. The spring 2020 syllabus for the course, "Writing Politics," reads in part:

> The focus of this course is on writing. It's intended to make those who participate self-conscious about language in order to encourage a perspective in which writing is a vehicle for theorizing. Our attention will be on details – e.g. even down to such punctuation as the dash, which as Denise Riley suggests, conveys a "theatrical hesitancy" – and on the structural aspects of an essay or chapter as a whole, e.g. on the way grammatical choices articulate the implicit temporality of the writer's relationship with the subject matter and on the way an overall compositional structure bears much of the burden of argumentative force. As the science fiction writer, Philip Dick discovered, there are no shortcuts. He schooled himself by reading. "I think

the best source for a writer," he remarked in an interview, "is to read good prose models." Accordingly, the course materials will be selected for the way they model good writing (in the variety of subject matter areas with which the seminar participants are concerned).

Because political science, like the other social sciences, is method-attentive, I have approached the course with a methodological emphasis based on Roland Barthes's suggestion that a text is a "methodological field." Welcoming critical engagement, it's a "fragment or substance occupying part of the space of books" [and manifesting a] ... subversive force in respect to old classifications."[2]

The textual selections in the chapters are influenced by another of Barthes's conceptual contributions to literary criticism, a phenomenology of reading that privileges "writerly" texts, those that engage a reader conceived as a producer rather than a passive consumer. It's a reader who is encouraged to extend the implications of the text. As he puts it, "The goal of literary work (of literature as work) is to make the reader no longer a consumer, but a producer of the text."[3]

To provide an example of a work that invites the reader to extend it imaginatively, I want to address a seemingly minor gesture in a novel by the Serbian expatriate, David Albahari. Concerned with the contemporary history of displaced migrants, Albahari's *Globetrotter* recounts a relationship between a nameless narrator, a painter from Saskatchewan, and a Serbian writer named David Atijas (giving the novel an autobiographical resonance). In a self-reflective moment, Albahari, referring to the ancestry of immigrant refugees to whom the word "background" has been applied, writes, "Background is the wrong word, but better that word than none at all."[4] Encouraged to reflect in response to Albahari's self-consciousness about the aporias of word choice, which runs throughout the novel, – As a commentator puts it, "Albahari ... [has] a way of letting his book provide its own analysis"[5] – I am casting myself as a "producer," provoked by Albahari's writerly text to think about alternative onto-political frames within which the value of word choice is located.

One that comes immediately to mind belongs to Martin Heidegger, who was especially concerned with the implications of word choice. While delivering one of his several lectures on Nietzsche, he raises the question, "What does Nietzsche mean by existence?" and proceeds to caution patience: "Waxing in confrontation with the matter itself, we must become capable of the capable word."[6] That remark reflects Heidegger's expressivist approach to language in which the adequacy of a word is a function of the comportment between the rhythms of the discourse in which it resides and the rhythms of the world to which it refers (hence his attachment to the poetry of Friedrich Hölderlin, which exemplifies that comportment).

In contrast, for William James the value of a word emerges from his philosophical version of pragmatism. It's a matter of the practical consequences that result from the selection. For Jean-Paul Sartre, it's the extent to which a word can cause something felt to be liberated. "Words wreak havoc," he writes, "when they happen to name something that is experienced but is not yet named."[7] For Franz Fanon, it's the way a word reveals a gap between one's self-understanding and the way one is (racially) interpolated by others. For Gilles Deleuze and Félix Guattari, it's not what a word signifies but rather the extent to which it contributes to "the possibility to express another possible community and to forge the means for another consciousness and another sensibility."[8] For Jacques Rancière, words are political resources for those who seek the

> fundamental ability to proliferate words ... [and are] unceasingly contested by those who claim to "speak correctly" – that is, by the masters of designation and classification who, by virtue of wanting to retain their status and power, flat-out deny this capacity to speak.[9]

Instead of searching for meanings, Rancière's "intellectual effort has been to think the distance between words differently: that is, neither on the model of a hermeneutics of suspicion nor on the deconstructive model of an interminable digging through the strata of metaphorical meaning." He concerns himself with inequalities with respect to the eligibility to speak. There is an "excess of words" he calls "literarity, [which] allows for a disruption in the relation between an order of discourse and its social function," opening a discursive space for those who have been politically disqualified.[10]

For Michel Foucault, who has a similar, politically attuned perspective (developed in his early emphasis on discursive practices), it's the extent to which a word (and the statement in which it is located) is an "asset that ... from the moment of its existence ... poses the question of power; an asset that is, by nature, the object of a struggle, a political struggle."[11] Importantly, to appreciate Foucault's work on discursive practices is to recognize that he, like Rancière, does not interpret texts to extract their meanings.[12] As is as evident in his literary criticism as it is in his archaeological and genealogical histories, Foucault's concern is with the objects that language privileges at particular historical junctures. The words comprising mental universes for him are events that reveal extant sociopolitical forces (a perspective I pursue in Chapter 2).[13]

At a minimum, word choice operates in a politically contentious context. As Vilém Flusser puts it (while hammering away at his computer keys), "The power of words is so great that each word evokes a whole chain of other words without my knowing it. A whole mob of words can rise up against me and against the keys of the machine."[14] M. M. Bakhtin offers a similar perspective, which he deploys on novels. Referring to Dostoyevsky's writing, he notes, "The human world exists as an ongoing dialogue in which multiple languages and chronotopes [time/space figures] engage and reshape each other perpetually."[15] "In Dostoevsky almost no word is without its intense sideward glance at someone else's word ... there are almost no objectified words in Dostoevsky, since the speech of his characters is constructed in a way that deprives it of all objectification."[16] The novels that are the featured texts in my investigations all embrace and reflect on the contingencies of word choice to which Bakhtin refers. As they rework the past of both the "world" and literature, they seek to come to adequate, politically attuned terms with violent historical events.

In what senses can words be regarded as adequate? The sociologist C. Wright Mills explicitly addressed the event-adequacy of words with respect to social theory. Writing during the rise of National Socialism in Germany, he wrote:

> When events move very fast and possible worlds swing around them, something happens to the quality of thinking. Some … repeat formulae; some … become reporters. To time observations with thought so as to mate a decent level of abstraction with crucial happenings is a difficult problem. Its solution lies in the *using* of intellectual residues of social-history, not jettisoning them except in precise confrontation with events.[17]

However, there is yet another issue with respect to "mating" words with events, the matter of temporal comportment, a concern with the relationship between the pace of events and the pace of writing. That problem was effectively discerned by Laura Marris, who found herself in the midst of the beginning of the 2020 COVID-19 pandemic while doing a new translation of Albert Camus's *The Plague*. She reports,

> Usually my work moves more slowly than the events of the moment, since translation involves lingering over the patterns of a sentence or the connotations of a word. But this time, the pace of my work and the pace of the virus were eerily similar. That's because I'm translating Albert Camus's novel "The Plague."[18]

Tellingly, Marris says at one point that she has to cope with the affective ambiance as well as the pacing involved in matching words with worlds while translating a particular sentence:

> I felt a fissure open between the page and the world, like a curtain lifted from a two-way mirror. When I looked at the text, I saw the world behind it – the ambulance sirens of Bergamo, the quarantine of Hubei province, the odd disjunction between spring flowers at the market and hospital ships in the news. It was – and is – very difficult to focus, to navigate between each sentence and its real-time double, to find the fuzzy edges where these reflections meet.

Marris's observation points to a significant contrast. Unlike social theorists who seek conceptual adequacy, fiction writers struggle to express embodied experience, to create a syntax within which there is an affective and emotional adequacy of the words and their positioning. The novelist Edward Lewis Wallant puts it this way, "There must be words which – in proper sequence – can make solid shapes of my feelings."[19] Wallant's reflection on word adequacy is effectively incorporated as a drama in a Roddy Doyle novel. On the surface the plot of his *Love* is a reencounter after a long hiatus between two 50-ish acquaintances, Joe and Davy, who go on a pub crawl together throughout the city of Dublin. As they reminisce, exchange sentiments, and make judgments about their own and each other's life choices (primarily romantic choices, hence the novel's title, *Love*), it becomes evident that words as well as characters are the plot's protagonists. Early in the conversation, Davy, who is both a character and narrator, has asked Joe about his new romantic relationship and says (as narrator), "I watched his face as he pushed back words that wouldn't do."[20]

Joe's struggle for adequate words proceeds despite his having, he says, "packed the words with my clothes and toothbrush when I was coming to Dublin for a few days."[21] After Joe reveals that he may have fathered a child he's never met, Davy says, "Does she [Joe's paramour] say you're the father – Not in so many words," says Joe, who then adds his perplexity about what to say: "It's tricky, Davy look – just tricky. I'm not doing it justice. The words are letting me down."[22] While together they struggle to apply words to their romantic relationships, they wonder at several moments (nine times in fact) in their conversation if the word salacious is a proper one to describe some of them, e.g., "I looked up the word salacious – a while ago," Joe says, "I googled it. I've been hearin' the word all my life and I knew what it meant, and I didn't exactly. If you know what I mean."[23]

Wallant's reflection and those of Doyle's characters encourage us to heed the poetic dimension of texts, which among other things connects the rhythms of language to the somatic rhythms with which the life world is being (co)experienced. A remark about what was achieved by Stéphane Mallarmé's innovative poetic graphology, which foregrounds the rhythm problem, is apropos: "Mallarmé freed the semiotic aspect of language concealed by traditional verse structure … through the 'scission of sense, of clause, of the word; the loss of their identity in favour of a rhythm, of a music, of a melody'."[24] Nevertheless, the word is not abandoned. Rather, a songlike poetic text "is not a proxy," as Steven Feld puts it, "for a denoted subject but self-consciously multiplies the intent of the word."[25] Julia Kristeva adds an important insight as well, distinguishing the semiotic disposition of poetic language from other language practices, e.g., denotatively oriented "scientific discourse" which aspires "to reduce as much as possible the semiotic component."[26]

Given its incorporation of a semiotic disposition, much of what fiction supplies is a somatically attuned poesis that thinks with "affects and percepts" rather than privileging concepts, as is the case in philosophical and social theory texts.[27] For example, while Giorgio Agamben expands our appreciation of the range of human subjectivity by capturing conceptually the concentration camp character, whom survivors (e.g., Primo Levi and Jean Améry) referred to as the *Muselmann*, "a staggering corpse ... mummy-men ... the living dead,"[28] Edward Wallant's novelistic version of such a character – his Sol Nazerman, in *The Pawnbroker*, a camp survivor who considers himself effectively dead – is constructed with affects and percepts, as are the other characters in the novel's milieu: New York City's Harlem, which Wallant fills with many who have been subjected to violence and humiliation.[29] Just as Primo Levi describes *Muselmanner* as "non-men who march and labour in silence,"[30] one of Wallant's characters, Cecil Mapp is experientially attuned to recognizing such a character. He captures the affective essence of "the pawnbroker"; as he watches him marching in silence toward the pawn shop, he manages for a local crime boss: "The sight of the big white man" – a "heavy. trudging man [who] resembled some kind of metal conveyance" – "lifted Cecil's spirit perceptibly; the awkward caution of his walk indicated misery on a different scale from his own ... He was actually moved to smile as Sol Nazerman approached, and he thought gaily, that man *suffer!*"[31]

There are some in Sol's working milieu whose suffering is on a similar scale. While the figure for Sol's dead emotions is ice: "Fifteen years ago today his heart had atrophied; like the mammoth, he had been preserved in ice,"[32] for the character "Robinson," an impoverished diabetic who frequents the pawnshop, turning in possessions for cash, it's fire:

> He lived almost entirely in moments. What had ground him down to that skull-like appearance was not just buried, but burned out beyond recognition ... He remembered the physical facts of a horrible life but had no sense of his past feelings. He knew he names and dates of the times of is beatings and humiliations. Of betrayals and obscene violations; he could recall every day he had spent in prisons and hospitals. Yet he had no emotional recall of any of it.[33]

And the milieu itself speaks of its accumulated misery; it is voiced by the pawnshop, which functions as an allegory for the neighborhood: "The shop creaked with the weight of other people's sorrows."[34]

Crucially, the contrast between Agamben's and Wallant's texts is not one between what is real versus what is fictive. Rather, it is a difference between what Rancière refers to as "unavowed" versus "avowed" fiction. As he puts it,

> Fiction, is a structure of rationality which is required wherever a sense of reality must be produced. It is firstly a form of presentation of things that cuts out a frame and places elements within it so as to compose a situation and make it perceptible ... The point is about the sense of reality produced by the cutting out of the scene, the identification of its elements and the modality of the description. Politicians, journalists or social scientists must use fictions, as well as novelists, whenever they have to say: this is the situation, these are the elements that compose it.[35]

There is, however, a difference in the grammar of articulation I want to emphasize. Whereas the tendency in social theory's approach to historical events and situations is to explain *what* has happened, literary texts tend to dwell on the phenomenology of experience; they emphasize *how* what has happened is experienced by those who make it happen and by those affected by what happens.

Nevertheless, as my investigations proceed, much of the political sensibility that emerges results from the interventions with which I impose concepts on the experiential flow of the literary texts I analyze. Such interventions constitute a method that Cesare Casarino characterizes as "philopoesis," the staging of engagements between conceptual discourses and literary texts. In Casarino's words, philopoesis "names a certain discontinuous and refractive interference between philosophy and literature."[36] What results is a mode of critical thinking that becomes available because the interference between genres – between those that privilege concepts and those that privilege affects and percepts – opens up "emergent potentialities that disrupt the status quo of the history of forms."[37] Philopoesis-as-method delivers critical thinking by de- or refiguring of the "figurative givens" that have dominated artistic forms.[38]

I want to note as well an important crossover between literary and social texts not only because literature often provides exemplary types for social theory to adopt, but also because literary texts that think critically function as social theory on their own. In addition to their poesis, in which they convey the phenomenology of experience, they deliver a politics of aesthetics by unsettling usual frames of intelligibility, connecting events and personae that are ordinarily seen as disparate. They typically do so by inventing characters whose mentalities and actions alter the thinkable, seeable, and possible. What a literary text can offer in this regard is treated elaborately by C. L. R. James. In his close reading of Herman Melville's *Moby Dick*, James raises the question of where one can find treatments of the mentalities of historically "original characters … who seem to demand for their creation an extension of the range of consciousness of their creators." They serve as models for rethinking "human character." Among the literary characters James identifies are Shakespeare's King Lear and Aeschylus's Prometheus.[39]

However, it is Melville who according to James supplies the most relevant exemplar for purposes of treating the historical moment in which he, James, was writing. Pondering Captain Ahab's monomaniacal thirst for revenge at the expense of his whaling ship, the Pequod's commercial mission, James asks, "Who is this extraordinary character?" He responds to that query by assiduously eliciting the persona Melville has constructed. He's a man, James observes, who is "socially inaccessible,"[40] and self-obsessed; "never for a moment does it cross his mind to question his relations with the people he works with. Those relations he accepts. *His* personality is suffering …."[41] "*He* is concerned only with what life has done to him …." As a result, "He is the most dangerous and destructive social type that has ever appeared in Western civilization."[42]

As regards the contemporary relevance of such a character type, James has Hitler and Nazism on his mind as he contemplates Ahab's mentality. He says that except for a few German writers who have understood the type, the contemporary political leaders have remained in the dark:

> not one ruler … despite all the preparations for war yesterday against Nazism … shows the slightest sign that he understands the enemy against whom he is preparing … It is the unique and solitary greatness of Melville that he saw and understood the type to the last degree and its relation to all other social types.[43]

James's critical reading of Melville's novel provides an important threshold for my investigations. Much of the analysis in the chapters enlists literary exemplars (Melville's help shape Chapter 3).

The Chapters

Although I had not planned it that way, as I sought texts to engage that would help me pursue my concern with the intimacies of violence – the way it has inhabited the mentalities of perpetrators and how it has been experienced by victims – the novels I selected and analyzed fit within the genre Linda Hutcheon famously calls "historiographic metafiction." As Hutcheon characterizes it,

> Historiographic metafiction works to situate itself within historical discourse without surrendering its autonomy as fiction ….it is a kind of seriously ironic parody that effects both aims: the intertexts of history and fiction take on parallel (though not equal) status in the parodic reworking of the textual past of both the "world" and literature.[44]

The main texts featured in each of the chapters are essayistic; their meta-textual interventions accompany the novels' physical terrains with what Deleuze and Guattari call "thought's territories."[45] Like the essayistic feature of the novels I analyze, the chapters in this investigation are essays. As for what that implies for one's participation in inquiry, I have found myself endorsing a passage from John O'Neill's book on the essayist (Michel de) Montaigne:

> The essay, is "an experiment in the community of truth and not a packaging of knowledge ruled by definitions and operations. The essay is a political instrument inasmuch as it liberates the writer and reader from the domination of conventional standards of clarity and communication [it's an] expression of literary initiative … accomplished against the limits of received language."[46]

I get similar instruction from Theodor Adorno for whom the essay is a "specu-lative investigation of specific, culturally predetermined objects."[47] It seeks to be neither comprehensive nor to make definitive knowledge claims: "It does not begin with Adam and Eve but with what it wants to discuss. It says what is at issue and stops where it feels itself complete – not where nothing is left to say."[48] The essay, he adds, privileges the "dreamer" rather than the "technician"; it resists "the positivist tendency to set every possible examinable object in rigid opposition to the knowing subject."[49]

Chapter 1: "A War of Words: Edna O'Brien's The Little Red Chairs"

The focus of Chapter 1 is on the violent political career of the architect of the Bosnian genocide, Radovan Karadžić, who once installed as President of Republika Srpska, fueled and exploited a patriotic fervor that led to the Bosnian War (1992–1995). I approach the Karadžić mentality and the effects of his violence through imaginative recreations in Edna O'Brien's novel *The Little Red Chairs*, which brings a fictional version of Karadžić to the small Irish village of Cloonoila in disguise as a healer and sex therapist named Vladimir Dragan. The narrative begins in a Gothic mood, which models "Dr. Vlad's" initial appearance in the village on the literary Dracula made famous by another Irish author, Bram Stoker. Thereafter, Karadzic's men-tality and that of his primary victim, Fidelma McBride, with whom he has an affair before abandoning her to live in disgrace (once his identity has been exposed), are articulated with literary exemplars. As the novel explores the gestation of Karadžić's mentality and Fidelma's coping with the traumatic after effects of his duplicity, literary characters are invoked to model their mentalities. One applied to Karadžić is voiced by one of his old school mates, K, who was subsequently a political crony. K informs him that as a young student he, Karadžić, was likened to Robert Musil's character (in his eponymous debut novel) "Young Törless," "You had been christened Young Törless," says K, "because of the two terribly contrasting aspects of your character, the sane, the reasonable and the other so dark, so vengeful." As for the literary exemplars modeling Fidelma, one likens her, in her recovery period, to Dido in Virgil's *Aeneid*.

With O'Brien's novel in the midst of the chapter, the analysis is bookended with nonfiction accounts of Karadžić, one at the outset of the chapter by the Bosnian writer/poet Semezdin Mehmedinović, whose lyrical writing discloses the ironies involved in the emergence of the prewar Karadžić effect on interethnic relations in Bosnia Herzegovina, and one near the end of the chapter by Jessica Stern, a bio-ethnography based on interviews with the jailed Karadžić awaiting trial. The Karadžić who tries (unsuccessfully) to bully Stern during the interviews strikingly resembles the one O'Brien invents. Noting the way Karadžić emerges in O'Brien's and Stern's texts, the chapter ends with a reflection on the differen-tial epistemological yields of novelistic versus ethnographic approaches. By way of transition, Chapter 1's emphasis on modeling mentality by drawing from literary history sets up the analysis in Chapter 2, which contrasts psychological and psychoanalytic with literary approaches to fascist mentalities.

Chapter 2: "Scripting Mentality"

Chapter 2 continues the analysis of the way mentalities are conceived and scripted but within a broader range of literatures, addressed to a broader range of questions. In addition to pursuing what a dangerous mentality is and how it thinks – what its "inner footage" is like, as O'Brien's character, Fidelma McBride, puts it in her novel – I also pursue questions about mentalities from the outside. Some of the texts I treat view mentality as an event. What that requires is analyzing the historical forces involved in making a kind of mentality an object of attention. After explicating mentality-as event disclosed in Michel Foucault's analysis of the legal career of nineteenth-century psychiatry, which shows how "the criminal" became a persona with a dangerous mind and accordingly an object of analytic rather than merely punitive attention, I raise that question in an extended reading of Robert Musil's epic *The Man Without Qualities*, a novel that is an exemplar of the historiographic metafiction genre.

The chapter situates Musil's essayistic novel within a variety of texts – philosophical, historical, cultural, and psychoanalytic – all of which seek to make sense of Nazi and proto Nazi mentalities whose emergence was anticipated in Musil's novel. Those texts – both literary and cinematic – are events as well as analyses of minds. They are reactions to the twentieth century's main event, the political ascendency of Hitler's National Socialism. Those texts include, among others, Klaus Theweleit's two volumes on the mentality of the members of the proto Nazi Freikorps, the famous Adorno et al. investigation of the fascist personality, and cinematic treatments of the political vacuum that Nazi supporters filled during the economic trauma of the Weimar period (the subject matter of the two films I discuss, *Cabaret* (1972) and *Babylon Berlin* (2017)).

However, the text that is most central to the chapter's focus on mentality is Musil's novel, which, with an innovative style, develops characters that are windows on a historical period. The chapter ends with attention to two texts from which I draw analytic insights on the way minds amplify fear – Brian Massumi's analysis of the Bush administration's post 9/11 color coded alerts, which discloses the reflexive temporal structure of fear, and Don DeLillo's novel *White Noise* which, in a different genre, parallels Massumi's analysis. Both texts analyze in their different stylistic ways, the intermediations of television broadcast and mental processing in an age in which, as Massumi puts it, television is "the *event* medium." Similarly, as one of DeLillo's characters remarks, "For most people there are only two places in the world. Where they live and their TV set."

Chapter 3: "Scripting 'America'"

The main focus of this chapter is an extended engagement with Thomas Pynchon's novel *Mason & Dixon*, which has a nonlinear temporal structure and multiple narrators. However, its narrative polyphony, which although an important part of Pynchon's commitment to a reality that shifts as alternative perspective pursue it, is less important than the way a subjunctive grammar – an emphasis on what might or could have been with respect to American history – and re-inflected repetitions shape the novel. With respect to the former, the novel's key phrase suggests that Mason and Dixon's survey "turns possibilities into simplicities," and with respect to the latter, the violence of their survey is figured early in the novel when they are described as "mark[ing] the earth with geometrick scars," a trope the novels picks up later when the Reverend Cherrycoke (one of the novel's main narrators) refigures a spatial effect as a temporal one. He says that a calendar reform instigated by England's head astronomer is "a chronologik wound."

The novel's most significant re-textualization is its way of figuring Philadelphia's role in America's founding story. Challenging the canonical story of American exceptionalism, the novel renders Philadelphia as an anti-Philadelphia. It is referred to in the text as "unchosen Philadelphia," an expression that surfaces as the Reverend Cherrycoke tells a story, while repeating the scar metaphor, in a room that begins to fill up with

> Black servants, the Indian poor, the Irish runaways, the Chinese sailors, the overflow'd from the mad hospital [all of whom] … bring their Scars, their pox-pitted Cheeks, their Burdens and Losses, their feverish eyes, their proud fellowship in a Mobility that is to be, whose shape none inside this House may know.

Fulfilling the requirement of historiographic metafiction as Hutcheon identifies it, the novel re-textualizes not only the traditional version of American history, but also some of the literary fiction that has supported that version. With respect to the latter, the chapter suggests that Pynchon's *Mason & Dixon* is an anti-James Fenimore Cooper text. While Cooper's elegiac Leatherstocking novels participated in what Patrick Brantlinger calls a "dark vanishing" (of Native America), Pynchon has his version of the surveyors, Mason and Dixon recognize what has vanished. They discover "other civic entities," and realize that the lines their survey is imposing constitute violent trespass. I end the chapter by noting Reverend Cherrycoke's allegorical remark that there's a story that "none inside the House may know." The "House" is America.

Chapter 4: "Czech Connections: Scripting the Epicenter of the Holocaust"

The chapter begins with an analysis of Laurent Binet's novel *HHhH* (Hitler's Brain is Named Heydrich), which tells two simultaneous stories. One is the drama of "Operation Android," the planning and execution of the assassination of Reinhard Heydrich, Protector of Czechoslovakia and Architect of the Final solution. The other follows the writer, Binet's decisions about how to write the story. Like Pynchon, Binet privileges the subjunctive to reflect on the historical contingencies shaping the terrain his novel is addressing. However, while Pynchon's might-have-beens are alternative Americas, Binet's might haves and could haves are associated with Heydrich's career and with his (Binet's) decisions as a writer about how to tell the story of Heydrich's career ascent and his assassination. While Pynchon is asking the more epic question, what kind of world might have been, Binet is asking the smaller question, what kind of Heydrich might have been; he might, for example, have been a more benign version as a navy officer if his naval career had not ended in a scandal. Concerned with getting the facts of his characters' roles in the story of the assassination correctly, Binet continually intrudes in the narrative to explain his choices of coverage. Even though he invents dialogues and imagines what his protagonists are experiencing, he is more focused on telling the reader what happened than with the aesthetics of writing. As he describes the writing process, what he conveys is the difficulty of making the composition adequate to the events. He figures out at one point the genre in which he is writing "I think I'm beginning to understand. What I'm writing is an *infranovel.*"

I follow the analysis of Binet's *HHhH* with treatment of a series of Czech novels that have been grouped under the rubric of "Holocaust laughter," noting how their turn to humor way challenges dominant assumptions about the Holocaust and its representational limits. I suggest that laughter-inducing Czech Holocaust fiction restores a sense of humanity to those who had been deprived of it as it moves the past into the future anterior, altering its will-have-been. Summoning and analyzing three Czechoslovakian Holocaust fictions, I allow those texts to participate once again in the meaning the event *will have had.*

The first of the three is Jiří Weil's *Life with a Star.* While much of Weil's focus is on the identity-confiscation and social obloquy a star-wearing Jew faced after the Nazi annexation of Czechoslovakia – e.g., his protagonist Roubicek, a former bank clerk says, "I was no longer one of them … I had become a special person whom everyone looked at and made way for" – what stands out as well is the novel's literary geography. It maps the change in the urban cartography that star-wearing entails. The novel covers the incessantly expanding prohibitions constraining the Jewish population's uses of space, both outside throughout the city and within their own dwellings. In Weil's novel, rather than a mere background, Prague's architecture and urban map are narrative elements. Moreover, an ironic and parodic style turns the novel into a tragicomedy.

With the turn to the chapter's next novel, one finds a very different cast of characters. The protagonist in Ladislav Grosman's *The Shop on Main Street*, Tono Brtko, is a Slovak everyman, a carpenter forced to participate in the Nazi expropriation of Jewish property. He is structured as a camera rather than, like Weil's Roubicek, as a first-person voice. Brtko delivers scenes the reader sees through his eyes. The button and ribbon shop to which he is assigned as an "Aryanizer" has belonged to an elderly Jewish widow, Rosalie Lautman. Mrs. Lautman, who is rheumatic and virtually deaf, never understands Brtko's explanation of his role. Once she realizes he's not a customer, she assumes he's come to assist her. Brtko gives up trying to explain his role and instead carries on with the pretense of being Mrs. Lautman's assistant. As a result, the conversations between the two are hilarious until, like Weil' *Life with a Star,* the novel turns into a tragicomedy. Brtko, who has been resisting his wife's demand that he bring home the shop's valuables (of which there are in fact none) and the Nazi-collaborating Hlinka-Guard commander, his brother-in-law's demand that he assert his authority, tries at the last minute to save Mrs. Lautman from deportation. Looking out of the shop window at the city square where the town's Jews are being rounded up to be transported to a concentration camp, Brtko, seeing the demoralized line up of victims, cannot bring himself to send Mrs. Lautman (who thinks that his agitation is due to his drinking after a quarrel with his wife) out to join them. Trying to hide her, he thrusts her into a small cubby hole, where her head hits the back wall. He has inadvertently killed her.

The novel's opening scene provides a transition to the chapter's next text, Bohumil Hrabal's *Closely Observed Trains.* As Grosman's novel opens, Tono Brtko is watching in confusion what turns out to be an ominous sign. He sees something strange. Having lived near the local train station, he had never seen the train that is passing at that time of day, a special train, not in the timetable is roaring past. As I go on to note, trains and train stations are pervasive in Holocaust literature for obvious reasons. A train station is the scene of the plot (in two senses) in Hrabal's comedic novel, which registers a later time period than Grosman's novel. It's 1945 and the German air force has lost control of the air space over Czechoslovakia. Having already deported the Jewish population, the Nazi's are using the railway system to transport troops and munitions.

To read Hrabal's *Closely Observed Trains* after reading Grosman's *The Shop on Main Street* is to enter a very different life world. The aspects of Czechoslovakian mentality that Hrabal's characters manifest are at the opposite end of the continuum from Grosman's head of the Hlinka Guards, Brtko's brother-in-law, and his acquisitive wife (who welcomes the destruction of the Jewish population so she can acquire its valuables). With the exception of two bureaucratically inclined collaborators with the Nazi occupation, Hrabal's protagonists are resistant to Nazism in both spirit and deed. The novel is structured as both a playful and humorous Bildungsroman and a celebration of the Czechoslovakian mentality. What is in evidence as the interpersonal relations in the plot proceed is a model of life-as-shared-pleasure in each other, managed despite being in the midst of the final days of the Nazi orchestration of death.

The novel's two interwoven narrative threads follow the endeavors of young train dispatcher, Miloš. His experiences reveal the situation on the ground, a growing Czech resistance to the last stages of the German occupation (to which he ultimately contributes by blowing up a German munitions train), and at the same time chronicle Miloš's ultimately successful effort to overcome his sexual malfunction, premature ejaculation (*Ejaculata Praecox*). The ethos that shapes Hrabal's writing is entangled with its form. In a monograph on writing, he refers to his style as the "Leica style," with which he "captured reality at peak moments of people talking and then composed a text out of it all."[50] What results is a Rabelaisian narrative that accords with his view "that it is only within the 'low' world of the plebeian, the world of the 'little Czech' that real beauty or nobility emerges."[51]

Train stations are also central to the next novel as the chapter exits from Czech writers and engages W. G. Sebald's *Austerlitz*, a novel that follows the process by which its protagonist, Austerlitz recovers the identity he had lost when sent to the UK as a child in a *kindertransport* that rescued middle European Jewish children. The book is a composite of multiple genres: photographs, a film, zoological speculations, and an inter-articulation between colonial and Holocaust histories. Here, I want to stress just two aspects of the analysis in the chapter. First, I figure the novel's narrator, who meets Austerlitz off and on during the novel, as a curator who assembles the material and leaves the reader to make sense of Austerlitz story as a whole. With a writing style that has been appropriately characterized as a "poetics of suspension," the novel shapes its politics of history and with a curational structure that opens Austerlitz story to readers in a way that solicits their active participation in sense making, much the way Daniel Libeskind designed his Berlin Jewish Museum, an ambiguous text that is realized through the way visitors select trajectories.

The second aspect I want to note is the way the novel turns the protagonist Austerlitz into a film editor. After Austerlitz acquires a copy of a 14-minute documentary the Nazi's made in the Theresienstadt camp, hoping to catch a glimpse of his mother who was imprisoned there, he manages to find her after he reedits the film, slowing it down so that it runs for an hour. What the slowed-down version reveals as well is an entirely different mood among the inmates of the camp. Unlike what appear to be people enjoying their work in the 14-minute version is a population unhappily sleepwalking through their tasks. What emerges is both an insight about the value of slowness (a feature of filmmaking that the chapter ascribes to Andrei Tarkovsky) and the way creative cinema work can re-textualize historical moments to reveal the violence sequestered within what is initially produced as a legitimating product. Sebald's curating of Austerlitz's film work achieves an attunement to the Czech experience of the Holocaust that accords the way his text as a whole enacts it: slowly, painstakingly, and with an innovative approach to visuality.

The chapter ends with a coda, a brief reading of Jáchym Topol's novel *The Devil's Workshop*, which I include as a challenge to my subtitle. While the novel's dark humor provides a critique of horror tourism (e.g., a group involved in turning the Theresienstadt camp into a Holocaust museum sells t-shirts inscribed with the logo, "Theresienstadt: If Kafka hadn't died, they would have killed him here"), its contribution to Holocaust history is cartographic. The novel extends the map of the Holocaust eastward to include the extermination of millions of Slavs along with Jews and gypsies and, as I suggest as well, downward to the mass graves of those exterminated. It puts pressure on the notion that the Holocaust has an "epicenter."

Chapter 5: "Inventing Assassins"

Three texts, all examples of the historiographic metafiction genre analyzed in earlier chapters, share the space of Chapter 5. The three – Justin Cartwright's *The Song Before It Is Sung*, Leonardo Padura's *The Man Who Loved Dogs*, and Don DeLillo's *Libra* – are novels with assassination plots. Each of the novels concerns itself with the agency through which assassins are constructed. When read together, it becomes apparent that some assassins emerge primarily through their own self-fashioning and some are owed more to the shaping efforts of others. Cinema provides a bridge between Sebald's novel and Cartwright's. His novel (hereafter *Song*) is pervasively cinematic. From the outset, the reader sees the world through the eyes of the character, Conrad Senior, who serves as the plot's main camera. His wide angle, depth of focus, and *mise en scène* observations conduct the reader through the narrative. As the novel opens, Conrad functions as a camera filtering what another camera shows. He's recalling a film he's watched of the trial of the would-be Hitler assassin, Axel Von Gottberg (the historical Adam von Trott) 60 years after it took place. He is haunted by images from the trial, having seen Axel "standing in a capacious suit before the People's Court with his hands folded in front of him." Like Sebald's *Austerlitz*, Conrad edits the film. However, in his case the editing is in his imagination. As he aestheticizes the courtroom scene, likening it to a Dutch painting, its impression changes markedly. He sees a courtroom

> beautifully lit…as though the windows of the court are admitting a soft, warm light, a Dutch light, containing the texture of paint, to coat the defendant, the judge himself, and the upstanding members of the public, who, in contrast to the decadents on trial, are mostly uniformed. The unintended aesthetic effect is to make von Gottberg look heroic.

Song's nonchronological narrative crisscrosses a global map that includes cities in England, German, Palestine/Israel, the US, Czechoslovakia, Latvia, Switzerland, and the Netherlands, as it interweaves history with the novel's plot. Its spatial mapping jumps back and forth between the events associated with the assassination attempt on Hitler and the subsequent trial of the plotters and a contemporary plot concerned mostly with Conrad's search for the execution film. Ultimately, however, the main story is about what happens in Conrad's head as he attempts to come to critical philosophical terms with the mentalities of two characters – the Hegel-inspired von Gottberg and the Nietzsche-inspired Mendel – who locate themselves differently with respect to one's obligations to place and history. Although the plot ranges over a broad array of geopolitical territories, its main concern is with what Deleuze and Guattari call "thought's territories." What the novel ultimately negotiates are the implications of the different onto-political approaches to life embraced by von Gottberg, a man of "deep belief," and the philosophically dispassionate Mendel, whose response to Europe's "growing tensions" is "to look more closely at ideas."

While Cartwrights *Song* is a well-composed essayistic novel, Leonardo Padura's *The Man Who Loved Dogs* is an epic. Borrowing from Milan Kundera's characterization of the novels of Proust, Musil, and Mann, among others, I suggest that Padura's novel is a fresco, a composition that paints a large-scale view of the life world.[52] It's also a triple biography that explores the lives of Lev Davidovic (Leon Trotsky) during the period of his exile, his assassin Ramón Mercader (who adopts several aliases throughout his life) while he is preparing to consummate the assassination, and the writer, Ivan Cardenas (representing Padura), while he attempts to overcome his apathy and write the story he has gotten from Mercader, whom he meets on a beach in Cuba near the end of his life.

Without going into an extended summary of a novel that spans many years and covers extensive territory, I want to note an important aspect of its style, which I refer to as one of its compositional strategies, re-inflected repetitions (much like the way they are used in Pynchon's *Mason & Dixon*). For example, As Iván begins to tell that multilevel story in Chapter 2, it becomes apparent, for example, why Chapter 1 featured dogs and gravediggers. (In the chapter, Iván's wife, Ana loses a beloved dog before she dies, and her death scene features gravediggers.) In Chapter 2, a dog and a gravedigger are featured. As Trotsky, in Siberian exile, is being forced to move on to Turkey, Stalin's agent threatens to make him leave his beloved dog behind, before the chapter ends. Trotsky refers to Stalin as "the grave digger of the revolution."

What becomes apparent as the novel follows the territorial movements of Trotsky and his assassin Mercader is a pedagogy about identity. As Stalin's agents work to invent a Mercader who can make his way into Trotsky's Mexico household (his last place of exile), we learn that the Mercader they fashion is preceded by what Deleuze calls an "a priori other," a virtual subject that anticipates the identity events in which a person is actualized to fill the virtual subject position. Padura's novel performs that insight, not only with the way Mercader becomes the assassinating subject, but also through what happens to Trotsky. At one point, he has Trotsky realize why "Stalin still hadn't broken his neck" (having already eliminated many other rivals with his show trials). After pondering that, he understands that Stalin still needed his existence because "his back had to serve as a springboard in Stalin's race to the most inaccessible summit [until such time as]…his usefulness as the perfect enemy was exhausted." The other main subject position that is ultimately filled is that of a writer, a role that Iván manages to fill after he is gifted the story of the man who loved dogs by Mercader (disguised as Jaime Lopez), whom he meets on the Cuban beach where Mercader daily walked with his two Russian wolfhounds.

Cuba, as it is constructed in different imaginaries, is a bridge from Padura's *Dogs* to DeLillo's *Libra*. DeLillo's novel follows the careers of two main characters,

Lee Harvey Oswald, the alleged Kennedy assassin, and Win Everett, a retired CIA operative who heads a group plotting to create a failed assassination attempt in order to renew attention to Cuban hemispheric subversion. As is the case with the way Russian agents script Mercader before he assumes his role, Everett and his associates invent an Oswald prior to his showing up as the character they've invented. While for Padura's Iván, Cuba is experienced as a place of institutionalized fundamentalism and demoralizing restrictions, hence the lassitude he feels until energized by Mercader's story, for *Libra*'s conspirators it's an ideologically fueled abstraction, a bastion of subversive, region-endangering communism.

Style-wise, rather than working with re-inflected repetitions, DeLillo's *Libra* thinks not only with a proliferation of the diverse metahistorical imaginaries of his characters, but also with a wide variety of popular media voices, film, and television especially. For example, early in the novel DeLillo has Oswald and his mother sitting in front of the TV screen "where blue heads spoke to them,"[53] and as he did in *White Noise* he has the TV voice staging interruptions "'Natures spelled backwards' the TV said"[54] and character whose perceptions are media-mediated, for example, one of Oswald's army friends, Bushnell makes sense of Oswald's remarks by conjuring popular media: "He thought Ozzie's remark sounded historical and charming, right out of a movie or TV play."[55]

In a new introduction to the novel, DeLillo offers an observation that resonates with my investigation's overall pedagogy. Noting how traumatic historical events persist, he writes

> Some stories never end even in our time, in the sightlines of history, in the retrieved instancy of film and videotape, there are stories waiting to be finished, opened to the thrust of reasoned analysis and haunted speculation. These stories...undergo a kind of condensation, seeping into the texture of everyday life, barely separable from the ten thousand little excitations that define a routine day of visual and aural static processed by the case-hardened consumer brain.

In accord with DeLillo's remark, I want to suggest that the methodology in this book, centers on re-textualizations of a variety of stories, all involved with mentalities and events that have been told and retold in different idioms and from varying loci of enunciation, treat events that cannot be closed. To invoke again Adorno's remark quoted above, what I have written "stops where it feels complete" to me but not "where nothing is left to say."

Notes

1 Félix Guattari, *The Three Ecologies*, trans. Ian Pindar and Paul Sutton (London: Athlone, 2000), 37.

2 Roland Barthes, "From Work to Text," in *Image, Music, Text*, trans. Stephen Health (New York: Hill and Wang, 1977), 157.

3 Roland Barthes, *S/Z*, trans. Richard Miller (New York: Hill and Wang, 1974), 4.

4 David Albahari, *Globetrotter*, trans. Ellen Elias Bursac (New Haven, CT: Yale University Press, 2014), 50.

5 I am quoting a review by Daniel Goldman, "David Albahari's "Globetrotter," *Words without Borders* October 2014, on the web at: www.wordswithoutborders.org/book-review/david-albaharis.

6 Martin Heidegger, *Nietzsche 2: The Eternal Recurrence of the Same*, trans. David Farrell Krell (San Francisco: Harper and Row, 1984), 27.

7 Jean Paul Sartre, *The family Idiot: Gustave Flaubert 1821–1857*, trans. Carol Osman (Chicago: University of Chicago Press, 1989), 127.

8 Gilles Deleuze and Felix Guattari, *Kafka: Toward a Minor Literature*, trans. Dana Polan (Mineapolis: University of Minnesota Press, 1986), 17. Despite Deleuze's position that language should be treated as a non-signifying machine, he, along with Guattari are attentive to literary texts and confess to introducing novelistic methods into philosophy. See Gilles Deleuze and Felix Guattari, *A Thousand Plateaus* trans. Trans. Brian Massumi (Minneapolis: University of Minnesota Press, 1988), 25. And for elaboration on Deleuzian literary criticism, see Daniel Haines, *From Deleuze and Guattari's words to a Deleuzian Theory of Reading* (Edinburgh, UK: Edinburgh University Press, 2015).

9 Davide Panagia, "Dissenting Words: A Conversation with Jacques Rancière," *Diacritics* (Summer, 2000), 30: 2 115.

10 *Ibid.*

11 Michel Foucault, *The Archaeology of Knowledge*, trans. A. M. Sheridan Smith (New York: Pantheon, 1972), 120.

12 Rancière notes that he pays a "different sort of attention to language than that found in the tradition of 'critique'… [a] practice of interpretive suspicion guided by the idea that words always hide something profound below the surface; the hermeneutic imperative is thus to examine these substrata of meaning in order to get at some even more profound secret.": Panagia, "Dissenting Words," 114.

13 For an extended treatment of this aspect of Foucault's literary criticism, see Chapter 3, "Literature and Literary Theory," in Simon During, *Foucault and Literature: Towards A Genealogy of Writing* (London: Routledge, 2015), 67–89.

14 Vilém Flusser, *Gestures*, trans. Nancy Ann Roth (Minneapolis: University of Minnesota Press, 2014), ebook, loc. 535.

15 I am quoting Stacy Burton's succinct summary of Bakhtin's view: "Bakhtin, Temporality, and Modern Narrative: Writing the Whole Triumphant Murderous Unstoppable Chute," *Comparative Literature* 48: 1 (1996), 48.

16 M. M. Bakhtin, *Problems of Dostoevsky's Poetics*, trans. Caryle Emerson (Minneapolis: University of Minnesota Press, 1984), 203.

17 C. Wright Mills, "Review of Franz Neumann's *Behemoth: The Structure and Function of National Socialism 1933–1944*," *Partisan Review* online at: www.wbenjamin.org/Behemoth.html.

18 Laura Marris, "Camus's Inoculation Against Hate," *The New York Times*, April 16, 2020, on the web at: www.nytimes.com/2020/04/16/books/review/the-plague-albert-camus-coronavirus.html?searchResultPosition=2.

19 Wallant quoted in Nicholas Ayo, "The Secular Heart: The Achievement of Edward Lewis Wallant," *Critique: Studies in Contemporary Fiction* Volume 12: 2 1970), 86.

20 Roddy Doyle, *Love* (New York: Viking, 2020), 18.

21 *Ibid.*, 20.

22 *Ibid.*, 107.

23 *Ibid.*, 116.

24 The quotation belongs to Julia Kristeva, *La Revolution du Langage Poetique*, quoted in Nicholas Chare, *Auschwitz Afterimages* (New York: I. B. Tauris, 2011), 3.

25 Steven Feld, *Sound and Sentiment: Bird, Weeping, Poetics and Song in Kaludi Expression*, (Philadelphia: University of Pennsylvania Press, 1982), 34.

26 Julia Kristeva, *Desire in Language*, trans. Thomas Gora, Alice Jardine, and Leon S. Roudiez (New York: Columbia University Press, 1980), 134.

27 I am following the distinction that structures much of the analysis in Deleuze and Guattari, *What is Philosophy?*

28 Giorgio Agamben, *Remnants of Auschwitz: The Witness and the Archive*, trans. Daniel Heller-Roazen (New York: Zone, 2002), 41.

29 Edward Lewis Wallant, *The Pawnbroker* (New York, Manner Books, 1962).

30 Quoted in Agamben, *Remnants of Auschwitz*, 44.

31 Wallant, *The Pawnbroker* 5.

32 *Ibid.*, 13.

33 *Ibid.*, 149.

34 *Ibid.*, 22.

35 Jacques Rancière, "Fictions of time" in Grace Hellyer and Julian Murphet eds. *Rancière and Literature* (Edinburgh: Edinburgh University Press, 2016), 1.

36 Cesare Casarino, "Philopoesis: A Theoretico-Methodological Manifesto," *boundary 2* (2002), 86.

37 The quotation is from Gilles Deleuze, *Foucault* trans. Sean Hand (Minneapolis: University of Minnesota Press, 1988), 86.

38 The expression "figurative givens" is from Deleuze's analyses of the de-figuring effects in the canvases of Francis Bacon. See Gilles Deleuze, *Francis Bacon: The Logic of Sensation*, trans. Daniel W. Smith (Minneapolis: University of Minnesota Press, 2003). And for a supportive commentary on Deleuze's approach to Francis Bacon, see Jacques Rancière, "Is There a Deleuzian Aesthetic," *Qui Parle* 14: 2 (Spring/Summer, 2004), 1–4. Rancière points out, for example, that the de-figuring that Deleuze ascribes to Bacon's canvases applies as well to Flaubert's novels, a "clearing the terrain, which undoes, line by line, the grammatical conjunctions and semantic inferences that make up the ordinary substance of a story," 12.

39 C. L. R. James, *Mariners, Renegades and Castaways: The Story of Herman Melville and The World We Live In* (New York: Allison & Busby, 1953), 123.

40 *Ibid.*, 13.

41 *Ibid.*, 17.

42 *Ibid.*, 15.

43 *Ibid.*

44 Linda Hutcheon, *A Poetics of Postmodernism: History, Theory, Fiction* (New York: Routledge, 1988), 124.

45 Gilles Deleuze and Felix Guattari, *What is Philosophy?* trans. trans. Hugh Tomlinson and Graham Burchell (New York: Columbia University Press, 1994), 69.

46 John O'Neill, *Essaying Montaigne* (Chicago: University of Chicago Press, 2001), 9.

47 Theodor Adorno, "The Essay as Form," *New German Critique* No. 32 (Spring-Summer, 1984), 151.

48 *Ibid.*, 152.
49 *Ibid.*, 152–153.
50 Bohumil Hrabal, *Why I Write* (Prague: Karolinum Press, 2019), 15.
51 The quotation is from Jonathan L. Owen, "Closely Observed Bodies: Corporeality, Totalitarianism and Subversion in Jiri Menzel's 1960s Adaptions of Bohumil Hrabal," *Canadian Slavonic Paper* 51: 4 (December, 2009), 498.
52 Milan Kundera, *The Art of the Novel*, trans. Linda Asher (New York: Harper, 2000), 47.
53 *Ibid.*
54 *Ibid.*, 5.
55 *Ibid.*, 90.

Bibliography

Adorno, Theodor (1984) 'The Essay as Form,' *New German Critique*, No. 32, pp. 151–171.

Agamben, Giorgio (2002) *Remnants of Auschwitz: The Witness and the Archive*, trans. Daniel Heller-Roazen, New York: Zone.

Albahari, David (2014) *Globetrotter*, trans. Ellen Elias Bursac, New Haven, CT: Yale University Press.

Ayo, Nicholas (1970) 'The Secular Heart: The Achievement of Edward Lewis Wallant,' *Critique: Studies in Contemporary Fiction* Vol. 12 (2), pp. 86–94.

Bakhtin, M. M. (1984) *Problems of Dostoevsky's Poetics,* trans. Caryle Emerson, Minneapolis: University of Minnesota Press.

Barthes, Roland (1974) *S/Z*, trans. Richard Howard, New York: Hill and Wang.

Barthes, Roland (1977) 'From Work to Text,' in *Image, Music, Text*, trans. Stephen Health, New York: Hill and Wang, pp. 155–164.

Burton, Stacy (1996) 'Bakhtin, Temporality, and Modern Narrative: Writing the Whole Triumphant Murderous Unstoppable Chute,' *Comparative Literature* 48: 1, pp. 39–64.

Casarino, Cesare (2002) 'Philopoesis: A Theoretico-Methodological Manifesto,' *boundary 2* Vol. 29 (1), pp. 65–96.

Chare, Nicholas (2011) *Auschwitz Afterimages*, New York: I. B. Tauris.

Deleuze, Gilles (1988), *Foucault*, trans. Sean Hand, Minneapolis: University of Minnesota Press.

Deleuze, Gilles (2003) *Francis Bacon: The Logic of Sensation*, trans. Daniel W. Smith, Minneapolis: University of Minnesota Press.

Deleuze, Gilles and Guattari, Félix (1986) *Kafka: Toward a Minor Literature*, trans. Dana Polan, Minneapolis: University of Minnesota Press.

Deleuze, Gilles and Guattari, Félix (1988) *A Thousand Plateaus*, trans. Brian Massumi, Minneapolis: University of Minnesota Press.

Deleuze, Gilles and Guattari, Félix (1994) *What is Philosophy?* trans. Hugh Tomlinson and Graham Burchell, New York: Columbia University Press.

Doyle, Roddy (2020) *Love*, New York: Viking.

During, Simon (2015) *Foucault and Literature: Towards a Genealogy of Writing*, London: Routledge.

Feld, Steven (1982) *Sound and Sentiment: Bird, Weeping, Poetics and Song in Kaludi Expression*, Philadelphia: University of Pennsylvania Press.

Flusser, Vilém (2014) *Gestures*, trans. Nancy Ann Roth, Minneapolis: University of Minnesota Press.

Foucault, Michel (1972) *The Archaeology of Knowledge*, trans. A. M. Sheridan Smith, New York: Pantheon.

Goldman, Daniel (2014) 'David Albahari's "Globetrotter,"' *Words without Borders, October* 2014, on the web at: www.wordswithoutborders.org/book-review/david-albaharis.

Guattari, Félix (2000) *The Three Ecologies*, trans. Ian Pindar and Paul Sutton, London: Athlone.

Haines, Daniel (2015) *From Deleuze and Guattari's Words to a Deleuzian Theory of Reading*, Edinburgh, UK: Edinburgh University Press.

Heidegger, Martin (1984) *Nietzsche 2: The Eternal Recurrence of the Same*, trans. David Farrell Krell, San Francisco: Harper and Row.

Hrabal, Bohumil (2019) *Why I Write*, trans. David Short, Prague: Karolinum Press.

Hutcheon, Linda (1988) *A Poetics of Postmodernism: History, Theory, Fiction*, New York: Routledge.

James, C. L. R. (1953) *Mariners, Renegades and Castaways: The Story of Herman Melville and The World We Live In*, New York: Allison & Busby.

Kristeva, Julia (1980) *Desire in Language,* trans. Thomas Gora, Alice Jardine, and Leon S. Roudiez, New York: Columbia University Press.

Kundera, Milan (2000) *The Art of the Novel*, trans. Linda Asher, New York: Harper.

Marris, Laura (2020) 'Camus's Inoculation Against Hate,' *The New York Times*, on the web at: www.nytimes.com/2020/04/16/books/review/the-plague-albert-camus-mcorona virus.html?searchResultPosition=2.

Mills, C. Wright (1944) 'Review of Franz Neumann's *Behemoth: The Structure and Function of National Socialism 1933–1944,*' *Partisan Review*, on the web at:www.wbenjamin.org/ Behemoth.html.

O'Neill, John (2001) *Essaying Montaigne*, Chicago: University of Chicago Press.

Owen, Jonathan L. (2009) 'Closely Observed Bodies: Corporeality, Totalitarianism and Subversion in Jiri Menzel's 1960s Adaptions of Bohumil Hrabal,' *Canadian Slavonic Papers* Vol. 54 (4), pp. 495–511.

Panagia, Davide (2000) 'Dissenting Words: A Conversation with Jacques Rancière,' *Diacritics* Vol. 30 (2), pp. 113–126.

Rancière, Jacques (2004) 'Is There a Deleuzian Aesthetic?', *Qui Parle* Vol. 14 (2), pp. 1–14.

Rancière, Jacques (2016) 'Fictions of Time' in Grace Hellyer and Julian Murphet eds. *Rancière and Literature,* Edinburgh: Edinburgh University Press, pp. 1–19.

Sartre, Jean Paul (1989) *The Family Idiot: Gustave Flaubert 1821–1857*, trans. Carol Osman, Chicago: University of Chicago Press.

Wallant, Edward Lewis (1962) *The Pawnbroker*, New York: Manner Books.

1

A WAR OF WORDS

Edna O'Brien's *The Little Red Chairs*

On the 6th of April 2012, to commemorate the twentieth anniversary of the start of the siege of Sarajevo by Bosnian Serb forces, 11,541 red chairs were laid out in row along the eight hundred metres of the Sarajevo high street. One empty chair for every Sarajevan killed during the 1,425 days of siege.[1] I wanted to take a dreadful situation, and the havoc and harm that it yields, and show how it spirals into the world at large.

Edna O'Brien, "The Spirit of the Gothic"

Poesis/Counter-Poesis

In an interview during the 1990 presidential election campaign in Bosnia-Herzegovina the candidate, Radovan Karadžić reports, "A simple sentence brought me to the fore of the Serb Democratic Party…I stated: 'Serbs you still exist and are allowed to be Serbs…'; he adds, 'We are teaching Serbs to be Serbs'."[2] As is well-known, that "teaching," which launched Karadžić's political career, precipitated a patriotic fervor that led to the Bosnian War (1992–1995) and the Karadžić-run ethnic cleansing that ultimately landed him in prison with a 40-year sentence (rendered on Mar 24, 2016 after a trial at the ICJ in the Hague). Karadžić's inspiration for the atrocities was articulated within what Slavoj Žižek refers to as a "military-poetic complex."[3] Along with his "simple sentence" Karadžić, who "was not only a ruthless political and military leader but [also] a poet," fueled Serbian violent enmity with poetry, for example:

> Convert to my new faith crowd
> I offer you what no one has had before
> The one who won't have bread will be fed by the light of my sun

People nothing is forbidden in my faith
There is loving and drinking
And looking at the sun for as long as you want
And this godhead forbids you nothing
Oh obey my call brethren people crowd[4]

In addition to using the media "to incite Serbian troops or legislators [for example] with lines from ancient poems of genocidal destruction," – while also reciting "his own eerily prophetic poetry about the fiery destruction of Sarajevo" over broadcast media – he participated in the destruction (e.g., "exhorting a Russian writer to take a turn firing a machine gun at the city)."[5] Much of the defensive response from Sarajevo was artistic. A film festival and theatrical productions went on during the siege, and especially notable was an extraordinarily heroic artistic response by the famous cellist of Sarajevo, Vedran Smajlovic a former musician in the Opera and Philharmonic orchestras of Sarajevo. In defiance of the snipers in the hills he played his cello in the public square; "I never stopped playing music throughout the siege," he said. "My weapon was my cello."[6]

Throughout the Karadžić-promoted war there were also other counter-weapons, most notably literary responses by the exilic Bosnian writers, Aleksandar Hemon, Semezdin Mehmedinovic, and Ismet Prcic, whose texts constituted a counter-poesis to Karadžić's violent poetic rants.[7] All three are characteristically attentive to the nuances of selecting words adequate to the capture of personal experiences, whether violent or mundane. Hemon puts it this way:

> The hard part in writing a narrative of someone's life is choosing from the abundance of details and microevents, all of them equally signifi-cant, or equally insignificant. If one elects to include only the important events: births, the details, the lives, the humiliations, the uprisings, the ends and the beginnings, one denies the real substance of life: the ephemera, the nether moments, much too small to be recorded…But you cannot simply list all the moments when the world tickles your senses, only to seep away between your fingers and eyelashes, leaving you alone to tell the story of your life to an audience interested only in the fireworks of universal experiences, the rollercoaster rides of sympathy and judgment.[8]

At a minimum, an effective aesthetically rendered political intervention requires entering "profoundly into the lives and worlds of others" in order to illuminate the micropolitics of individual experience in ways that also produce collective, macropolitical (i.e., structural) insights.[9] It rests on an "ability to reveal possible worlds lodged within the apparent banality of the actual."[10] In this chapter, which is focused on literary treatments of the violent career of Radovan Karadžić, I examine (briefly) the contribution of one of the Bosnian exilic writers, Mehmedinovic, whose *Sarajevo Blues* is a poetic response to the Karadžić-directed siege of Sarajevo, and complement his counter voice to Karadžić's violence-inspiring words with an extensive analysis of another literary genre, a novel which (like Hemon) "sees banal details and lingers over them, viewing them in the shadow of warfare,"[11] while it invents a fictional western migration of that same perpetrator. Featured as a protagonist in Edna O'Brien *The Little Red Chairs*, Karadžić, masquerading as a holistic healer and sex therapist, travels to the fictional Irish town of Cloonoila in a disguise similar to the one that he used to hide in plain sight in Belgrade and elsewhere for 12 years prior to being brought to trial at the ICJ in the Hague.

> At the time of his arrest, [using the name] Dragan Dabic [he] was fast becoming a minor celebrity in Belgrade. He had his own column in a national magazine. He was a rising star in a Connecticut-based vitamin company. And he was collaborating with a well-known sexologist on a novel form of sperm-rejuvenation therapy.[12]

"Literary Justice"

Featuring a version of the man whose "architecture of enmity"[13] inspired the atrocities perpetrated on thousands of Bosnians during the Bosnian war, O'Brien's novel invents an elaborate series of encounters between Karadžić and Cloonoila's residents. Disguised, relocated and re-self-fashioned under an assumed name, O'Brien's version of Karadžić perpetrates a different kind of violence. He is still killing, albeit more "softly with his words," as he exploits the vulnerabilities of the town's residents, most notably Fidelma McBride with whom he has an affair. I locate the novel within Shoshana Felman's conceptual frame, which distinguishes literary from legal justice and compare O'Brien's rendering of the Karadžić – justice relationship with Jessica Stern's ethnographic version, based on her conversations with him in The Hague (in which the Karadžić who emerges sounds very like the one who deludes and cynically uses Fidelma McBride). To elaborate the Felman framing,

> [I]n contrast to the "legal justice," dispensed at trials ("physical theaters of justice"), "literary justice is a dimension of concrete embodiment and a language of finitude that in contrast to the law, encapsulates not closure but precisely what…. refuses to be closed…It is to this refusal of the trauma to be closed that literature does justice."[14]

For purposes of illustration of the non-closural aspect of literary justice, I want to rehearse a section of a text I have analyzed previously, a novel concerned with a post-apartheid trial presided over by South Africa's Truth and Reconciliation Commission. Imagining an encounter between a former torturer, Dirk Hendricks and one of his victims, Alex Mpondo, Gillian Slovo's *Red Dust* dwells on the ambiguities of a perpetrator's identity and the traumatic legacy of his career as a torturer rather than celebrating a verdict. Rendering Hendricks as one seeking to "cross the line" from "perpetrator to reconciled," her emphasis is on how he is perceived by his victim rather than on the jury's decision about whether he is to be reconciled rather than convicted. For Mpondo, Hendricks is a divided subject. Under his gaze, Hendricks appears in some moments as "an ordinary man brought down by history" and in others as the sadist who victimized him. At one point, as Mpondo looks into Hendrick's "grey eyes… the man whom Alex had known… seem[s] to have vanished," only to show up at another point, after Alex mentions his (Hendrick's) estranged wife. At that moment Alex sees "a glimmer…in the flashing of the stranger's eyes" of the Hendricks he had previously known.[15] As for the novel's actualization of literary justice, I put it this way:

> The novel does not help the reader decide if Hendricks is a liar, a problem that the tribunal would have to solve. Rather, it leaves open the issue in order to both render identities and relationships ambiguous and to treat the issue of the atrocities by the white apartheid regime's functionaries experientially by pondering the continuing emotional damage to both perpetrators and victims.[16]

In O'Brien's novel there's a similar perceptual drama, in this case experienced by a different kind of victim. Fidelma McBride, vulnerable because she is feeling trapped in a childless and failing marriage, is deceptively courted and seduced by the character Karadžić impersonates, Dr. Vladimir Dragan ("Twice in her married life she was pregnant and [her husband] Jack bought her pieces of jewelry, but she lost it both times, and believing the failure to be hers, she grieved alone"[17]). In Part Three of the novel, "On a quest for truth, justice, and atonement," Fidelma visits Karadžić in "the conjugal room" in the Hague, where he is imprisoned while awaiting trial. After she resists his attempts to intimidate her (as he had done so effectively in Cloonoila), he asks "Who sent you…what organization is behind this…this dirty work?" She answers, "No one…I came alone…I had to." She then asks, "When we made love, what was on your mind?" After Karadžić responds, "Pleasure," she asks, "When you were carving up your pure homeland, with your guns opening fire even on ambulances, what was on your mind, or did the sheer numbers, the hundreds of thousands, deaden the truth of it all?" In response to that question, "he freezes."[18]

Near the end of the novel, Fidelma, still at The Hague attending Karadžić's trial, meets another trial attendee, a Serb from Bosnia Herzegovina, who joins her at her table in a bar. As their conversation ensues, she tells him, "I knew your president…I had a part in his life, a walk on part…but still significant…he came to our village as a healer." Asked if she "came for him," she responds, "I wanted to believe he would show some grain of remorse…*a single word* (my emphasis)…what goes on inside him…the inner footage."[19] When the novel ends, it has become evident that words cannot provide closure. As the literary critic, M. M. Bakhtin suggests, words are perpetually open to resignification because they function within "the dialogic fabric of human life" and are thus open to changing nuances in interpersonal encounters.[20] Illustrating that insight in his analysis of polyphony in Dostoevsky's novels, he writes,

> In Dostoevsky almost no word is without its intense sideward glance at someone else's word. At the same time there are almost no objectified words in Dostoevsky, since the speech of his characters is constructed in a way that deprives it of all objectification.[21]

O'Brien's novel incorporates that insight. As it concludes, Fidelma, living in London and having said, "I am not a stranger here anymore"[22] (applied not only to others perceptions, but also to her self-regard) is attending a play in which, "For the finale, the word *Home* was to be sung and chanted in thirty-five different languages of the performers." Eleven lines later, the very last sentence of the novel reads, "You would not believe how many words there are for *home* and what savage music there can be wrung from it."[23] However, the novel offers much more as it develops an equivalence between two types of atrocity: the Karadžić-led murder of thousands in the Balkans and (an imaginative version of) his softer killing in his disguise as a holistic healer, exploiting people's vulnerabilities. Before analyzing that and the other "generic veins"[24] of O'Brien's novel, I want to return to Mehmedinovic's *Sarajevo Blues*, which like O'Brien's novel, concerns itself with the vagaries of words.

Mehmedinovic's Sarajevo

> Shells are constructed so shrapnel can't be cleaned out of the flesh, that's why there are so many amputations. Their power is a great stimulant to the soldier, that corpse in a trench coat, to his military autism.
>
> *Semezdin Mehedinovic, Sarajevo Blues*

> Nationality; this thing or idea, or reality for which so many have fought, spilling so much blood, is the thing that least belongs to you, the most accidental, the most dangerous part of one's self...
>
> *Jorge Semprún, Literature or Life*

Well into the blues motif of his poetic rejoinder to President (of Republika Srpska) Radovan Karadžić's discourse on the need for ethnic separation, Mehmedinovic, an activist in the resistance of Sarajevo's artistic community to "the genocidal attack of Serbian nationalists,"[25] points out that Bosnian literature defies Karadžić's rants against ethnic mixing.

> In the case of Bosnia, you could not say that the literature in Sarajevo or Bosnia-Herzegovina was Bosnian or Croatian or Serbian. But this is

precisely what happened as a result of war, that on the borders of culture all kinds of divisions and separations have been made.[26]

That making, in which Karadžić was the primary protagonist, was an ideological imposition of a model of cultural separation that was contradicted by what existed "on the ground (culture-as-lived), but is not in accordance with the [ideological] prescription."[27]

In a literary montage of poems and commentary, Mehmedinovic supplies a counter ideology, what he calls "an urban ideology," which flourished in artistic genres shared across ethnicities in Sarajevo, a "common aesthetic" derived from the "comic book art, rock music and film with which," he says, "my generation educated ourselves."[28] Because the blues addresses not only the pain of victimization, but also the redemptive exercises of memory, which reveal forms of solidarity against attempts to impose antagonistic difference, Mehmedinović's writing, an anti-violence poesis and politically framed aesthetic that refigures the war, recovers memories of experiences that nationalists had tried to efface, and laments the exile into which he and many others were forced:

> Once I too will depart alone
> Into the darkness of the grave –
> On Alikfakovac
> Or on another hill, the city
> I knew everyone in
> And now only two or
> Three remain –
> And only night, alone
> I look out from the past
> On the city's darkness
> From someone else's
> Home, I, stranger –
> I a stranger[29]

Antagonistic toward the shared "word abundance"[30] on which Sarajevo's multiethnic artistic community thrived, Bosnian Serb nationalists practiced what Mehmedinovic's translator, Ammiel Alcalay calls a "reductive vocabulary."[31] Impoverishing figuration and constricting the lexicon, they killed "word abundance" as well as people. As Mehmedinovic puts it, "It is not only my world that has been deconstructed but language as well."[32] With a rich and compelling assortment of words, Mehmedinovic's literary intervention into Karadžić's and his fellow nationalist's war restores what their "reductive" vocabularies evacuated. Moving back from the "critical exigencies of [Mehmedinovic's extended] essay" to "the affective pull of [O'Brien's] novel," we can observe a similar displacement.[33] In *The Little Red Chairs*, O'Brien provides a word abundance, in her case words and a composition as a whole that expose the softer as well as the harder violence that a fictional albeit very realistic and unrepentant Karadžić practices. The novel's "heteroglossia"[34] (its many contending voices) conveys the sensibilities associated with diverse forms of victimhood while at the same time discrediting the lies with which the actual/historical Karadžić has attempted to justify the "ethnic cleansing" he directed.

Cloonoila: "The Wolf Is Entitled to the Lamb"[35]

> The subjective life of all readers is peopled, not only by those one has known, but also by literary figures...possessed of a much higher degree of reality than many people we have been introduced to in the course of our lives.
>
> *Jean Améry*

The novel's initial introduction of the disguised Karadžić evokes a Gothic mood. With cinematic detail it suggests something uncanny about a visitor who seems incongruous in the sights and sounds of a wintry Cloonoila:

> The town takes its name from the river. The current, swift and dangerous, surges with manic glee...From the slenderest twigs of the overhanging trees in Folk park, the melting ice drips, with the soft susurrus sound and the hooped metal sculpture, an eyesore to many locals, is improved by a straggling necklace of icicles, bluish in that frosted night...He stays by the water's edge, apparently mesmerised by it. Bearded and in a long dark coat and white gloves, he stands on the narrow bridge, looks down at the roaring current, then looks around...his presence the single curiosity in the monotony of the winter evening[36]

O'Brien's Gothic-inspired opening, with its introduction of the vampiric looking "Vlad" recalls the literary Dracula made famous by another Irish author, Bram Stoker. The Vlad in his *Dracula* (1897) takes his name from the infamous fifteenth-century Romanian prince, Vlad III Dracula (the infamous "Vlad the Impaler"). The Gothic scene O'Brien constructs is also Hitchcockian. In many of his films, Alfred Hitchcock displaced the Gothic genre from its traditional architectural venues (the gloomy and dark castles and mansions of traditional gothic literature) to cinematic landscapes:

> Hitchcock's camera typically only begins by enacting a survey of a seemingly natural scene. Eventually, as the filming proceeds, it become evident that there is a perverse element in the landscape..."The film's movement invariably proceeds from landscape to stain, from overall shot to close-up, and this movement invariably prepares the spectator for the event."[37]

The Hitchcockian Gothic effect that Karadžić's initial presence conveys to the reader, a strange intrusion in an otherwise uneventful scene (a landscape that reflects a small town mired in the traditional rhythms of everyday life), has also registered itself broadly in the town, whose residents experience signs of Gothic horror:

> Long afterwards there would be those who reported strange occurrences on that same winter evening: dogs barking crazily, as if there was thunder, and the sound of the nightingale, whose song and warblings were never heard so far west. The child of a gipsy family, who lived in a caravan by the sea, swore she saw the Pooka Man coming through the window at her, pointing a hatchet.[38]

Hitchcock effects are pervasive in the novel. Hitchcockian Gothic landscapes are always accompanied by a Gothicism present in his destabilized or divided subjects, whose intrusions haunt traditional domestic spaces. Exemplary of this aspect of Hitchcock's Gothicism is Uncle Charley (Joseph Cotton) in his *Shadow of a Doubt* (1943). *Shadow*'s Charley Oakley (whom O'Brien's Dr. Vlad echoes), known to authorities as The Merry Widow Killer, is pursued by police detectives. He manages to escape on a train traveling from the notably non-picturesque, "seedy and sinister" back streets of an Eastern city, where his crimes were perpetrated, to the sunny, "clean and friendly" California town of Santa Rosa, where he plans to hide indefinitely among family members.[39] His niece, Charlotte Newton (Teresa Wright) – nicknamed Charley (one of the film's main Gothic doubling effects[40]) – greets her seemingly benign and appealing uncle (her mother's younger brother) warmly as he alights from the train.

However, like the opening of O'Brien's novel, a Gothic mood disrupts a seemingly tranquil domestic scene early on, conveyed not only by Uncle Charlie's ever-changing facial expressions, which at some moments makes him appear avuncular and at others mysteriously withdrawn, but also by the haunting sounds of Dimitry Tiomkin's soundtrack, which is playing bars from The Merry Widow Waltz during a family dining scene. At the dinner in which "Uncle Charlie" is auditioning for the extended family, his alternating facial expressions are accompanied by alterations between his small talk and some disturbingly hostile sentiments. However, despite those alarming moments, Charlotte/Charley (like O'Brien's Fidelma) is initially deceived by a man whose criminal history remains hidden until late in the story. He's an exemplary prototype for the disguised Karadžić, a vampiric monster, disguised as someone with charming innocence. And as is the case with O'Brien's novel, *Shadow* has Dracula references, e.g., a moment when one character, "half-jokingly," asks another to "tell the story of Dracula."[41] Like the vampiric, charming, and seductive Uncle Charley, to whom women are drawn, the vampiric Dr. Vladimir Dragan uses his charm (and in his case diverse discursive assets as well) to exercise power over women. As is noted at the beginning of a chapter well into Dr. Vlad's sojourn in Cloonoila, "His name is on everybody's lips, Dr Vlad this and Dr Vlad that. He has done wonders for people, women claiming to be rejuvenated after two treatments."[42]

The Hitchcockian Gothic effects in O'Brien's novel thus operate both at the outset, as Dr. Vlad's appearance is a disconcerting presence ("stain") in the landscape, and subsequently as his beguiling manner (much like Uncle Charley's in *Shadow*) temporarily holds people in thrall to his words. His exotic charm is in evidence in his first human contact. While seeking information about his lodging, he enters a bar and meets the prolix barman, Dara, "a blatherer by nature…[who] unfolds his personal history, just to keep the ball rolling."[43] However, in the midst of his blather, Dara also provides another disclosure of O'Brien's Gothic framing; he mentions having recently seen "a great fillum with Christian Bale" and says that although [Bale/Batman] is "the Dark Knight…I wouldn't be into *horror* [my emphasis], no way."[44] At this point in the encounter all that the blathering Dara can elicit from the stranger is a single word. When he finally pauses for a moment and asks, "And where would your part of the world be," "Vladimir Dragan" responds, "Montenegro."[45]

However, once "the stranger" has managed to seize an interlocutory place in the conversation, he overwhelms the barman with his eloquent polysemic phrasings. Dara, a man who lives in a geographically small place and resides as well in a linguistically restrictive vernacular, is stunned by the words of the well-travelled and linguistically talented visitor. He is "gobsmacked, as he would later put it, by the sagacity of this man, the knowledge, a walking university to himself."[46] In that encounter, as throughout the novel, O'Brien recreates the discursive power of a Karadžić who has had a medical education, has been a practicing psychotherapist, has published poetry and other literary forms, and has founded a political party. Sagacity is of course only part of the Karadžić package. How it translates into performance is central to the story. In the small world of the Irish village, his words are to be used to beguile and seduce rather than (as was the case in the larger world from which he had fled) inciting ethno-national enmity. Dara and the others whom he subsequently awes with his discursive proficiency are not privy to the violent dimension of his literary acts; for example, these lines from an untitled poem written before his political career had positioned him to implement his ethno-national-fueled enmity:

> …I am disgusted by the souls who radiate nothing
> Like a small nasty puppy puny death
> Is approaching from afar
> I don't know what to make of all these things
> But I can't stand the sight of you you file of scum
> You file of snails
> Well hurry up in your slime
> Because if I can turn my words into thunder

I can turn you into a pool of stagnant water
…So your stupid rotten your vain souls
Wouldn't stare at me with their stupid peaceful eyes
…I don't even know what
These slimy creatures are for
What all their words are for…
What their lectures are for…
Without a purpose and with no beauty
Without a purpose
And no soundness[47]

Holding back from revealing the cynically violent Karadžić, until well into the novel, at the outset O'Brien's portrayal of Dr. Vlad hints at his dark side and stages a clash of "sociolects."[48] The initial focus is on how one who is able to exercise linguistic dominance can exploit a village population in which some are functioning within the local vernacular and others, for example, migrants from other countries, also lack the words that would enable effective discursive resistance. Nevertheless, there is a public sphere in (among other places) Dara's bar where at one point several patrons, who are less in awe of Dr. Vlad than Dara, express skepticism of his abilities and motives ("Was the newcomer one of those sharks, speculating for gas or oil," one of them wonders[49]). There is also a character whom Dr. Vlad's manner does not wholly deceive. Mujo, a Bosnia refugee, recognizes his voice, "the voice he had heard on television [giving him and the reader a sense] that something he did not know, or…half knew, is happening."[50]

There is also another episodic public sphere which weighs against Dr. Vlad's linguistic dominance. Fidelma is chairperson of a book club, which has enriched her and her club members' linguistic world in ways that help them contextualize the presence of the predatory "wolf" roaming their village. Why "wolf"? After introducing himself as Dr. Vladimir Dragan, Karadžić tells Dara that he is known as "Vuk, meaning wolf," a name taken, he says, from a popular legend in his homeland.[51] Doubtless O'Brien has him adopt that sobriquet (used in fact by generations of Karadžić's) because it participates in her Gothic framing of the story. In Bram Stoker's *Dracula*, wolves (and bats), commanded by Dracula, participate in the story, not only to help to carry out Count Dracula's violent mission, but also to represent symbolically the animalistic drives through which he and other vampires pursue their conscienceless desires.

The Seductive Trail Begins

Later in the novel (while Fidelma is in exile in London), there are disclosures about the siege of Sarajevo by former victims she meets. One is initiated with a metaphor that connects them with what has transpired during the Vuk's predatory practices in Cloonoila. Zelmic, a Bosnian war survivor, tells Fidelma that

"Sarajevo, her city [is] not the same any more, the heart has gone out of it."[52] That figure recalls what has taken place during the Vuk's Cloonoila sojourn, his capture of Fidelma's heart. To connect the two kinds of violence, we can heed an insight Jacques Rancière provides in an analysis of Jean-Luc Godard's film *Histoire(s) du Cinema*. Rancière points out that the film's "clash of heterogeneous elements...provide[s] a common measure." It creates an equivalence between "two captivations,"[53] that of the "German crowds by Nazi ideology" and that of the "film crowds by Hollywood."[54] Similarly, the heterogeneous clashes in O'Brien's novel create an equivalence, in that case between two kinds of violence – the Karadžić-directed siege that (temporarily) took the heart out of Sarajevo and Karadžić/Vuk's seduction that (temporarily) captures Fidelma's heart.

In the runup to that particular capture is a drama in which the newly arrived "Vladimir Dragan" insinuates himself into the village with eloquence and guile. First, against initial resistance, he secures a room in "Fifi's" guest lodgings (ordinarily not available during the winter season) by helping her find her missing dog and then extoling the "enjoyable" morning he has spent in her presence; "it was all it took to sway her."[55] Subsequently to promote his "holistic healing" enterprise he has to overcome the local "moral economy,"[56] initially by overcoming staunch resistance from a cleric, Father Damien, who is wary of how a vocation that includes "sex therapy," will go down with the local Bishop. To co-opt him the Vuk, revises his business card, eliminating the sex therapy reference and further ingratiating himself by agreeing to a community conversation, a Q & A. and saying (mostly to himself as he exercises his wolf-like predatory sense), that, "He is anxious to get acquainted with the local people because he intends to make Cloonoila his home, sensing in it that primal innocence lost to most places in the world."[57] The next hurdle in the local moral economy is easily leaped. He convinces a nun, "Sister Bonaventure," that his healing massage treatment is medical rather than sexual. His hands as much as his words accomplish the seduction ("His hands were so capable and so far reaching...she felt herself giving in to it").[58]

However, the next encounter turns out to be perilous. A police officer (a Garda) intercepts him while he's leading a group of children on a nature walk. The man, aiming to bully Dr. Vlad with the power of his policing position, threatens to arrest him and have him interrogated at the Garda Station. What succeeds for Karadžić, who faces exposure and thereafter a trip to the Hague if he's actually booked, is the words with which he creates a homosocial mood: "He plays a last, audacious card...openly admitting to having been a cheat once [in order to be] seen as a man of truth. 'I avoided military service,' he says with a colluding smile."[59] He follows that move by representing himself as a soccer fan ("soccer was [in fact] one of Karadžić's passions")[60], which he correctly suspects will ingratiate him with the Garda.

Emotionally exhausted by the close call, that evening he goes for a swim in "his secret cove" and thereafter "lies on the bank and drifts into a sleep" that brings on a very revealing dream.[61] To paraphrase *Hamlet* (which O'Brien clearly has in mind), the dream's the thing wherein she captures the conscience of Karadžić. The implied Hamlet reference with which O'Brien creates the dreaming Karadžić is but one moment in one of the novel's most pervasive narrative threads. *The Little Red Chairs* thinks with a trajectory of literary references through which O'Brien figures and captures Karadžić's mentality.

Literary Mentalities

Having already drawn on Bram Stoker's *Dracula* to figure Dr. Vlad as a wolf-like predator, O'Brien proceeds to invoke additional literary types both to shape the novel's drama and to capture (what she has Fidelma refer to as) Karadžić's "inner footage." The most important literary source of Karadžić's inner footage emerges when "Suddenly into the dream walks his old friend K,….all in black, altered through death." After K remarks on the "near thing today, you must have been shitting your pants,"[62] they proceed to reminisce about their roles in the siege of Sarajevo, mentioning (without guilt), the deadly consequences and Karadžić's coverup, his lies in his attempt to counter media reports of the atrocities. What then ensues is a literary sequence. K mentions Samuel Becket's "Godot" play, performed during the siege (much to Karadžić's consternation) and then switches to the literature that had inspired them during their university days, Shakespeare among others.

Confirming O'Brien's oblique *Hamlet* moment, K mentions rereading the play during the siege and speculates that during Karadžić's ethnic purification drive, "Shakespeare must have come to mind – that *tide in the affairs of man* [from *Julius Caesar*], yet you mastered any doubts you might have had. So came the next Bonanza. Srebrenica. A killing spree. Eight thousand Bosniak men…"[63] Of course Shakespeare has another resonance for O'Brien's construction of the Karadžić mentality; the persistent binary in his plays between "seeming" and "being," with which he constructs his characters is proto-Gothic.[64] Having added that for them "Shakespeare was God," K remarks also on their shared "love of Goethe and [Robert] Musil." It is ultimately the latter whom O'Brien selects as the author of the most apropos literary prototype of Karadžić's mentality. "You had been christened Young Törless," says K, "because of the two terribly contrasting aspects of your character, the sane, the reasonable and the other so dark, so vengeful."[65] The implication O'Brien draws from the Törless character, the protagonist in Robert Musil's debut novel, *The Confusions of Young Törless* (1906), is that rather than a single "inner footage," the workings of Karadžić's Gothic mentality involves jump cuts between two separate streams.

Rather than going into a detailed synopsis of Musil's novel – set in a German school in which some young students brutalize a classmate – it suffices to note that the emphasis is on personalities rather than setting. As is noted in a preface to one edition, the school itself "simply acts as a funnel down which is poured a selection of personalities."[66] Törless, whose personality takes center stage, is constructed with a "dividing line" that separates "his own feelings and some innermost self that craved understanding of them."[67] He is often haunted by feelings that indicate a hidden and inaccessible reality that drives his often "feverish" feelings. While Törless is the Gothic subject that most closely models the Karadžić persona that O'Brien constructs[68] to incorporate Karadžić's theological tonalities, O'Brien had to create as well their inter-articulation with his Gothic personality, which realized itself as a violent ethno-nationalism (happening during his political career but hidden within his a pseudo-religious healing practice in the Irish village). The novel suggests that a dark, malignant narcissism, hidden within a benign social presentation and vehiculated with theological fervor, translates well between ethno-nationalism and the pseudo-medical practices of the healing guru.

It is a displaced theological fervor, for as one analysis of the emergence of Gothic texts – construed as "Romantic explorations of gothic subjectivity" – points out, they show up at a historical moment as "an alternative theology" when traditional religions are under pressure, creating "change" that for many is "radical and painful [however]…if gothic is a theology, then what is the object of worship?"[69] The answer, which is fundamental to the contribution of O'Brien's Gothic construction of Karadžić, is that the object is arbitrary. Weaponized theology works well on vulnerable targets, however and wherever they have become vulnerable. It can inspire a "holy war" or seduce a village population.[70] Where it operates, victims proliferate, thousands in the case of the Bosnian war, a few in O'Brien's fictional Cloonoila. However, the most notable victim on which the novel exercises most of its critical thinking is Fidelma.

The Seduction

With Fidelma, as is the case with Karadžić, literary references carry much the burden of the novel's thinking (in her case about the details of her vulnerable situation). At her reading group, for example, Fidelma suggests that Bridget, one of the members, might start the evening by reading from "the chapter called Dido," from *The Aeneid*, the chapter in which Aeneas abandons Dido (previewing Fidelma's abandonment by her lover, Dr. Vlad).[71] That literary moment is followed by a conversation about Emma Bovary's mental disposition, alerting the reader to Fidelma's entry into an extra-marital affair. Afterwards, while she is exploring the room she has arranged to begin the affair with Dr. Vlad, Fidelma is "sitting on one of the high chairs, far too restless to read the book she has opened – *The Kreutzer Sonata*," a novel in which Tolstoy disparages extra-marital affairs.[72] One of the novel's characters is a man, Pozdnyshev, who is described as a "fornicator" with a dissolute life-style, who marries, becomes discontent with his wife, beats her to death and ends up in prison (Karadžić's destination both in life and in the novel). And in a subsequent moment, while they are sitting on the bed about to make love, another violent literary character, whose profile also mirrors

Karadžić's, comes up. Dr. Vlad asks her, "what poem or of piece of literature in her country best expressed the wooing of a lady." She selects John Millington Synge's *Playboy of the Western World*; "it was a Playboy," she says, "who said he had killed his da and wandered into County Mayo to boast of his feats, where the women of Connaught fell for him."[73]

After they have sex, rather than tenderness, Dr. Vlad delivers an injunction: "We must not get your story mixed-up with my story Fidelma." When she asks, "And what is your story Vlad?" he reverts to his Karadžić persona and says "My sacred duty to God and my own people."[74] It is evident, however, that although they bring very different stories to their encounter, their stories share a consequence. Once it is known that she has been sexually intimate with Dr. Vlad, graffiti, "Where the Wolves Fuck" shows up on the sidewalk in front of her boutique and Dr. Vlad's car is vandalized. She has become a pariah in the town, and as a result, like Karadžić, she is to go into exile. Contrary to Vlad's injunction, in a crucial sense their stories converge. Nevertheless, in the dynamic of identity/difference that the novel enacts – one a perpetrator of violence and one a victim – O'Brien imagines a way that the murderous violence of Karadžić's architecture of genocide in Bosnia "spirals into the world at large" (to repeat her words from the epigraph). She uses the cultural receptivity within the world with which she is familiar to play out such consequences.

Once in exile in London (in Part Two of the novel), Fidelma undergoes a healing process in a venue with which O'Brien is familiar (having lived in London for over 30 years). Unlike Karadžić's exile in which he seeks to use the self he has made to exploit those he meets, Fidelma is on a re-self-fashioning mission to rid herself of the "counterfeit guilt" she has acquired because of her association with Karadžić. Here once again a literary reference carries the burden of situating a character's mentality. She says that before leaving Ireland she "spoke to the land-scape, itself, saying I wanted to cleanse my house and my soul, myself." Recalling that moment – outside a convent where she had been given shelter – she adds, "There is a poem, a beautiful poem by Emily Dickenson that says, 'When it comes, the landscape listens – Shadows – hold their breath – When it goes, 'tis like the distance on the look of death'."[75] Here, however, Fidelma is a benign shadow. Her landscape moment is part of the novel's formal structure, its use of "referential montage" (moments in which one scene recalls an earlier one).[76] This scene refers back to the one at the beginning of the novel in which "the stranger," Karadžić in disguise, is a dark shadow about to haunt Cloonoila. In contrast, the landscape in which Fidelma is situated in this scene positions her as one seeking to heal and to assist rather than haunt.

Where Karadžić's Ireland sojourn involves taking advantage of those he meets, Fidelma's involves compensating those she meets for the *dis*advantages they've experienced. As the story turns toward victims from diverse global venues now living in London, Fidelma's work on the self involves her as a helping professional. Joyce Carol Oates captures the motive of Fidelma's dedication to re-self-fashioning:

Determined to expiate the curse of a union with the Devil by dedicating herself to the aid of desperate, displaced persons at a shelter for the homeless in London [Fidelma says] "I could not go home until I could come home to myself."[77]

However, O'Brien's novel thinks well beyond the vagaries of an individual's experience. Fidelma's translation of her suffering into a practicing ethos is the place where the novel's ethico-political sensibility reveals itself. Rather than merely narrating a plot in which Fidelma suffers a misfortune and manages to survive it, while suggesting (as I've noted) an equivalence between Karadžić's softer and harder violence (adding her misfortune to the many misfortunes of the murdered Bosnians), in moving to the London scene the novel constructs a more elaborate equivalence. It is one between what Fidelma has suffered and the broader suffering of London's migrants, many of whom are invisible in London's peoplescape (they are "night people, one step away from ghosts"[78]). During a moment that acknowledges the equivalence, the "story" moment that Dr. Vlad articulates as he initiates his separation from Fidelma, is repeated but with a different valence. One of the "night people, Bluey from Mozambique says, 'A little bit of your story and a little bit of my story Fidelma....'."[79]

"Once Bitten...[No Longer] Shy"

In Bram Stoker's *Dracula*, the Count penetrates one of his victim's, Mina Harker's mind after biting her. During Karadžić's Ireland sojourn as the predatory Dracula-like Vlad he performs an intellectual (as well as a romantic) seductiveness; his version of Dracula's bite makes others his willing prey.[80] It's the softer violence of exploitation and cold abandonment after his harder genocidal violence. In contrast, Fidelma's intent is an absolute and caring hospitality to otherness. To achieve that hospitality, she has to strengthen herself by recognizing that (as I have put it elsewhere) "a hospitality to alterity...must be predicated on a hospitality to oneself."[81] In that way, her story becomes hospitable to the stories of the London others she engages (hence the "and" in Bluey's remark).

The London encounters help Fidelma come to terms with her violent fantasies. In another conversation with "Bluey," in which he tells her that he saw himself as "dirt" in the eyes of those whom he looked at through a window in a restaurant in Barcelona and that "'In those moments I wanted to kill' [and asks] … have you ever wanted to kill, Fidelma?", she responds, "Yes," much to his surprise.[82] It's doubtless, crafted by O'Brien, as another of Fidelma's Dido moments. Dido is a woman, who (as Elena Ferrante observes) had been "consumed by mad love," only to end up (after being abandoned by Aeneas) being turned from "the happy woman" into one "furious and raging," in a city she sees "distinguished by hatred and revenge."[83] However, unlike Dido who spills her own blood, Fildema has swapped her city for a London she experiences as redemptive, a place where she can heal herself and overcome her rage. To follow Fidelma's London sojourn is to be encouraged to observe "what is formidable about women" as Ferrante puts it in remarks that capture the significance of what O'Brien achieves in her construction of her protagonist:

> It's a short-cut to set aside what is formidable about women, to imagine us merely as organisms with good feelings, skilled master of gentility....but those who create literature have to make hostility, aversion, and fury visible, along with generous sentiments. It's their task, they have to dig inside, describe women from close up, feel that they are there, Aeneas or no Aeneas, Theseus or no Theseus.[84]

Ultimately, Fidelma's successful work on herself, aided by those who befriend her in London, enables her not only to return "home" (as a comfortably self-regarding subject), but also to confront Karadžić in The Hague with a fortitude she had lacked when he seduced and abandoned her in Cloonoila. That same kind of fortitude was very much needed by Jessica Stern, who had to ward off Karadžić's attempt to use his "energy healing" tactics on her when she spent 48 hours with him in preparation for writing a Karadžić bio-ethnography. "There were several times during our discussion," she writes, "that Radovan Karadžić wanted to demonstrate his skill at bioenergetic healing."[85] Stern's interviews with Karadžić (meeting him at one point in the "conjugal" room where O'Brien stages Fidelma's Karadžić encounter) and with those who know him (relatives among others) form the basis of her book *My War Criminal: Personal Encounters with an Architect of Genocide*.[86] The Karadžić whom she encounters is astonishingly like the one O'Brien invents, especially the way he emerges as Stern rehearses a struggle between a man bent on exercising dominance and a strong woman able to resist it. I turn here to Stern's account, not only to validate O'Brien's incisive political insights into a genocidal mentality (and how to confront it), but also to assess the similarity between two literary practices, fictional and ethnographic.

Literary Dramas

The political drama that O'Brien stages, in which forms of violence and types of victims are equated, takes place in a novelistic theater of repetition, which (as Gilles Deleuze suggests) "is opposed to the theater of representation."[87] Rather than merely representing types of characters and their entanglements, in O'Brien's "thinking *as* theater,"[88] many of the scenes she stages mimic, while re-inflecting, earlier scenes. For example, during the novel's treatment of London, an immigrant family is shaken when a "huge stone" is hurled through their front window as they are preparing their dinner.[89] Several pages later, it is noted that "the stone" in Fidelma's heart has been softened as a result of her encounters with some of London's immigrants.[90] What is achieved with such repetitions is an "intensification

[and] dramatization of events,"[91] which provide the reader with a challenging thinking space rarely available in chronologically organized nonfictional writing genres. Although O'Brien herself is off-stage, throughout the drama aspects of her autobiography provide templates for Fidelma's self-fashioning during her London stay. O'Brien is also a "country girl," whose self-making was liberated and intensified after she moved to London. As she puts it, "It was in London that I would find both the freedom and the incentive to write."[92]

In contrast, Stern is a player *within* her ethnography of Karadžić. That she has self-consciously written herself into the drama is immediately apparent in the "*My*" of her title. For purposes of comparison, like novels ethnographies are literatures. As such, those who compose them have to face "what it means to convey something" (e.g., in the translation of "field notes" into a written investigation) by being sensitive to "the density of certain words [and] turns of phrase…[in order] to produce worlds of life, worlds of thought, through a convergence with the literary and the lived, the philosophical and the aesthetic."[93] What distinguishes ethnographies from "avowed" fictional genres (e.g., O'Brien's novel) is that they are "unavowed" fictions. That binary is articulated by Jacques Rancière, who points out,

> 'fiction' is not restricted to the invention of imaginary things…avowed fiction… is the laboratory where fictional forms are experimented as such and which, for that reason, helps us understand the functioning of the forms of unavowed fiction at work in politics social science or other theoretical discourses. It does so because it is obliged to construct what is at the heart of any fictional rationality but easily can be presupposed in the forms of unavowed fiction: time, which means the form of coexistence of facts that defines a situation and the mode of connection between events that defines a story.[94]

Similarly, as regards the specifics of a comparison between a novel and an ethnography, "literature," as Didier Fassin points out, "is not the only domain claiming to capture life. Anthropology, and to some degree, the other social sciences share the same project…writers share ethnographers' endeavor to 'life and words'."[95] Accordingly, as Jessica Stern solicited the relationship between Karadžić's life and words, the character that emerges looks very like the one that O'Brien invents. "People like Radovan," she discovers, "become two people: their original personality – their true self – and the heroic personality they create."[96]

Jessica Stern's Story

As Walter Benjamin investigated an extravagant and rich artistic genre, German tragic drama, he reports that he had to strive to preserve his objectivity by practicing an "ascetic apprenticeship" in order to be able "to take in the whole panorama and yet remain in control of oneself."[97] Describing the challenge of *her* "ascetic apprenticeship," Stern recounts a moment in her 48 hours of conversation with Karadžić (in Scheveningen Prison between October 8, 2014 and November 11, 2016) when she

> saw from his eyes that he had recovered the upper hand…in the brief moment I had let down my guard, he had figured out one of the few tributes coming from him, that would mean something to me. He would repeat the phrase, "You're scaring me,", many times…But as soon as I realized he was trying to flatter me, "You're scaring me" became a useless weapon in his arsenal of seduction.[98]

She realizes ultimately that at no point should she relax her guard – for example on two occasions when he unexpectedly calls her on the phone, catching her unprepared, "unclothed," she says, "of my usual emotional armor." She then observes, "Until now I hadn't realized I needed to gird myself in order to speak with him."[99] Summing up the nature of the struggle she was undergoing in their face-to-face interactions, she writes,

> Both of us were locked up, together on the project of my learning about him…my challenge over time, was to surprise him, even surpass him…on the surface, we were polite. But if I examine myself closely, I realize that on a deeper level, we were like two animals fighting for our lives.[100]

Here Stern is acknowledging that despite the struggle between them for control, there's a sense in which they profoundly converge. As they participate in a contentious struggle, they both do so as divided subjects. As is the case with the encounter between Fidelma and "Dr.Vlad" in O'Brien's novel, Stern finds herself staging a play of identity/difference. Despite her attempt to abject the man she sees as a "psychopath,"[101] i.e., to place him within a singularly evil frame, Stern discovers that she shares an aspect of his mentality. While it becomes clear that she is dealing with a divided subject, one who was capable of "instantly mutating his personality and mood to suit the needs of the moment,"[102] she becomes privy to her own division. She recognizes that Karadžić was "forcing two parts of myself that normally operate on separate tracks to come into contact, to scrape against each other, to omit dangerous sparks."[103]

With her frequent remarks about moments of self-recognition, which punctuate the interview with Karadžić as it proceeds, it becomes evident to Stern (and her reader), that her ethnography of Karadžić's life and fate is also an autoethnography. While O'Brien articulates the condition of a becoming subject, contending with a cynically manipulative adversary, through her aesthetic subject, Fidelma, Stern is her own becoming subject. She shares the condition that Bakhtin ascribes to novelists: "Authors are open to themselves by seeing themselves as 'unconsummated,' as subjects who are always becoming, who are axiologically yet-to-be."[104]

Apart from what she learns about herself, while forced to develop an attentively self-conscious persona as she confronts a "formidable" subject/adversary, one able to "present himself, even to close observers, as holding different views from one day to the next," a "chameleon"[105] (as described by Robert Donia, a historian testifying at the trial), Stern is privy to critical insights into Karadžić's personality. Those insights are articulated in a narrative thread that relies on other observers, passed on in departures from her accounts of her meetings with Karadžić. Among what stands out analytically is an observation she quotes from a former Karadžić medical colleague, Dr. Angel, about the gap between the man who is rightly seen as the war criminal and is accordingly sentenced to a 40-year jail term and Karadžić's own self-understanding. Turning to literary exemplars, Dr. Angel says,

> Here is my take on who he was and how he became a Byronic hero, a Siegfried. When I knew him as a young doctor, he was still in the process of forming the heroic myth. He was not yet the Hero he became. He was already a poet in the public eye. But that was part of promoting the myth – but not yet being the hero of action.

Stern picks up the hero framing with a historical exemplar (to which she frequently turns in her account), Prince Lazar, a medieval Serbian ruler who created a powerful Serbian state: "To us he's a war criminal. But he views himself as a mythic hero, He feels that his trial was actually a trial of the Serbian people. He is a martyr for Serbia. Like Prince Lazar."[106] So, while for O'Brien Karadžić is modeled as Young Törless, for Stern, he's Prince Lazar. Whatever may be the best way to frame Karadžić's mentality, while his body is more or less locked up and immobilized – the result of legal justice – the framing of Karadžić as a mentality and the implications of that mentality's violent performativity always will-have-been; they remain open from the point of view of literary justice.

Justice Is Never Done

It is questionable, even from a legal point of view, whether the judgment of a court delivers justice. As Giorgio Agamben points out, "As jurists well know, law is not directed toward the establishment of justice...Law is solely directed toward judgment."[107] That observation is affirmed in a fictional version of the trial of another convicted war criminal from Balkan's wars, Tihomir Blaškić (a general who served in the Croatian Bosniak War), In his novel *Zone*, Mathias Énard invents a trial scene from the point of view of his protagonist, a reformed fighter, Mircovic, who had once served in a militia under *Blaškić's* command. Like Agamben, Mircovic sees a diremption between trials and justice.

Blaškić is in his box at The Hague among the lawyers the interpreters the prosecutors the witnesses the journalists the onlookers the soldiers of the UNPROFOR.... *Blaškić* in his box is one single man and has to answer for all our crimes, according to the principle of individual criminal responsibility which links him to history, he's a body in a chair wearing a headset, he is on trial in place of all those who held a weapon...[108]

Similarly, the O'Brien and Stern literary versions of Karadžić leave the question of justice open. To return to a consideration of the non-closural aspect of literary (as opposed to legal) justice, and apply it to the O'Brien and Stern texts, I want to again note Shoshana Felman's treatment of that binary, heeding especially the way she regards the trauma of victims as a "strange interruption...which the law tries to contain and translate...into legal-consciousness terminology."[109] It is evident, as Felman points out, that the law and trauma are on different temporal trajectories. Evoking one of the literary examples that O'Brien uses, Felman contrasts the O. J. Simpson's trial with the one in Tolstoy's *The Kreutzer Sonata*. While both are cases in which a husband has murdered his wife, there is a "striking" difference; "the husband in Tolstoy's work acknowledges his guilt, and is precisely telling us the story to explain not only why, but *how* he killed his wife."[110] With that contrast, Felman sorts the differences between a trial's and a literary text's conclusions and effects.

> A trial is presumed to be a search for truth, but, technically, it is a search for a decision, and thus, in essence, it seeks not simply truth but a finality: a force of resolution. In contrast, a literary text is a search for meaning, for expression, for heightened significance, and for symbolic understanding.[111]

Doubtless, Felman's juxtaposition of trials and trauma and her contrast between truth/finality-seeking and the search for meaning that she ascribes to literature apply well to Stern's literary (auto)ethnography. In her investigation, Stern's own bodily reactions effectively simulate the Karadžić effect. The temporal trajectory she provides for Karadžić's movement toward a conviction is continually interrupted by a different temporality, the process of her overcoming of what she describes as a traumatic "moral hazard," which imposes on her the task of keeping her "visceral responses" to herself, while facing the "impossible task involved [in] the effort to stay open to Karadžić's explication of why he behaved as he did."[112]

That dilemma imposed itself on another researcher inquiring into the mind and acts of a war criminal. In his investigation of the role of Nuon Chea, the man who presided over the torture killings of thousands in the infamous Tuol Sleng prison during the Cambodian genocide, Alvin Lim did his interview at Chea's home, having been invited to join him and his family for breakfast. Despite his "physical frailty," Lim writes, "this octogenarian, who is accused of the extermination of almost a third of Cambodia's population, terrified me." Lim reports that in the process of consuming a "delicious Sino-Khmer breakfast, my sense of fear clashed with but failed to kill, my gustatory enjoyment."[113] Then – as Deleuze suggests about one who must select among affects, which are "the dark precursors" of concepts[114] – Lim uses that clash to achieve a conceptual grasp of the meaning of the event. "My gustatory encounter with Nuon Chea – the very embodiment of Cambodia's recent memory of genocide – is an instance of the affective intersection of haptic space ['phenomenological space that the exterior senses constantly construct'] with places of memory." His search for meaning has him turning, he notes, to Deleuze and Guattari's "valorization of the haptic over the tactile" to explore that intersection.[115]

As for Stern's conceptual decision in her search for meaning (having selected among *her* clashing affects), it's assisted by Dr. Angel, who tells her, "He [Karadžić] felt obliged to be a killer because of fear." At that point the Karadžić mentality falls into place for Stern. "Now Karadžić's jumbled words come back to me," she says; "State of mind is very important…If one is presuming he will be killed he will kill."[116] Having thus fixed on fear as the extra-juridical part of the Karadžić puzzle, Stern proceeds to elaborate its relevance to her investigation. Observing that "The wars in Yugoslavia had not started with massacres. They started with someone talking about fear [and that]… Stoking fear is a powerful weapon," she repeats Karadžić's remark about someone who fears he will be killed may himself kill, and adds that "he knew how to drum up fear."[117] Subsequently, listening to Karadžić's rants about how "globalization" is a threat to "people [who] long for their own cultures," she becomes attuned to fear's structural element, which translates into the enmity that some threatened populations develop.[118] "Even worse than economic losses for people left behind by globalization are the losses of status and dignity" she suggests.[119] Those insights consummate Stern's search for meaning. Although O'Brien discloses a similar Karadžić, her literary effort works differently. It should *not* be construed as a *search* for meaning.

A Cinematic O'Brien

I want to suggest that in the case of O'Brien's novel we should heed what it does. In contrast with Stern's (auto)ethnography, what the novel does is create effects rather than search for meaning. To figure the contrast I want to recur to Deleuze's distinction between movement and time images. Although Deleuze patiently develops his view of the different kinds of image throughout his two volumes on cinema, a single remark on one page of *Cinema 2* sets up the analogy I want to stress. Discussing the film, *Story of a Love Affair*, he says it "exhibits a 'camera autonomy' when it stops following the movement of the characters or directing its own movement at them, to carry out constant reframings as functions of thought."[120] What that remark captures, as it refers to "reframings as functions of thought," applies well to O'Brien's *The Little Red Chairs*, which rather than searching for meaning thinks with the way it frames its narrative. Moreover, how and what it thinks invites another cinematic reference. The novel tracks very closely with the Stephen Frears film *Dirty Pretty Things* (2002), which is set in London and, as in Part Two of *The Little Red Chairs*, treats moments of solidarity among an immigrant population, many of whom, are "night people" who are exploitable because they work illegally. Early in the film, one of them, Juliette (Sophie Okonedo), a sex worker who meets her clients in the hotel at night, says that she "doesn't exist." Similarly, Fidelma's "night person" friend, Bluey, says to her (after she's denied something at work), "Look, forget it….as a night cleaner you are supposed to be invisible. You do not exist as a person."[121]

Bluey's remark applies to many of the precarious lives that are present in Frears's film. Juxtaposing haves and have nots in contemporary London, *Dirty Pretty Things* dwells on the difference between touristic central London and its more impoverished, immigrant-inhabited South London area. As a drama, the film has two of the have nots threatened to have their illegal status exposed unless they cooperate in an illegal organ harvesting and selling enterprise. Like Fidelma and her co-workers in O'Brien's novel. Frear's protagonists, the threatened refugees, Okwe (Chiwektel Ejiofor) a Nigerian Doctor and Senay (Audrey Tautou) a Turkish hotel worker, support each other. With the help of a group of marginalized people – the sex worker Juliette, a doorman from somewhere in Eastern Europe, and a Chinese immigrant who works in a morgue – they become transformed from victims into effective political subjects. Assisted by his friends, rather than extracting Senay's kidneys in exchange for passports, Okwe drugs the organ trade entrepreneur (the hotel manager Senior Juan (Sergei Lopez)), harvests his kidney, sells it, and flees from London back to Nigeria while the emancipated Senay heads to New York.

However, while the film thinks primarily with images – its diverse parts of the London peoplescape is composed with what Andre Bazin calls "image-facts,"[122] – for example juxtaposing in its montage of scenes a richly ornate, tourist filled hotel lobby on the one hand and a sweat shop with immigrant labor, and a taxi business run by immigrants on the other – O'Brien's novel (its cinematic qualities notwithstanding) thinks with literary vehicles, with what Roland Barthes calls "word-thoughts."[123] In the Part Two, South London section, which features a recovering Fidelma, the novel has Fidelma leaving the *Aeneid's* Dido behind as "the [aforementioned] stone in her heart" begins to "soften."[124] Her emergence as an emotionally fortified, confident self is reflected in the poetry to which she is exposed through an "aesthetic sociality."[125] She and a male friend ("A man called James"[126]) share a growing familiarity with the poetry of "John Clare, John Keats, Wallace Stevens, Elizabeth Bishop, Marianne Moore and many another." Edified and strengthened by poetic reflections on the vagaries of life, especially the precarities women face, O'Brien references them with lines from a Wallace Steven's poem:

> *O thin men of Haddam,*
> *"Why do you imagine golden birds?*
> *Do you not see how the blackbird*

Walks around the feet
Of the women about you[127]

Fidelma brings her poetry-strengthened emotional armor to her final encounter with Karadžić. She arrives at The Hague embodying a counter-poesis. Rather than asking what the novel means the reader is witness to something it does; it composes an event in which an erstwhile victim has become discursively empowered.

Notes

1 From the opening leaf of Edna O'Brien, *The Little Red Chairs* (New York: Little, Brown and Company, 2015).
2 Radovan Karadzic interviewed in *Oslobodjenje*, 2 October 1990, quoted in Gerard Toal and Adis Maksic, "'Serbs, You Are Allowed to be Serbs!' Radovan Karadzic and the 1990 Election Campaign in Bosnia-Herzegovina," *Ethnopolitics* 13: 3 (2014), 267.
3 Slavoj Žižek, "The Military-Poetic Complex," *London Review of Books* 10: 16 (August 14, 2008), on the web at: www.lrb.co.uk/the-[a[er/v30/n16.
4 Quoted in *Ibid.*
5 The quotation is from Jay Surdukowski, "The Sword and the Shield: The Uses of Poetry at the War Crimes Trial of Radovan Karadzic, the Poet-Warrior," *Law and Literature* 31: 3 (2019), 334.
6 Cited in Michael J. Shapiro, "Bosnian Blues," *Peace Review* 24: 4 (2012), 491.
7 I have analyzed their writing previously: Michael J. Shapiro, "Go West, Go East: War's Exilic Subjects," *Security Dialogue* 44: 4 (2013), 315–329.
8 Aleksandar Hemon, *Nowhere Man* (New York: Vintage, 2002), 41.
9 The quoted expression belongs to Anand Pandian and Stuart McClean, "Prologue" to *Crumpled Paper Boat: Experiments in Ethnographic Writing* (Durham, NC: Duke University Press, 2017), 8.
10 *Ibid.*, 5.
11 The quotation belongs to James Wood, "Stranger In Our Midst: A War Criminal Rusicates in Edna O'Brien's 'The Little Red Chairs," *The New York Times Magazine*, April 25, 2016, on the web at: www.newyorker.com/magazine/2016/04/25/edna-obriens-the-little-red-chairs.
12 Jack Hite, Radovan Karadzic's New-Age Adventure, *The New York Times* July 26, 2009, on the web at: www.nytimes.com/2009/07/26/magazine/26karadzic-t.html.
13 I am quoting an expression I use in an earlier study: Michael J. Shapiro, *Violent Cartographies: Mapping Cutlures of War* (Minneapolis: University of Minnesota Pres, 1997), xi.
14 Michael J. Shapiro, *War Crimes, Atrocity, and Justice* (Cambridge, UK: Polity, 2015), 41. The inner quotations are from Shoshana Felman, *The Juridical Unconscious: Trials and Traumas of the Twentieth Century* (Cambridge, MA: Harvard University Press, 2002), 8.
15 Gillian Slovo, *Red Dust* (New York: W.W. Norton, 2000), 184–185.
16 Shapiro, *War Crimes, Atrocity, and Justice*, 171.
17 O'Brien, *The Little Red Chairs*, 43.
18 *Ibid.*, 274–275.
19 *Ibid.*, 290–291.

20 See M. M. Bakhtin, "Author and Hero in Aesthetic Activity," in *Art and Answerability*, trans V. Liapunov (Austin: University of Texas Press, 1990), 42–56.

21 M. M. Bakhtin, *Problems of Dostoevsky's Poetics* trans. Caryle Emerson (Minneapolis: University of Minnesota Press, 1984). 203.

22 O'Brien, *The Little Red Chairs*, 293.

23 *Ibid.*, 297.

24 The expression belongs to James Wood, "Stranger In Our midst: A War Criminal Rusticates in Edna O'Brien's The Little Red Chairs," *The New Yorker* April 25, 2016, on the web at: www.newyorker.com/magazine/2016/04/25/edna-obriens-the-little-red-chairs.

25 Ammiel Alcalay, "Translator's Introduction to Semezdin Mehmedinovic, *Sarajevo Blues*, trans Ammiel Alcalay (San Francisco: City Lights, 1998), xii.

26 Mehmedinovic, *Sarajevo Blues*, 107.

27 The quotation is from Roger M. Hayden, "Imaged Communities and Real Victims: Self-determination and Ethnic Cleansing in Yugoslavia, "*American Ethnologist* 23: 4 (November, 1996), 784.

28 Mehmedinovic, *Sarajevo Blues*, 110.

29 *Ibid.*, 10.

30 *Ibid.*, 90.

31 Alcalay, "Translator's Introduction" xv.

32 Mehmedinovic, *Sarajevo Blues*, 23.

33 The quotations are from Michèle Richman's "Foreword" to Réda Bensmaïa, *The Barthes Effect: The Essay as Reflective Text*, trans. Pat Fedkiew (Minneapolis: University of Minnesota Pres, 1987), xx.

34 The term belongs to M. M. Bakhtin, which he ascribed to novels in general. See his "Discourse and the Novel," in *The Dialogic Imagination*, trans. Michael Holqvist (Austin: University of Texas Press, 1981), 259–422.

35 O'Brien, *The Little Red Chairs* – citing *The Mountain Wreath* (Serbian Saga), in a front leaf of the book.

36 Ibid., 3–4.

37 Michael J. Shapiro, *Deforming American Political Thought: Challenging the Jeffersonian Legacy* Second Edition (London: Routledge, 2016), 5. The inner quotation is from Pascal Bonitzer, "Hitchcockian Suspense," in Slavoj Žižek ed. *Everything You Wanted to Know About Lacan…But Were Afraid to Ask Hitchcock* (New York: Verso, 1992), 23.

38 O'Brien, *The Little Red Chairs*, 3–4.

39 Quotations are from Ronnie Scheib's reading of the film, "Charlie's Uncle," *Film Comment* 12: 2 (March/April 1976), 56.

40 For insight into the doubling effects in the film, see Donald Spoto, *The Art of Alfred Hitchcock* (New York: Doubleday, 1976), 119.

41 The quotations are from David Sterrett, *The Films of Alfred Hitchcock* (New York: Cambridge University Press, 1993), 74.

42 O'Brien, *The Little Red Chairs*, 75.

43 *Ibid.*, 5.

44 *Ibid.*

45 *Ibid.*, 7.

46 *Ibid.*

47 Karadzic poems, on the web at: www.pbs.org/wgbh/pages/frontline/shows/karadzic/radovan/poems.html.

48 The sociolect term is Bakhtin's in "Discourse and the Novel."

49 O'Brien, *The Little Red Chairs*, 11.

50 *Ibid.*, 109.

51 *Ibid.*, 9.

52 *Ibid.*, 249.

53 Jacques Rancière, *The Future of the Image* trans. G Elliot (New York: Verso, 2007), 55.

54 *Ibid.*, 53.

55 O'Brien, *The Little Red Chairs*, 20.

56 By moral economy I am referring to inhibitions about what kinds of commodities and what kinds of merchandising are regarded as are morally appropriate. I analyze and explicate moral economy in Michael J. Shapiro, "The Moralized Economy in Hard Times," *Theory & Event* 14: 4 (December, 2011).

57 *Ibid.*, 28.

58 *Ibid.*, 35.

59 *Ibid.*, 65.

60 Reported in Jessica Stern, *My War Criminal: Personal Encounters with an Architect of Genocide* (New York: HarperCollins, 2020), 112.

61 *Ibid.*, 67.

62 *Ibid.*

63 *Ibid.*, 70.

64 That binary is mentioned in Diane Hoeveler, "Inventing the Gothic Subject: Revolution, Secularization, and the Discourse of Suffering," in Larry H. Peer ed. *Romanticism and the Idea of Individualism* (Provo, UT: International Conference on Romanticism, 2002), 5–16.

65 *Ibid.*, 71.

66 Alan Pryce-Jones, "Preface" to Robert Musil, *Young Törless*, trans. Elthne Wilkins and Ernst Kaiser (New York: Noonday Press, 1958), vi.

67 Musil, *Young Törless*, 28.

68 Robert Musil, *The Confusions of Young Törless*, trans. Shaun Whiteside (New York: Penguin, 2001).

69 Hoeveler, "Inventing the Gothic Subject, 6.

70 For an analysis that ascribes a "holy war" view to Karadzic's mobilization of Serbian nationalists, see Marcus Tanner, "Karadzic's 'Holy War,'" *The Guardian* 3/2/2010, on the web at: www.theguardian.com/commentisfree/belief/2010/mar/02/karadzic-holy-war-bosnia.

71 O'Brien, *The Little red Chairs*, 79.

72 *Ibid.*, 90.

73 *Ibid.*, 101.

74 *Ibid.*, 102.

75 *Ibid.*, 215.

76 I am borrowing the expression, "referential montage" from an analysis of Stanley Kubrick's film *Barry Lyndon* by John Engel, "*Barry Lyndon*, a Picture of Irony," *Eighteenth Century Life* 19 (1995), 83–88.

77 Joyce Carol Oates, "'The Little Red Chairs,' by Edna O'Brien," *The New York Times.* March 28, 2015, on the web at: www.nytimes.com/2016/04/03/books/review/the-little-red-chairs-by-edna-obrien.html.

78 O'Brien, *The Little Red Chairs*, 175.

79 *Ibid.*, 173.

80 There's a complex sexuality associated with the vampiric in Stoker's *Dracula*. His Count's bite tends to "cancel out" gender difference, and he is as possessive of males as he is of females. See Nancy Armstrong's reading in her chapter, "The Necessary Gothic" in *How Novel's Think* (New York: Columbia University Press, 2006), 137–186.

81 Michael J. Shapiro, The Politics of Globalization," in *Cinematic Political Thought* (Edinburgh, UK: Edinburgh University Press, 1999), 120.

82 O'Brien, *The Little Red Chairs*, 172.

83 Elena Ferrante, *Frantumaglia: A Writer's Journey*, trans. Ann Goldstein (New York: Europe Editions, 2016), 150.

84 *Ibid.*, 152.

85 Jessica Stern, "Why Did I Let a Convicted War Criminal Practice Energy Healing on Me?: My 48 hours with Radovan Karadzic," *The New York Times*, January 16, 2020, on the web at: www.nytimes.com/2020/01/16/opinion/sunday/radovan-karadzic.html.

86 Stern, *My War Criminal: Personal Encounters with an Architect of Genocide*.

87 Gilles Deleuze, *Difference and Repetition* trans. Paul Patton (New York: Columbia University Press, 1994), 10.

88 I am borrowing that expression from Mark D. Jordan, "Foucault's Philosophical Theaters," in Tony Fisher and Kelina Gotman eds. *Foucault's Theaters* (Manchester, UK: Manchester University Press, 2020), 27.

89 O'Brien, *The Little Red Chairs*, 162.

90 *Ibid.*, 185.

91 Jordan, "Foucault's Philosophical Theaters," 31.

92 Edna O'Brien, *Country Girl: A Memoire* (New York: Back Bay Books, 2012), 138.

93 The quotation is from the "Introduction," to *Crumpled Paper Boat*, 13.

94 Jacques Rancière, "Fictions of Time," In Grace Hellyer and Julian Murphet eds. *Rancière and Literature* (Edinburgh: Edinburgh University Press, 2016), 1.

95 Didier Fassin, "True Life, Real Lives: Revisiting the Boundaries Between Ethnography and Fiction," *American Ethnologist* 41: 1 (2014), 41.

96 Stern, *My War Criminal*, 61.

97 Benjamin, *The Origins of German Tragic Drama* trans. John Osborne (London: Verso, 1998), 56.

98 Stern, *My War Criminal*, 54.

99 *Ibid.*, 195.

100 *Ibid.*, 197.

101 *Ibid.*, 271.

102 *Ibid.*, 111.

103 *Ibid.*, 197.

104 M. M Bakhtin, "Author and Hero in Aesthetic Activity," in *Art and Answerability* trans. V. Liapunov (Austin: University of Texas Press, 1990), 13.

105 Stern, *My War Criminal*, 111.

106 *Ibid.*, 211.

107 Giorgio Agamben, *Remnants of Auschwitz: The Witness and the Archive*, trans. Daniel Heller-Roazen (New York: Zone Books, 2002), 18.

108 Mathias Énard. *Zone* trans. Charlotte Mandell (Rochester, NY: Open Letter, 2010), 72–73.

109 Felman, *The Juridical Unconscious*, 5.

110 *Ibid.*, 54.

111 *Ibid.*, 54–55.

112 Stern, *My War Criminal*, 195.
113 Alvin Cheng-Hin Lim, "Breakfast with the Dictator," *Theory & Event* 13: 4 (2010).
114 Gilles Deleuze, "Spinoza and the Three Ethics," in *Essays Critical and Clinical*, trans. Daniel W. Smith and Michael A. Greco (Minneapolis: University of Minnesota Press,1997), 144.
115 *Ibid.*
116 *Ibid.*, 211.
117 Stern, *My War Criminal*, 240–241.
118 *Ibid.*, 244.
119 *Ibid.*, 245.
120 Gilles Deleuze, *Cinema 2: The Time Image* trans. Hugh Tomlinson and Robert Galeta (Minneapolis: University of Minnesota Press, 1989), 24.
121 O'Brien, *The Little Red Chairs*, 220–221.
122 See Andre Bazin, "An Aesthetic of Reality: Cinematic Realism and the Italian School of liberation," in *What is Cinema*, trans. Hugh Gray (Berkley: University of California Press, 1971).
123 See Roland Barthes, *Roland Barthes by Roland Barthes*, trans. Richard Howard (New York: Hill and Wang, 1977).
124 O'Brien, *The Little Red Chairs*, 185.
125 I am borrowing that expression from Fred Moten, who refers to "the aesthetic sociality of blackness" in his *Black and Blur* (Durham, NC: Duke University Press, 2017), 275.
126 O'Brien, *The Little Red Chairs*, 231.
127 *Ibid.*, 241.

Bibliography

Agamben, Giorgio (2002) *Remnants of Auschwitz: The Witness and the Archive*, trans. Daniel Heller-Roazen, New York: Zone Books.

Alcalay, Ammiel (1998) 'Translator's Introduction' to Semezdin Mehmedinovic, *Sarajevo Blues*, trans Ammiel Alcalay, San Francisco: City Lights, pp. xi–xvii.

Armstrong, Nancy (2006) 'The Necessary Gothic' in *How Novel's Think*, New York: Columbia University Press, pp. 137–186.

Bakhtin, M. M. (1981) 'Discourse and the Novel,' in *The Dialogic Imagination*, trans. Michael Holqvist, Austin: University of Texas Press, (1981), 259–422.

Bakhtin, M. M. (1984) *Problems of Dostoevsky's Poetics* trans. Caryle Emerson, Minneapolis: University of Minnesota Press.

Bakhtin, M. M. (1990) 'Author and Hero in Aesthetic Activity,' in *Art and Answerability*, trans. V. Liapunov, Austin: University of Texas Press, pp. 42–56.

Barthes, Roland (1977) *Roland Barthes by Roland Barthes*, trans. Richard Howard, New York: Hill and Wang.

Bazin, Andre (1971) 'An Aesthetic of Reality: Cinematic Realism and the Italian School of Liberation,' in *What is Cinema*, trans. Hugh Gray, Berkeley: University of California Press.

Benjamin, Walter (1998) *The Origins of German Tragic Drama*, trans. John Osborne, London: Verso.

Bensmaïa, Réda (1987) *The Barthes Effect: The Essay as Reflective Text*, trans. Pat Fedkiew, Minneapolis: University of Minnesota Press.

Bonitzer, Pascal (1992) 'Hitchkockian Suspense,' in Slavoj Žižek ed. *Everything You Wanted to Know About Lacan…But Were Afraid to Ask Hitchcock*, New York: Verso.

Deleuze, Gilles (1989) *Cinema 2: The Time Image*, trans. Hugh Tomlinson and Robert Galeta, Minneapolis: University of Minnesota Press.

Deleuze, Gilles (1994) *Difference and Repetition*, trans. Paul Patton, New York: Columbia University Press.

Deleuze, Gilles (1997) 'Spinoza and the Three Ethics', in *Essays Critical and Clinical*, trans. Daniel W. Smith and Michael A. Greco, Minneapolis: University of Minnesota Press, pp. 138–151.

Énard, Mathias (2010) *Zone*, trans. Charlotte Mandell, Rochester, NY: Open Letter.

Engel, John (1995) '*Barry Lyndon*, a Picture of Irony,' *Eighteenth Century Life* No. 19, pp. 83–88.

Fassin, Didier (2014) 'True Life, Real Lives: Revisiting the Boundaries Between Ethnography and Fiction,' *American Ethnologist* Vol. 41 (1), pp. 40–55.

Felman, Shoshana (2002) *The Juridical Unconscious: Trials and Traumas of the Twentieth Century*, Cambridge, MA: Harvard University Press.

Ferrante, Elena (2016) *Frantumaglia: A Writer's Journey*, trans. Ann Goldstein, New York: Europe Editions.

Fisher, Tony and Gotman, Kelina eds. (2020). *Foucault's Theaters: Idols of the Odeons*, Manchester, UK: Manchester University Press.

Hayden, Roger M. (1996) 'Imaged Communities and Real Victims: Self-determination and Ethnic Cleansing in Yugoslavia,' *American Ethnologist* Vol. 23 (4), pp. 783–801.

Hemon, Aleksandar (2002) *Nowhere Man* (New York: Vintage).

Hite, Jack (2009) 'Radovan Karadzic's New-Age Adventure,' *The New York Times*, on the web at: www.nytimes.com/2009/07/26/magazine/26karadzic-t.html.

Hoeveler, Diane (2002) 'Inventing the Gothic Subject: Revolution, Secularization, and the Discourse of Suffering' in Larry H. Peer ed. *Romanticism and the Idea of Individualism*, Provo, UT: International Conference on Romanticism, pp. 5–16.

Jordan, Mark D. (2020) "Foucault's Philosophical Theaters," in Tony Fisher and Fisher, Tony and Kelina Gotman, eds. *Foucault's Theaters: Idols of the Odeons*, Manchester, UK: Manchester University Press, pp. 25–37.

Karadzic, Radovan poems, on the web at: www.pbs.org/wgbh/pages/frontline/shows/karadzic/radovan/poems.html.

Lim, Alvin Cheng-Hin, 'Breakfast with the Dictator,' *Theory & Event* Vol. 13 (4), pp. 1–13.

Mehmedinovic, Semezdin (1998), *Sarajevo Blues*, trans. Ammiel Alcalay, San Francisco, City Lights.

Musil, Robert (2001) *The Confusions of Young Törless*, trans. Shaun Whiteside, New York: Penguin.

Moten, Fred (2017) *Black and Blur*, Durham, NC: Duke University Press.

Oates, Joyce Carol (2015) '"The Little Red Chairs", by Edna O'Brien,' *The New York Times*. on the web at: www.nytimes.com/2016/04/03/books/review/the-little-red-chairs-by-edna-obrien.html.

O'Brien, Edna (2012) *Country Girl: A Memoire*, New York: Back Bay Books.

O'Brien, Edna (2015) *The Little Red Chairs,* New York: Little, Brown and Company.

Pandian, Anand and McClean, Stuart (2017) "Prologue" to *Crumpled Paper Boat: Experiments in Ethnographic Writing,* Durham, NC: Duke University Press, pp. 1–10.

Pryce-Jones, Alan (1958) 'Preface' to Robert Musil, *Young Törless*, trans. Elthne Wilkins and Ernst Kaiser, New York: Noonday Press., pp. v–ix.

Rancière, Jacques (2007) *The Future of the Image*, trans. G Elliot, New York: Verso.

Rancière, Jacques (2016) 'Fictions of Time,' in Grace Hellyer and Julian Murphet eds. *Rancière and Literature* Edinburgh: Edinburgh University Press, pp. 1–19.

Scheib, Ronnie (1976) 'Charlie's Uncle,' *Film Comment* Vol 12 (2), pp. 55–62.

Shapiro, Michael J. (1997) *Violent Cartographies: Mapping Cultures of War*, Minneapolis: University of Minnesota Press.

Shapiro, Michael J. (1999) 'The Politics of Globalization,' in *Cinematic Political Thought*, Edinburgh, UK: Edinburgh University Press, pp. 82–135.

Shapiro, Michael J. (2011) 'The Moralized Economy in Hard Times,' *Theory & Event* Vol. 14: (4).

Shapiro, Michael J. (2012) 'Bosnian Blues,' *Peace Review* Vol. 24 (4), pp. 490–497.

Shapiro, Michael J, (2013) 'Go West, Go East: War's Exilic Subjects,' *Security Dialogue* Vol. 44(4), pp. 315–329.

Shapiro, Michael J. (2015) *War Crimes, Atrocity, and Justice*, Cambridge, UK: Polity.

Shapiro, Michael J. (2016) *Deforming American Political Thought: Challenging the Jeffersonian Legacy* Second Edition, London: Routledge.

Slovo, Gillian (2000) *Red Dust*, New York: W. W. Norton.

Spoto, Donald (1976) *The Art of Alfred Hitchcock*, New York: Doubleday.

Stern, Jessica (2020) 'Why Did I Let a Convicted War Criminal Practice Energy Healing on Me?: My 48 hours with Radovan Karadzic,' *The New York Times*, on the web at: www. nytimes.com/2020/01/16/opinion/sunday/radovan-karadzic.html.

Stern, Jessica (2020) *My War Criminal: Personal Encounters with an Architect of Genocide*, New York: HarperCollins.

Sterrett, David (1993) *The Films of Alfred Hitchcock*, New York: Cambridge University Press.

Surdukowski, Jay (2019) 'The Sword and the Shield: The Uses of Poetry at the War Crimes Trial of Radovan Karadzic, the Poet-Warrior,' *Law and Literature* Vol. 31 (3), pp. 333–355.

Tanner, Marcus (2010) 'Karadzic's "Holy War",' *The Guardian* on the web at: www. theguardian.com/commentisfree/belief/2010/mar/02/karadzic-holy-war-bosnia.

Toal, Gerard and Maksic, Adis (2014) '"Serbs, You Are Allowed to be Serbs!" Radovan Karadzic and the 1990 Election Campaign in Bosnia-Herzegovina,' *Ethnopolitics* Vol. 13(3), pp. 267–287.

Wood, James (2016) 'Stranger In Our Midst: A War Criminal Rusticates in Edna O'Brien's 'The Little Red Chairs,' *The New York Times Magazine*, April 25, 2016, on the web at: www.newyorker.com/magazine/2016/04/25/edna-obriens-the-little-red-chairs.

Žižek, Slavoj (2008) 'The Military-Poetic Complex,' *London Review of Books* Vol. 10 (16), on the web at: www.lrb.co.uk/the-paper/v30/n16/slavoj-zizek/the-military-poetic-complex.

2

SCRIPTING MENTALITY

Mentality as Event

The featured text in Chapter 1, Edna O'Brien's novel *The Little Red* Chairs, is a fictional rendering of a dangerous mentality. It figures personal styles and situations by turning to literary prototypes to illuminate the functioning of minds: the violence that some actualize, the susceptibilities of their victims, and the resiliencies the victims manage to evince. In this chapter I continue to pursue the way mentalities are conceived but within a broader range of literatures, addressed to a broader range of questions. Rather than asking only about what a dangerous mentality is and how it thinks – what its "inner footage" is like, as O'Brien's character, Fidelma McBride puts it – I also pursue questions about mentalities from the outside by locating them as a series of historical events in which they become objects of attention.

To elucidate the event question, I begin with reflections on Michel Foucault's brief inquiry into a notable moment in the management of "criminal danger," the entry into history of "the criminal." Foucault's approach to that new subject is initiated with quotations from a conversation in "the Paris criminal courts," where a man accused of five rapes and six attempted rapes between February and June, 1975 was being tried. While the accused remains virtually silent, the presiding judge questions him in an attempt to discover what he has (and has had) in mind: "Have you tied to reflect on your case"; "Why at twenty-two years of age do such violent urges overtake you"; "Why would you do it again?"[1] To situate the conversation in a critical historical frame, Foucault points to what is peculiar about the judge's questioning. Whereas up to the middle of the nineteenth century, there was no attempt to inquire into the mind of a perpetrator, – the courts concerned themselves only with crimes and penalties – "legal justice today has at least as much to do with criminals as with crimes."[2]

As the analysis proceeds, Foucault, without concerning himself with the clinical perspectives from which their questions are derived, calls attention to the presence of psychiatrists' testimony about the mentality of the accused. Whatever the psychiatrists' particular views of the unconscious might have been, what a critically oriented (genealogical) history concerns itself with is not the theories they embrace but their presence as knowledge agents in juridical space. Psychiatrists had become part of a complex apparatus serving a newly institutionalized *political* mentality, a "governmentality" whose biopolitical problem had shifted from the body of the sovereign to a newly recognized collective body, the "population."[3] The event, in short, is one in which criminal motives had become relevant and as a result, "Crime became an important issue for psychiatrists."[4] To summarize the critical significance of the event in historical terms, whereas law-breakers had once been targets of sovereign retaliation, they were now objects of knowledge (and bodies to reform rather than discard). The new character, the "criminal" had become a subject reflecting a new form of governance. To put Foucault's intervention grammatically, quite apart from questions about the nature of mentalities – a "what" question – is a "when" question, one about the circumstances of their becoming a concern. Those circumstances elicited a broad range of mentality-theorizing and produced apparatuses of surveillance.

In a follow-up remark, Foucault provides a threshold for introducing William James, whose vocation as a psychologist fit within the new governmentality. Foucault notes, "If psychiatry became so important in the nineteenth century, it was not simply because it applied a new medical rationality to mental or behavioral disorders, it was because it functioned as a sort of public hygiene," applied to a new target of governance, the social order.[5] By the mid to late nineteenth century, when James had decided to give up a career as an artist and enter medical school, the medical "gaze," a focus of Foucault's archaeological approach to medical perception, had shifted. The individual-focused art of the healer had been replaced by the teaching hospital. A science of health had turned medical perception into a "loquacious gaze,"[6] trained on the population as a whole. Accordingly, doctors had become part of the apparatus charged with maintaining public rather than merely individual health. By way of transition, I want to suggest that what Foucault calls "the birth of the clinic," was a condition of possibility for the (scientific) nature of William James's medical training.[7]

William James's Scripted Mentalities

When James decided to turn from medicine to psychology, he brought medicine's modern scientific mentality to his new vocation. Launching his monumental study, *Principles of Psychology*, he dedicated himself to the development of a pure science of the brain, albeit with an "epistemological humility"[8] (He said, for example, "the best mark of health that a science can show is [an] unfinished-seeming front").[9] Epistemological humility notwithstanding, James began his writing venture with a commitment to a pure, metaphysics-free science of the mind. "All attempts to explain our phenomenally generated thoughts as products of deeper lying entities [he includes 'soul,' 'transcendental ego,' 'ideas,' and 'elementary units of conscious'] are metaphysical."[10] "I have treated our passing thoughts," he says, "as integers, and regarded the mere laws of their coexistence with brain-states as the ultimate laws of our science."[11]

Nevertheless, during the writing process of his *Principles* James made two important discoveries that were recalcitrant to his scientific aspirations. First, despite his commitment to a science of mentality,

> after more than fourteen years of research and two thousand pages of psychological writings which fall ostensibly under the natural-scientific program, [he] confessed that he did not know what a mental state is [or]… what could count as a mental state.[12]

Second (which followed from the first), he became more of a philosophically oriented phenomenologist than a psychologist. As Bruce Wilshire points out, "Phenomenology enters *The Principles of Psychology* exactly at the point where the explicit program of the work [the scientific correlation of 'mental states with brain states'] breaks down."[13]

If not a science of mentality, how then should one characterize *Principles*? Certainly, the knowledge discipline in evidence as the text proceeds is more philosophical than psychological. However, what stands out are the text's rhetorical rhythms and figures of speech. The writing in *Principles*, "is charged with the kind of metaphor that strives to rescue consciousness from the somberly boring fact of its flatly existing in process."[14] Accordingly, the psychologist Wilhelm Wundt, whose writings had influenced James, famously remarked that James's *Principles* is a beautiful piece of literature and is not psychology. Of course, Wundt's presumption of an epistemic gulf between literature and science is belied by the histories of many scientific fields. It has been demonstrated, for example, that the epistemic cogency of Darwin's *The Evolution of the Species* is inextricably connected to his "plots"[15] And more generally, as "Gillian Beer has shown, [there is] a 'shared discourse' that allows ideas, metaphors, myths and narrative patterns to move 'rapidly and freely to and fro between scientists and non-scientists'."[16]

Nevertheless, Wundt was on to something in his reading of James's *Principles*. Throughout the text, James represents mentality with literary flourishes, rendering the mind with a wide variety of figures of speech. While all scientists and philosophers must write to publicize their work, James stands out as one who was unusually adept with figuration. For example, in his explication of his most famous psychological representation of the dynamics of mind, the "stream of consciousness," he turns to theatricality: "The mind is a kind of theatre, where several perceptions successively make their appearance, pass, repass, glide away and mingle in an infinite variety of postures and situations."[17] James was attentive as well to how to figure the writing process. Having trained to be a painter before he entered a medical curriculum and thence shifted to psychological science, career-wise he had turned from art to science but stylistically he never abandoned art. It is therefore unsurprising that he likens the compositional aspect of writing to the process of adding shape and color to a painter's canvass. "Philosophers," he says, "paint" their "views."[18]

Ultimately, James *writes* his way toward a view of mentality. He stages an encounter between compositions; his written composition engages the dynamic of cognitive composition he ascribes to mentality. The way James figures the writing process as a slowly developing artistic composition compares with the way Paul Cézanne created his canvasses, gradually adding "color difference, otherwise known as color interval [to] build the space."[19] James's literary (and painterly) construction of the dynamics of mentality is a creative and compelling "unavowed" fiction, which compares structurally with the "avowed" fictional approach to mentality of one of his contemporaries, Robert Musil, who also stages a compositional encounter, in his case with a novel that creates a mentality-world engagement within a subjunctive ontology (a commitment to yet unrealized possibilities).[20]

My turn to Musil's most famous work, *Der Mann ohne Eigenschaften / The Man Without Qualities* (hereafter *Qualities*), is intended once again to address a "when," question, which complements the "what" questions with which the novel is concerned. Musil renders mentality as a historically shaped event as well as a nuanced, eloquently figured philosophy of mind. His *Qualities* is a novel that thinks both with its plot and with the meta-commentary with which a third person narrator interprets the scenes and events.

Musil's "Hero of the Mind"[21]

What distinguishes literary fiction is the fact that the reality of the situations and the linkage of the events cannot be supposed to be already known, that they are the object of an explicit construction.

Jacques Rancière, Fictions of Time

Whereas imaginative writing *does* often try to give shape to something that has never existed before, the essay tries to understand the implications of such shape – its latent structure. The essay reaches out for what lies behind the image.

György Lukács, On the Nature and the Form of the Essay

[T]his…essayistic novel…is the mode for depicting a mind so active that it nearly constitutes a character independent of the man whose mind it is.

Roger Kimball, The Qualities of Robert Musil

Two remarks by Maurice Blanchot capture the inter-articulation of essay and novel in Musil's *Qualities* (which Blanchot translates as *Particularities*). He sees the protagonist Ulrich, "The Man without particularities" as "not a hypothesis that is little by little embodied," but as "the opposite: a living presence that becomes a thought."[22] In the novel-as-essay, Ulrich, he says, becomes "a theory of himself."[23] The lack of "particularities" ascribed to Ulrich is by his estranged artist friend, Walter in a conversation with his (Walter's) romantic partner, Clarisse. Jealous of Ulrich's seeming appeal for Clarisse, Walter says,

> His appearance gives no clue to what his profession might be, and yet he doesn't look like a man without a profession either…He always knows what to do. He knows how to gaze into a woman's eyes. He can put his mind to any question at any time[24] He's a man without qualities…there are millions of them nowadays…It's the human type produced by our time.[25]

If we heed the German word for qualities, *Eigenschaften*, we can better appreciate Walter's "millions of them." As a man of his time, Ulrich is without his *own* qualities. However, Ulrich has a demeanor – cynical and ironic – if not a singular quality. The novel's "normative mentality"[26] matches that demeanor; "the mind of the work is precisely mind under the form of irony."[27] Ulrich's lack of his own qualities reflects a general malaise in response to a moment of flux in the nature of the ideational supports for coherent personhood. To summarize the historical moment, "Set in Vienna in 1913 [the novel] depicts a world on the edge of a precipice – the moral, cultural, political precipice that was to give way to the abyss of World War I the following year."[28] That lack of ideational stability is acknowledged by Ulrich: "He suspects that the given order of things is not as solid as it pretends to be; no thing, no self, no principle, is safe, everything is undergoing an invisible transformation."[29] Accordingly, he approaches that order from an ironic distance. At one point he says to himself,

> what was keeping him spellbound in this aloof and nameless way of life was nothing other than the compulsion to that loosening and binding of the world that is known by a word we do not care to encounter by itself: spirit or mind.[30]

To heed the phenomenology of Ulrich's encounter with his world, we have to recognize the way Musil lends the world itself a potential scripting force. The novel's form-as-essay does not construct mentality as a "function of a rarefied subjective consciousness"[31] but as an interaction of essays; "the world itself as an essay,"[32] i.e., the world as a reservoir of virtuality containing as yet unrealized possibilities, is engaged by mind-as-essay. However, the novel also consists in a meeting of *minds*, most pervasively as an inter-articulation between Musil's and Ulrich's. Ulrich, as Musil's "conceptual persona"[33] performs in the text as a series of "thought-events"[34] that animate Musil's ethico-political ontology. However, rather than wholly identifying with Ulrich, Musil stands in a "zone of proximity"[35] with him as well as other characters. While Musil's sensibility is articulated in part through that of his protagonist, the overall compositional structure of *Qualities* exceeds a simple author-protagonist connection. "Musil is linked anxiously to Ulrich,"[36] but Ulrich also shares his affective and thought worlds with other characters, those through whom his "impulses" play themselves out a "second time."[37]

Although there are several characters who perform a "second time," I want to focus on one, the carpenter Christian Moosbrugger, a sex murderer whose mentality arguably "represents the dark, unconscious viciousness and irrationalism" of the world Musil's novel is observing.[38] Moosbrugger, who shows no remorse for his violent acts, is effectively a repetition of Musil's Törless (the protagonist of his first novel, treated in Chapter 1), who is also "a product of his age." Törless's "darkness within"[39] anticipates the bifurcated mentalities in *Qualities.* However, apart from the nature of Moosbrugger's mentality is the mentality-scrutiny that he elicits. Moosbrugger, whose murders make him an object of psychiatric attention, is another instance of the "when" of mentality that Foucault elaborates in his analysis of criminal danger in the nineteenth century. Like the official reactions to Foucault's rapist, the Moosbrugger event represents the governmentality of Musil's contemporary age; he's a mind that must be understood rather than a body to be disposed of. However, unlike Foucault's silent rapist, Musil's perpetrator has a lot to say.

Moosbrugger's mentality is engaged as thoroughly by Musil as it is by the fictional psychiatrists charged with uncovering his motivations, albeit not within a psychological idiom. The Moosbrugger he invents doesn't deny his crimes; instead, he "wanted his deeds understood as the mishaps of an important philosophy of life."

> He hated no one as fervently as he hated psychiatrists who imagined they could dismiss his whole complex personality with a few foreign words... [and] never missed a chance to demonstrate in open court his own superiority over the psychiatrists, unmasking them as puffed up dupes and charlatans who knew nothing at all.[40]

Musil, with an expansive language that exceeds the reductive protocols of psychiatry, does not dismiss complexities. Like Foucault, he links the problem of Moosbrugger's case to the juridical practices it elicits. As the text puts it, "As always in such cases, the medical diagnoses of his mental condition fluctuated under the pressure of the superior world of juridical concepts."[41]

For Musil's compositional purposes, Moosbrugger therefore serves to affirm and double aspects of Ulrich's mentality. "Ulrich was especially taken with the fact that Mooseburger's defense was evidently based on some dimly discernible principle."[42]

His fascination with Moosbrugger's case activates him. Seeing Moosbrugger as part of the "invigorating fever [that] rose all over Europe (out of the becalmed mentality of the nineteenth century's last two decades")), Ulrich intercedes with a magistrate in behalf of leniency, arguing that "our penal code, dating from the middle of the last century, is outdated." The argument is to no avail, but the passage conveying the failure of his intervention gives rise to one of the novel's most enviable, metaphorically delivered moments:

> Just a few words, adroitly planted, can be as fruitful as rich garden loam, but in this place their effect was closer to that of a little clump of dirt one has inadvertently brought into the room on the sole of one's shoe.[43]

That sequence in the novel is part of Musil's ongoing theorization of language, an aspect of his essayistic style that is expressed by the oft-used words, possible and possibility. Alienated from the world in which the novel is situated, Ulrich is continually focused on a possible, yet unrealized world. Looking "upon the aesthetic as the ethical…since my youth…he wrote in his diary,"[44] Musil has the character Walter express his (and thus Ulrich's) ethically oriented subjunctive ontology:

> What he thinks of anything will always depend on some possible context – nothing is, to him, what it is; everything is subject to change, in flux, part of a whole, of an infinite number of wholes…So every answer he gives is only a partial answer, every feeling only an opinion, and he never cares what something is, only "how" it is [and one could appropriately add, "and what it *could* be"].[45]

Accordingly, Musil has Ulrich at one point lamenting the situation which, "in the course of time commonplace and impersonal ideas are automatically reinforced while unusual ideas fade away."[46] Thereafter, imagining how life *could* be figured, Musil evokes literary genres; could "a life's work…be imagined as consisting of three poems or three actions as of three treatises, in which the individual's capacity for achievement is intensified to its highest degree."[47] Living in continual "uncertainty," Ulrich recognizes that "uncertainty is sometimes nothing more than a mistrust of certainty" and thinks that "a conscious human essayism would face the task of transforming the world's haphazard awareness the into a will."[48] Ultimately, Musil's ethico-political task, expressed by Ulrich and some of the characters who second Ulrich's perspective (e.g., Arnheim,[49] who disparages those who, "with a single note muffle a thousand possibilities"[50]), is exemplified in a chapter heading: "Dethroning the Ideocracy."[51]

Musil's evocation of ideocracy underscores the ironic dimension of his text, which is concerned with the gap between ideology and reality. While Ulrich evinces empathy for the nonconformist Moosbrugger, who resides at the bottom of the society's status hierarchy, those at the top are targets of his irony, Count Leinsdorf especially. Director of a Parallel Campaign designed to celebrate Austria's exemplary role in global peace, the Count is part of a clueless aristocratic class whose practices represent the negation of Ulrich's/Musil's subjunctive ethos. It's an ethos succinctly expressed by Thomas Pynchon, who refers (in his novel *Mason & Dixon* treated in Chapter 3) to the way "subjunctive hopes" are effaced by the surveying task of Mason and Dixon, whose westward moving survey reduces "Possibilities to Simplicities that serve the ends to Governments."[52]

Attributing such a reduction to the mentality of Leinsdorf and his class, Ulrich represents him with caustic irony as a man who

> had never known "the people" in any other respect, except on Sundays and holidays, when they poured out from behind the scenery as a cheerful, colorful throng, like an opera chorus…Brought up in a religious and feudal spirit, never exposed to contradiction…he knew the outlook of more up-to-date people only from the controversies in Parliament or in the newspapers.[53]

The contrast Musil invents between Moosbrugger and Leinsdorf is central to the way he approaches a dangerous historical moment. Jane Smiley expresses it well:

> The chapters on Moosbrugger and Count Leinsdorf are contrasting masterpieces of empathy – on the one hand, with a murderer whose grasp of reality is utterly logical but scarily tenuous, on the other, with an aristocrat who has no idea what is going on in the nation he is responsible for.[54]

It becomes evident that Musil, who is writing in a world on the edge of disaster (the social alienation in the interwar period that leads to a welcoming of authoritarian messages that helped precipitate the second world war), views the mentality of a Leinsdorf as far more dangerous than that of a Moosbrugger. As he fashioned his novel, which is (to recur to Ulrich's words) "an essay [that], in the sequence of its paragraphs, explores a thing from many sides without wholly encompassing it,"[55] Musil nevertheless offers an ethical lesson that prepares us for an issue that many textual treatments of mentality subsequently explored, the susceptibility of Germany's and Austria's societies to the rise of Hitler's National Socialism. To pursue an analysis of some of them, I turn first to Kenneth Burke's, which begins with a statement of urgency on the appearance of Hitler's *Mein Kampf* (in translation). "Exasperating" and "nauseating though it is, [it] must be approached analytically," he says, "for it is written by a man who has 'swung a great people into his wake'."[56]

The Rhetorical Strategy of *Mein Kampf*

A bridge from Musil's *Quality* to Burke's "Rhetoric of Hitler's 'Battle'" is provided by the philosopher Johann Gottlieb Fichte. Inspired by Martin Luther's German translation of the bible, Fichte wrote a nationalistic treatise, *Addresses to the German Nation* (1808), in which he extols the development of a shared national mentality owed to the German language. Its "supersensuousness," he says, comprehends "the sum total of the sensuous mental life of the nation deposited in language…[which] proceeds from the whole previous life of the nation."[57] And he adds,

> What an immeasurable influence on the whole human development of a people the character of its language may have – its language, which accompanies the individual into the most secret depths of his/[her] mind…united within its domain in the whole mass…who speaks it into one common understanding.[58]

Musil treats Fichte's religious nationalism ironically, entering Fichte's book into a conversation associated with Count Leinsdorf's "Parallel Campaign." He inclines Leinsdorf's attention to Fichte's *Addresses* as his secretary reads a passage:

> To be freed from the original sin of sloth and the cowardice and duplicity that follow in its wake, men need models, such as the founders o the great religion actually were, to prefigure for them the enigma of freedom. The necessary teaching of moral conviction is the task of the church, whose symbols must be regarded not as homilies but only as the means of instruction for the proclamation of eternal verities.[59]

Thus inspired by an articulation of religious with nationalist sentiments, the Count proceeds to speculate about the aim of his "Campaign," the restoration of his country's honor among "the family of nations," after having lost its "place of eminence" because of a Prussian "Stab in the back," which had "thrust Austria down" (in 1866).[60]

Hitler's *Mein Kampf* is replete with the inter-articulation of religious and nationalist sentiments that Fichte's treatise initiated. As was the case with Leinsdorf's "Parallel Campaign," the occasion for Hitler's book was a national disgrace, in his case the one Germany experienced as a result of losing a war. However, in Hitler's text Germany's primary enemies are not the victors in World War I; they are within. On Burke's reading, Hitler's call to battle constructs an internal devil with a perverse mentality, Jewish economic cunning, which is juxtaposed to Aryan virtuous sacrifice; "The 'Aryan' is constructive; the Jew is 'destructive'."[61] Not an astute reader of the bible, "Hitler appeals by relying on a bastardization of fundamentally religious patterns of thought"[62] Nevertheless the "remnants of [his] personal library reveal a deep but erratic interest in religion and theology."[63] Fichte was one of Hitler's "philosophical enablers."[64] Although not embracing the virulent anti-Semitism that Hitler was to adopt, Fichte was adverse to giving those Jews, "who retained their religious identities and failed to assimilate," civil rights.[65] Whether or not Hitler read Fichte closely (the collected works were in his library), as one commentary puts it, "From Fichte, Hitler learned of German exceptionalism and nationalism."[66] In any case, *Mein Kampf* follows Fichte's textual strategy of articulating religion with nationalistic sentiments (albeit in his case with a "corrupt use of religious patterns"[67]). Hitler selects the aspects of "[c]hurch thought" that are concerned with "personality" in order to emphasize Christianity's commitment to a "moral betterment" that "elevates" the "Aryan" above the mentalities of "racially inferior groups" (e.g., "Jews" and "Negroes").[68]

Burke identifies an aspect of the text that likely generated its widespread influence. "Hitler," he suggests, "provided a 'world view' for people who had previously seen the world but piecemeal."[69] In his crime novel *Lucky You* (about a couple of bigoted scammers who plan to rob a lottery winner), Carl Hiaasen provides the same insight. As the two, Bode Gazzer a poacher, and Chub a counterfeiter are in conversation early in the novel, Bode provides Chub with what Hitler offers his readers; he helps Chub

> organize his multitude of hatreds into a single venomous philosophy.... [e.g.] "Oklahoma," Bode Gazzer said sharply, "and that was the government did it, to frame those two white boys. No, I'm talking 'bout a militia. Armed, disciplined and well-regulated, like it says in the Second Amendment."[70]

The influence of Gazzer on Chub and Hitler on his readers is well captured in Jean Paul Sartre's remark, "Words wreck havoc when they happen to name something that is experienced but is not yet named."[71] In the case of Hitler's *Mein Kampf*, however, Sartre's remark needs a supplement, a specification of the historical context that yielded the ideational susceptibilities of Hitler's readers (already noted above) and the rhetorical forms within which the words were embedded. Burke supplies those, most notably in what he discerns as the way Hitler develops spiritual – material connections; he "knows when to 'spiritualize' a material issue, and when to 'materialize' a spiritual one."[72] However, apart from what Burke identifies as the persuasive aspect of the text (what J. L Austin designates as "perlocutionary force"[73]), is Burke's conceptual contribution. He supplies "the event adequacy of theoretical discourse"[74] that C. Wright Mills called for during the emergence of National Socialism. Mills referred to the need "To time observations with thought so as to mate a decent level of abstraction with crucial happenings."[75]

Burke's essay achieves that precisely. However, his essay goes beyond mere theorizing; it's also a call to treat Hitler's scripted mentality as a dangerous event that must be both heeded and challenged. Given, he says, what we "learn from the Hitler's book,"[76] "our anti-Hitler Battle, is to find all available ways of making the Hitlerite distortions of religion apparent in order that the politicians of his kind in American are not able to perform a similar swindle."[77] Burke was prescient; there was a "similar swindle" underway by a politician of his kind, US President Donald Trump, an "aspirational fascist," as William Connolly puts it. He used Hitler's strategy, incitement of "fanatical intolerance against his own constituencies of choice: Muslims, Mexicans, the news media, feminists, African Americans, ecologists, the film industry, and the professorate."[78] And like Hitler, Trump engaged in "the repetition of Big Lies," which have consisted in his case in:

> The birther charge against Obama, the first African American president; the assertion to have seen "thousands of Muslims on TV celebrate 9/11 when there were no such celebrations; the campaign charge that the 2016 election was rigged; the false repetitio that he won by a landslide; the constant refrain that the media always lies about him; the persistent denial or deflection of Putin's election hacking…"[79]
>
> Subsequently, there was his biggest lie, that the election he lost, running for a second term, was stolen,

In the conclusion, I address a textual response to a prior swindle, Brian Massumi's analysis of the Bush Administration's post 9/11, color-coded terror alert system. Here I begin a transition from the literatures concerned with the expressed "inner footage" of a dangerous mind to some literatures – specifically Theodor W. Adorno et al.'s survey research approach to "authoritarian personalities" and Klaus Theweleit's psychoanalytic investigation of the texts containing "male fantasies" – concerned with minds that are susceptible to fascistic demagoguery.

"Theorizing in the Shadow of the Holocaust"[80]

In the Preface to Adorno et al.'s book, Max Horkheimer identifies the dangerous historical moment that has motivated the investigation:

> The central theme of the work is a relatively new concept – the rise of an anthropological species we call the authoritarian type of man. In contrast with the bigot of the older style he seems to combine the ideas and skills which are typical of a highly industrialized society with irrational or anti-rational beliefs. He is at the same time enlightened and superstitious, proud to be an individualist and in constant fear of not being like all the others, jealous of his independence and inclined to submit blindly to power and authority.[81]

The investigation is among other things an attempt at a *counter*-anthropology to challenge the Nazi ideational program, which contained a *perverse* anthropology.

In the aftermath of World War II as the international community sought to achieve an oppositional ideational coherence, various aspects of Nazi anthropology were targeted. One significant arena for the targeting developed during the Nuremberg trials. Because the Nazi death apparatuses were legitimated in part by anthropological concepts, based on hierarchical versions of human nature (e.g., Alfred Hoche's notorious gloss on "life unworthy of life"[82]), the Nuremberg war crimes trials sought to establish a counter-anthropology in order to create a collective victim/plaintiff. That subject turned out to be "humanity." What enabled the prosecution of the Nazi collaborators tried for war crimes was "the conceptual development of a notion of 'crimes against humanity'" (even though that new collective subject, "humanity as a whole," as an object of a crime fit uneasily within established legal discourse).[83]

The anthropological initiative that Horkheimer attributes to the Adorno et al. investigation also obliquely references Nazi anthropology. One perverse anthropological legitimation for the National Socialist racial laws was supplied by the psychologist E. R. Jaensch in his 1938 book, *Der Gegentypus* (The Anti-Type). Jaensch also referred to The Anti-Type as an S-Type, a "synaesthetic: one who enjoys concomitant sensation, a subjective experience from another sense that the one being stimulated, as in color hearing."[84] He viewed such types as characterized by "perceptual slovenliness," and as he "filled out his characterization of the S-Type more from his imagination than evidence," he added a political framing: "The S-Type would be a man with so-called 'liberal' views; one who ... would take childish wanton pleasure in being eccentric."[85] Jaensch invented a "contrasting personality," the "J-Type," a type that "made definite, unambiguous perceptual judgments and persisted in them [one who is] tough, masculine, firm... [and politically one who]...made a good Nazi Party member."[86]

At the outset Adorno et al. identify their target as an individual's "mentality," which they conceive as "a broad and coherent pattern...[which is] an expression of deep lying trends in his personality."[87] Their conception of mentality turns out to resemble Jaensch's J-Type, albeit scripted within a radically different political perspective. Their F-scale interview questions are designed to disclose a type dangerously susceptible to fascist appeals. In contrast with what Jaensch saw as a fascist-friendly mentality, their investigation is based on a counter-anthropological model, invented to promote a contrasting political agenda, one seeking to inhibit the flourishing of a Jaensch type. In short, what for Jaensch was a promising political type, scripted within his pseudo anthropology, was for Adorno et al. worrisome, one who could be recruited in authoritarian campaigns that disseminate bigotry and hatred.

Apart from the details of their method and the way they construed the content of the mentalities they sought to illuminate is Adorno et al.'s location in an ongoing historical event. Their scrutiny of the fascism-susceptible mentality participates in a scholarly history, which began in the early 1930's and extended into the 1960s as scholars began investigating the personality bases of susceptibility to fascist or, more generally, authoritarian appeals. Among those comparable to the approach of Adorno et al. are the investigations of Milton Rokeach and H. J. Eysenck, seeking to disclose "closed" versus "open" and "tough" versus "tender" minds respectively. Theirs, like Adorno et al.'s was part of the post–World War II attempts to understand how to intervene lest a Hitler event be repeated.[88]

However, *The Authoritarian Personality* investigation stands out for its explicit normative aims and its presumption that science might possibly save us. As Horkheimer notes, the authors of the Authoritarian Personality study were "imbued with the conviction that the sincere and systematic scientific eluci-dation of a phenomenon can contribute directly to an amelioration of the cul-tural atmosphere in which hatred breeds."[89] Nevertheless, as an investigation that looked intensively at individual mentalities, it did not adequately assess the "cultural climate" in which they developed, the historical moment that contains the structural fault lines within which cultural antagonisms emerge. With that concern in mind, I want to review briefly, Sven Ranulf's analysis of moral indignation, which is context-sensitive and exemplary among the early investigations aimed at understanding the interpersonal enmity that fueled Hitler's rise to power.

Ranulf begins with the question of why one finds a "disinterested demand" to punish people whose life styles and behaviors create no material "deprivation" for those making the demands.[90] Writing in the period of the rise of National Socialism in Germany, Ranulf refers to the "resentment of pious, thrifty, debt-ridden peasants at urban creditors bankers, atheists, and liberals," coupled with the reaction of psychologically impoverished lower middle class experien-cing a "recrudescence of the bitter memories of the lost war." In that context, fascists offered a "channel for the discharge of the long-accumulated aggressions of the many botched and bungled personalities who had flocked to the swas-tika banner."[91] Although he doesn't elaborate the culture war that was brewing in Weimar Germany, Ranulf, whose main focus is on how "in human societies [there is]…the more or less pronounced disposition to assist in the punishment of criminals," provides a threshold for recognizing its significance with his suggestion that "moral indignation (which is the emotion behind the disinterest tendency to inflict punishment) is a kind of disguised envy."[92] What is there to envy? Likely the answer, which was outside of the scope of Ranulf's analysis, was the exuberant acting out within Weimar's Cabaret Culture, which flourished in an open and tol-erant cosmopolitan Berlin in which gender bending and a wide variety of other identity improvisations were featured.

Reinforced by an artistic environment – in the theatrical events of the period, e.g., the Brecht/Weil *Three Penny Opera*, *Avant guard* film and Jazz clubs – in the gatherings in Cabaret clubs androgynous and wildly decorated bodies were works of art, canvasses upon which alternative dispositions were being scripted. Those who participated were the essence of the S-Type personality, engaging

FIGURE 2.1 A cross-dresser on stage in the Netflix series *Babylon Berlin*.

in the "wanton pleasure," the "gender-bending and ambiguous…sexuality…cross dressing" and so on that the Nazi psychologist E. R Jaensch disparaged as an "Anti-Type" (in contrast with the "stability" and "rigidity" of the J-Types that Jaensch valorized as the potential Fascist). Cabaret Culture thrived on a "Berlinisch attitude of ironic bemusement and a slightly curled lip (see Figure 2.1 a cross-dresser on stage)"[93] until the Nazis came to power to give that attitude a fat lip, shutting clubs and theaters, burning books, and engaging in "fierce campaigns against feminism, jazz, modern architecture and much else."[94]

The juxtaposition between Cabaret Culture and the Nazi thuggery that attacked it is presented rhythmically in an opening scene of the Bob Fosse-directed film *Cabaret* (1972), located in Weimar Berlin in 1931. While a song and dance routine, stylized "slapping," by the Emcee (Joel Grey) proceeds on stage within the Kit Kat Club, Nazi thugs are beating the club owner (who had earlier expelled them) in an alley outside the theater. The rhythms of the beating match those of the music/dance routine.

The Netflix series, *Babylon Berlin* (2020) portrays Weimar Berlin similarly. It's a noir detective drama transpiring within last vestiges of Berlin's Cabaret culture (accompanied by a soundtrack that expresses the social rhythms of the period) at a moment in which a fascist emergence is underway. The mentality of both *Cabaret* and *Babylon Berlin* are shaped by an anti-fascist aesthetic. Rather than treating mentalities as psychological traits, they show them as temporalized dramas and locate them in the historical-cultural context that shaped the fascist mentality, which was activated as the "discharge of the long-accumulated aggressions" to which Ranulf refers.

Freudianism

> There is no domain of the psychic without text
>> *Jacques Derrida, Freud and the Scene of Writing*

In contrast with *Cabaret's* and *Babylon Berlin's* location of mentality within rhythmically articulated dramas that connect mind and world, as mentality is dramatically actualized, mentality is treated in terms of its psychological depth for Adorno et al. in their *Authoritarian Personality* study and by Klaus Theweleit in his two-volume study, *Male Fantasies*. Both investigations sought to disclose that depth by relying (in varying ways) on a Freudian psychoanalytic perspective. However, I want to note that, "Freudianism" (V. N. Volosinov identifying term in his extended criticism of Freud's neglect of the socioeconomic milieu[95]) is more a literary production than the science of the mind that Freud's biologisms imply. As Jacques Derrida has shown, "at the decisive moments of his itinerary [Freud] has recourse to metaphorical models."[96]

Although he produced innovative and influential constructions of mentality, with a narrative of its etiology and hermeneutics of its coded manifestations,[97] like William James (albeit without confessing), Freud's version of mentality is a series of metaphors rather than a discovery of its neurological basis. One in particular is central to his construction of the mind. While drawing on the language of scientific inquiry to construct a "neurological fable," what Freud created instead is an elaborate metaphor, a "writing machine."[98] While James likens the dynamics of mentality to a theatrical drama, Freud employs a "psychographic metaphor."[99] He likens the breaches between consciousness and the unconscious to the operation of a mystic writing pad, a "*Wunderbloc*, a writing machine…into which the whole of the psychical apparatus will be projected."[100]

Along with his construction of mentality as a graphology is the temporality Freud lends to way the machine operates. His "writing machine" functions as a series of deferrals of threatening affects (what he calls cathexes). While Freud's psychical graphology relies on a "space of writing," there is also, as Derrida points out, "*a time of writing*," a discontinuous process in which the writing proceeds as "the interruption and restoration of contact between the various depths of psychical levels."[101] Given the complex spatio-temporality with which Freud figures the "depth" of consciousness, it's clear that Freudian psychology has a tenuous purchase in Adorno et al.'s. analysis of fascist-susceptible mentality. It has a stronger purchase in Theweleit's account of the "male fantasies" of the proto Nazi *Freikorps*, which more consistently relies in on a Freudian psychoanalytic frame, albeit re-inflected in Deleuze and Guattari's critique of Jacques Lacan on desire.

Figuring the Already Figured

To observe the use of Freudian psychology in Adorno et al.'s and Theweleit's investigations one has to work through two levels of figuration, that which constructs the Freudian mind, whose metaphorical basis is disguised in a meta language of scientific discovery, and what is overlaid on Freudianism by the figures in their applications. While Theweleit applies an elaborate set of explicit metaphors to the "male fantasies" with which he is concerned, the metaphors in Adorno et al.'s approach to fascist-susceptible mentalities are as disguised in a scientific metalanguage as are many of Freud's interpretations. Treating Freudian psychology as theoretical rather than as a literary production, they state, "For theory as to the structure of personality we have leaned most heavily upon Freud." *Not* in fact very heavy. After noting their dependence on Freud they refer to "personality forces," among which are the Freudian concepts, "drives," "needs," "wishes," and "emotional impulses," which they derive from "academic psychology."[102] In particular the Freud-inspired concept of the drive, as well as the one's introduced later: e. g., the "superego" and the "syndrome," play no role as variables in the social psychological framing of their investigation, which is composed of a "widening circle of covariance"[103] that treats the social correlates of the attitude clusters disclosed. With regard to Adorno's et al.'s reference to the "drive" (*Trieb* in German), it should be noted that "drive" is a metaphor which, as Jacques Lacan points out, is a "pulsion" (i.e., a physics metaphor). Alternatively, when Freud translates it as "instinct," it becomes a "biological observation."[104]

Ultimately, as a social science investigation *The Authoritarian Personality* yielded "findings," i.e., the typically weak but nevertheless suggestive associations one finds within attitude clusters and between cognitive attributes and social positioning (the typical results of well-designed research in social psychology). To the extent that the investigation reached the "depth" of the fascist-susceptible mentalities it sought to illuminate, it relied on some supportive clinical work – interviews which the authors admit are too cursory to compare with what is elicited in the case work of psychoanalysts. In contrast, as a literary production, the investigations "unavowed" Freudian fictions, on which they layer many others, such as anthropological ones (e.g., the ethnocentric mentality) and sociological ones (e.g., alienated types) adds up to a compendium of metaphorically framed fascist appeal-susceptible traits. Nevertheless, as Rancière has suggested, that something is an "unavowed fiction" does not imply that it has no epistemological value. The relevant question about fiction is not "whether the description is true or not" but whether it composes a coherent "sense of reality" and illuminates "the consequence that can be drawn from it."[105]

What I want to suggest is that the occasion and motivation of the authoritarian personality investigation is more telling than what we can learn by perusing its findings. Likely the study would have yielded a more illuminating Freudian framing (and a better assessment of consequences) had it focused on desire (central to Theweleit's approach to dangerous mentalities) instead of turning to a health metaphor, which shapes the concluding chapter, "Psychological ILL Health and Potential Fascism." Importantly, however, by focusing on the kind of mentalities that are likely most susceptible to fascist appeals, the investigation issued an alert that the conditions for the success of a fascist political movement remain. Since the forces that shaped the movement-susceptible mentalities before the "Second World War" persist, there are good reasons to look nearby for minds that a fascistic movement can mobilize by helping a wide variety of bigots "organize [their] multitude of hatreds into a single venomous philosophy" (to repeat the imagery in Hiaasen's crime story).

Klaus Theweleit's investigation into male fantasies, which is located in the national space of the rise of National Socialism, relies more elaborately on Freudian psychology. However, as an event in which a type of mentality has become an object of investigation, it is motivated by a different national problematic, and it draws on a different intellectual framing, a critical re-inflection of Freudian/Lacanian desire influenced by Deleuze and Guattari's first volume on Capitalism and Schizophrenia, their *Anti-Oedipus*.[106] In contrast with Adorno et al.'s focus on a dangerous future, Theweleit is concerned with the past, specifically Germany's experience of generation conflict, which begins in the 1960's with a generation's "refusal to accept responsibility for their role in the recent Nazi past [in contention with]...students obsessed with their parent's guilt."[107] Like Adorno et al, Theweleit is concerned with the psychology of fascists and authoritarians. However, while Adorno et al. elicited and scripted that psychology working mostly with interviews, Theweleit worked with the texts of soldier males, a large corpus of Freikorps literature, mined to disclose their "psychic *processes*."[108] And while Freud's primary metaphor for mentality is a "writing machine," Theweleit, drawing on Deleuze and Guattari, figures mentality as a "desiring machine." "The unconscious," he writes, "is a desiring-machine and the body parts, components of that machine."[109] Unlike the descriptive style of *The Authoritarian Personality* text, the style of *Male Fantasies* displays a rich poesis. In the words of one commentator, it is "at once cultural history, critical theory, and gory, Gothic prose poem."[110]

Figuring the body/mind of the "soldier male" Theweleit refers to "a new man...whose physique has been mechanized, his psyche eliminated – or in part displaced into his body armor."[111] As he proceeds to describe the new man as one with a "machinelike periphery, whose interior has lost its meaning...[a] mechanized body [with a]..compulsion to subjugate and repulse what is specifically human within," crucial to his analysis is what his "incarcerated interior"[112] is protected against; it's "all that can be identified with the female body: with liquidity, with warmth, and above all with a sensuality that is responsive to other human beings."[113] In short, "The warrior utopia of the [the fascist's] mechanized body is...erected against the female self within."[114]

To situate the radical lack of empathy that characterizes the soldier male's total abjection of the feminine and other forms of difference within, I want to juxtapose a moment in a novel that provides a counter ethos, one that acknowledges and embraces the woman (and other forms of otherness) within. In Russell's Banks's *Continental Drift*, one of his main protagonists, Robert Dubois, a married man and father who had hitherto lived in the predominantly white world of

the state of New Hampshire, begins an affair in Miami with Marguerite Dill, an
African American woman. In an essayistic intervention that conveys the challenge
that Marguerite's world presents to Robert – who is constructed as the "type of
man" that avoids introspection – Banks offers this reflection:

> To understand your children, you attend to the child in you…to imagine
> Elaine [his wife] and Doris [a former paramour] and now Marguerite, the
> three women who in recent years have mattered most to him, all Bob has
> to do is pay attention to the woman in himself. It's harder in the case of
> Marguerite, but all the more interesting to him for that, because with her he
> has to pay attention to the black man in himself as well.[115]

Although not blocked by the "psychosis" Theweleit extracts from Freikorps texts,
"Robert" fails to achieve that kind of attention. In contrast, for the Freikorps it's a
militant inattention to the forms of internal otherness that they are steeled against.
"The most urgent task of the solder male," Theweleit writes, "is to pursue, to dam
in, and to subdue any force that threatens to transform him back into the horribly
disorganized jumble of flesh, hair, skin, bones, intestines, and feelings that calls itself
human."[116] What is subdued turns their psychic energy outward as an urge to violently obliterate perceived enemy-others, whom they figure with the same fleshly
attributes they suppress in themselves.

   The fraught and violent fantasies that animate Freikorps texts supply much the
figuration that shapes Theweleit's. For example, "blood," which Theweleit suggests,

> may be substituted for almost any part of the fascist's psychic apparatus…
> [and is] the productive force of his unconscious [is symptomatically expressed
> as a dread of women's fluids (a "red flood") and is externalized as what]…
> the war-machine need to continue functioning,[117]

as it migrates from the fascist mentality to his weapons: "The gun barrel bundles all
the energy of 'hissing' blood into eruption, a shot…impelled by a single drive: to
speed from the gun barrel…and to penetrate other bodies."[118] When Theweleit
refers to desire as a "productive force," he is using Deleuze and Guattari's perspective not only to figure desire as a productive machine – realized as the engine of
war, the only engine that produces the desired satisfaction – but also to generate
the ethos and occasion for his project as a whole. Accordingly, I want to suggest
that (as is the case for Adorno et al.'s investigation of a fascist-susceptible mentality),
quite apart from the nuances of his theorizing of the mentality of his subjects, in
which he shares Deleuze and Guattari's rejection of the Freudian family romance
in favor of the subject's "desiring production," Theweleit is providing the political
significance of his entire project.

   As becomes apparent in the conclusion to "volume two," Theweleit's use of
Deleuzian desire-as-productive is more important for the way it allocates collective

responsibility for Nazi violence than it is as a re-inflection of Freudian psycho-analysis. After all his extensive work on texts that disclose fascism's inaugurating and enabling mentality, his focus turns to "the reality of fascism as it lives beyond the inter-war period of its gemination."[119] Referring to the "main generalizations" with which he will conclude, Theweleit refers to

> two tendencies identifiable among many Germans under fascism. First despite their many differences, large numbers of Germans were united in a common understanding of the German situation…[seeing themselves as] German men…as such their demands for forms of self-realization that pitted them against other human beings. Their second unifying trait was to rid themselves of their own tormenting feelings – the bodily stirrings that could never again be integrated once released [and were] united in the anti-eroticism of their marital relations, the formal quality of their neighborly relations; in the chilly distinctions demanded by Germany's ubiquitous hierarchical systems…They were united as the wearers of granite expressions.[120]

His scripting of collective mentality – a population-wide desiring production that he ascribes to much of Germany – is a response to a popular self-justifying proposition that fascism was "simply a form of seduction or misrecognition." Rather, he insists, the desiring machine was a collective "production of reality…Followers, in other words, do more than simply 'follow'," a proposition, he says he is "offering… [as a] hypothesis whose plausibility seems to me substantial."[121]

In what is his primary concern, a political intervention into how the fascist experience is to be understood, Theweleit is reacting against, "a widespread assumption that the war created men of this physical and psychic construction; and, though the assumption itself is severely mistaken, its effects are clearly visible in attempts to understand and combat contemporary fascism in Germany." Theweleit was therefore writing himself into historical time. His attention to mentality is a "when" and "how" as much as a "what" analysis. As an event it is intended to affect the will-have-been of fascism. He insists that the fascist mentality, however psychotic its more extreme manifestations registered in the Freikorps texts he analyzed, was a collective mind event. Most importantly for Theweleit, rather than assuming, as the contemporary historical framing of the period would have it, that the fascist mentality was produced by the war, that mentality was a primary, widespread condition of possibility for allowing it to happen. "The Problem of fascism has to be seen as the 'normal'; organization of our lived relations – a problem for which, as yet, we have no resolution."[122]

It is therefore instructive to pursue the implications of the way Theweleit stages an encounter between "the micro-politics of his theory of fascism,"[123] the nuances of the working of proto-fascist mentalities, and Germany's macro-political situation, the struggle to allocate responsibility for a shameful past and manage what remains of the impulses that created it. To take up the challenge and extend the implications of Theweleit's micro-to-macro composition, I turn to a contemporary encounter between minds and media. Whereas the media aggregation of susceptible mentalities during the rise of National Socialism featured an encounter between the radically alienated minds/bodies of proto-fascist supporters and (among other media) Hitler's mass rallies aimed at unifying their disparate anxieties and enmities into a political movement, the contemporary exploitation of anxieties and enmities are assembled in a different media landscape.

From Heimat to Homeland Security

> Every people in search of itself thinks about where to locate the margin between its own home and the rest of the world.
>
> *Milan Kundera, Encounters*

> I've come to understand that the medium [TV] is a primal force in the American home. Sealed off, timeless, self-contained, self-referring. It's...like something we know in a dream-like and preconscious way.
>
> *Don DeLillo, White Noise*

Responding to "the Bush Administration's" Homeland Security's Department's "introduction of its color-coded terror alert system" early in this millennium, Brian Massumi analyzes the complex relationship between mentality and media, emphasizing television's role in broadcasting that alert system.[124] "Television," he writes, "has become the *event* medium."[125] As the above epigraph implies, Don DeLillo develops that insight as well, in his case in a literary genre. For example, one of the novel's characters (functioning in a novel whose time precedes today's social media tsunami) says, "For most people there are only two places in the world, where they live and their TV set."[126] Noting the parallels between the two texts, I proceed to read Massumi's analysis along with parts of DeLillo's novel. As I note in an earlier reading of *White Noise*, the media – radio and television in particular – are among the novel's protagonists. "The ever-present television set [which is often the speaking subject in sentences] produces news of danger within its continuous stream of simulated experiences."[127] Massumi's essay develops its argument with a similar style. As his title implies the media constitute a primary voice. While DeLillo punctuates his plot with such lines as, "the television said: 'And other trends that could dramatically impact your portfolio'."[128] Massumi's title reads in part "The Spectrum Said." And crucially, by way of reconnecting with the trajectory of texts in the analysis thus far, DeLillo and Massumi evince similar thematizations. Hitler appears in *White Noise* as the basis of an academic discipline. An educational institution, College-on-the-Hill has a Department of Hitler Studies, a symptom of its founding faculty member, the novel's main protagonist, Jack Gladney's, preoccupation with death. Massumi, also with fascism in mind, summarizes the import of his analysis,

> The grounding and surrounding fear that the system [of color-coded alerts] helps develop tends toward an autonomy that makes it an ontogenetic force to be reckoned with. That reckoning must include the irrational, self-propelling mode of fear-based collective individuation we call fascism.[129]

While Homeland Security's alerts were a response to 9/11, in DeLillo's novel the fear arousing event is the accidental release of a toxic cloud (of Nyodene gas), which the media treats with a variety of euphemisms, referring to it, for example, as "an airborne toxic event." However, inasmuch as DeLillo text is heteroglossic, there is a clash of voices. Gladney's son Heinrich continually challenges the family's and media's disconcertingly ambiguous reassurances. At one point, while watching the dark cloud, which "the radio calls…a feathery plume," he says to his father, "It's like a shapeless growing thing. A dark breathing thing of smoke. Why do they call it a plume?"[130] Massumi provides a similar account of the media effect. He describes the functioning of the alert system as designed to "modulate" fear:

> The alert system was introduced to calibrate the public's anxiety. In the aftermath of 9/11, the public's fearfulness had tended to swing out of control in response to dramatic, but mainly vague, government warnings of an impending follow-up attack. The alert system was designed to modulate that fear.[131]

DeLillo and Massumi also contextualize the media-consciousness connection similarly. Remarking that "TV offers incredible mounts of psychic data," *White Noise's* character Murray – one of the novel's "conceptual personae"[132] (who allegedly is able to "know so much" because, as he says, "I'm from New York"), refers to the reception of that "data" as preconceptual:

> I've come to understand that the medium is a primal force in the American home, Sealed-off, timeless, self-contained, self-referring. It's like a myth being born right there in the living room, like something we know in a dream-like and preconscious way.[133]

While DeLillo's novel thinks about the way media impacts consciousness through the voices of his characters, Massumi uses a philosophical framing to develop a similar view of how a television-transmitted alert impacts the viewer:

> Addressing bodies from the dispositional angle of their affectivity, instead of addressing subjects from the positional angle of their ideations, shunts

government functions away from the mediations of adherence or belief and toward direct *activation*, what else is a state of alert?[134]

There are also shared constructions of the temporalities of minds/bodies; the future looms large in both texts. In *White Noise* Gladney at one point imagines himself in a "tabloid future," having "become part of the public stuff of media disaster." He follows that observation by lending a nonlinear temporality to cognition: "The small audience of the old and blind recognized the predictions of the psychics as events so near to happening that they had to be shaped *in advance* [my emphasis] to our needs and wishes."[135] Similarly, Massumi points out that the threat conveyed by the color-coded alerts "is not a substantial form, but a time form: a futurity [that]…has a capacity to fill the present."[136] Adding temporal imagery he writes, "Since its object is virtual, the only actual leverage the security operation can have is on threat's back-cast presence, its pre-effect of fear."[137]

That similarity notwithstanding, the two textual approaches figure the dynamic of mentality differently. The characters in *White Noise* are Proustian (in Deleuze's sense). They undergo an "apprenticeship," a "sensitivity to [dangerous] signs,…[as] the world [has become] an object to be deciphered."[138] Involved in a search for signs, at one point Gladney says, "In my current state, bearing the death impression of the Nyodene cloud, I was ready to search anywhere for signs and hints, intimations of odd comfort."[139] Because Gladney and the others are fearful enough to be available for domination by a fascist type, Murray steps in and coaches Gladney to fashion himself as one who could usurp that role by, for example, "surviving an assassination attempt." "The situation is ripe," he adds, "for a charismatic type to take over…Helpless and fearful people are drawn to magical figures, mythic figures, epic men who intimidate and darkly loom." "You're talking about Hitler," I take it," Gladney replies, to which Murray responds, "Some people are larger than life. Hitler is larger than death."[140]

Massumi by contrast evokes the temporal priority of the body, citing William James argument that "fear strikes the body and compels it to action before it registers consciously." What dominates is not a larger than life autocrat but the signs themselves. "Threat strikes the nervous system with a directness forbidding any separation between the responsiveness of the body and its environment."[141] Massumi follows that model of the temporal priority of the body with a series of temporal tropes that, assembled as a whole, comprise a fear narrative in which the body-mind complex participates in its subjection to signs by becoming routinized. The fear "emotion becomes enactable in anticipation of itself [it]… has revirtualized [emerging] as an end effect…looped back to the beginning as its cause." Thus "revirtualized," it "becomes *a way of life.*"[142]

The DeLillo and Massumi texts therefore share a focus on mentality-sign dynamics but within different philosophical frames. Whereas DeLillo's aesthetic subjects are Proustian – they're involved as noted in a *search* for signs, – Massumi are Peircean. He enlists Charles Sanders Peirce's philosophy of perception to develop a model in which Homeland Security's media-suborned subjects are activated to evoke their *own* signs. It's an "autonomization of fear" in which "fear is fear of itself." "According to Peirce," Massumi writes, "every thought beyond immediate perception *is* a sign";[143] the effect of the alerts is thus to make fear become "self-comprehending."[144] Massumi figures his construction of that compelling mentality "timeslip" in a travel metaphor. Homeland Security's subjects are on a "journey through fear,"[145] a "self-propelling mode of fear-based collective individuation…[that enfranchises] fascism."[146] In contrast, DeLillo's fear-aroused subjects are ultimately enervated and disconcerted rather than self-activated. His metaphor for their destination (after a hopeless search for signs) is a supermarket whose shelves have been rearranged. There is "panic in the aisles, dismay in the faces of older shoppers…[who are] frozen in the aisles, trying to figure out the pattern, discern the underlying logic."[147] Ultimately both texts figure mentality to frame an anti-fascist politics of aesthetics. In contrast with fascism's "aestheticization of politics," which offers symbols of collective solidarity (as Walter Benjamin famously puts it),[148] each text "suspends the ordinary coordinates of sensory experience and reframes the network of relations between spaces and times, subjects and objects, the common a and the singular."[149] One (Massumi's) is a scripting of mentality within a philosophical medium that features innovative temporal tropes, the other (DeLillo's) scripts mentality within a novel that proliferates clashing aesthetic subjects. As was the case for Walter Benjamin, when he issued his warning, they make mentality an object of analysis to alert us to political crisis, thus sharing the ethico-political impetus of the other texts in this chapter.

Notes

1 See Michel Foucault, "About the Concept of the 'Dangerous Individual' in 19th-Century Psychiatry," *International Journal of Law and Psychiatry,* Vol. 1: 1 (1978) On the web at: http://schwarzemilch.files.wordpress.com/2009/02/foucault_dangerous_individual.pdf.
2 *Ibid.*
3 Michel Foucault, *The History of Sexuality Vol I: An Introduction* trans. Robert Hurley (New York: Pantheon, 1978), 25. In a subsequent investigation, based on his lectures under the title, *Security, Territory, Population,* Foucault refers not only to an emerging governmentality – connected to new techniques of power focused on managing the new collective object, the "population" (a collectivity subject to calculations) – but also to the role of the "human sciences." He shows that at the same time that governance had shifted from a focus on sovereign power to one of managing the social order, those "sciences" became concerned with the population's individual subjects, whose living, working, and speaking had to be comprehended: Michel Foucault, *Security, Territory, Population* trans. Graham Burchell (New York: Palgrave Macmilllan, 2007), 79.
4 Foucault, "About the Concept of the 'Dangerous Individual' in 19th-Century Psychiatry."
5 *Ibid.*

6 Michel Foucault, *The Birth of the Clinic: An Archaeology of Medical Perception* (trans. A. M. Sheridan Smith (New York: Pantheon, 1973), xii.

7 See *Ibid.*.

8 The expression is attributed to James by John Kaag, *Sick Souls, Healthy Minds: How William James Can Sve Your Life* (Princeton: Princeton University Press, 2020), 137.

9 William James, *Principles of Psychology – Vols 1–2* (Leamington Spa: Pantianos Classics 2017) ebook loc 116.

10 *Ibid.*, loc. 96.

11 *Ibid.*

12 The quotation is from Bruce Wilshire, "Protophenomenology in the psychology of William James," Transactions of the Charles S. Peirce Society, Vol. 5, No. 1 (Winter, 1969), 26.

13 *Ibid.*, 25.

14 Frederick Hoffman, "William James and the Modern Literary Consciousness," *Criticism* 4: 1 (Winter, 1962), 7.

15 See Gillian Beer, *Darwin's Plots: Evolutionary Narrative in Darwin, George Eliot and Nineteenth-Century Fiction* (Cambridge: Cambridge University Press, 2009).

16 Vanessa L. Ryan, "Reading the Mind: From George Eliot's Fiction to James Sully's Psychology," *Journal of the History of Ideas* 70: 4 (October, 2009), 620. The inner quotations are from Beer *Ibid.*, 7.

17 James, *Principles of Psychology*, loc. 5810.

18 William James, *Pragmatism: A New Name for Some Old Ways of Thinking* (New York: Longmans, Green & Co., 1910), 275.

19 The quotation is from Norman Turner, "Cezanne, Wagner, Modulation," *Journal of Aesthetics and Art Criticism*, 56: 4 (Fall, 1998), 10.

20 The avowed versus unavowed fiction binary, which I treat also in Chapter 1 is developed by Jacques Rancière, "Fictions of Time," in Grace Hellyer and Julian Murphet eds. *Rancière and Literature* (Edinburgh: Edinburgh University Press, 2016).

21 The quotation is from Maurice Blanchot, "Musil," in *The Book to Come*, trans. Charlotte Mandell (Stanford: Stanford University Press, 2003), 141.

22 Blanchot, "Musil," 140.

23 *Ibid.*, 142.

24 Robert Musil. *The Man without Qualities* (Collingdale: Diana Publisher, 2018), ebook loc., 1203.

25 *Ibid.*, 1186.

26 The expression belongs to Georg Lukács, *Theory of the Novel* trans. Anna Bosock (Cambridge: MIT Press, 1971), 84.

27 The quotation belongs to Blanchot, "Musil," 138.

28 I am borrowing the summary from Jane Smiley, "Nowhere man," a review of *The Man Without Qualities* in *The Guardian*, June 17, 2006, on the web at: www.theguardian.com/books/2006/jun/17/featuresreviews.guardianreview28.

29 Musil. *The Man Without Qualities*, loc. 4925.

30 *Ibid.*, loc. 2950.

31 The quotation is from Mark B. N. Hansen's rendering of Jan Patočka's materialist version of phenomenology: *Feed Forward: On the Future of Twenty-First-Century Media* (Chicago: University of Chicago Press, 2015), 68.

32 The expression belongs to Harrison, "The Essayistic Novel and Mode of Life: Robert Musil's The Man without Qualities."

33 The concept of a conceptual personae is developed in Gilles Deleuze and Felix Guattari, *What is Philosophy?* trans. Hugh Tomlinson and Graham Burchell (New York: Columbia University Press, 1994), 61–83.

34 *Ibid.*, 70.

35 The phrase belongs to Gilles Deleuze, "Literature and Life," *Critical Inquiry* 23: 2 (Winter, 1997), 226.

36 Blanchot, *Musil*, 139.

37 *Ibid.*, 138.

38 Quotations from Kimball, "The Qualities of Robert Musil."

39 The quotations are from J. M. Coetzee's "Introduction" to the Penguin edition of *The Confusions of Young Törless*, trans. Shaun Whiteside (New York: Penguin, 2001), xii.

40 Musil, *The Man without Qualities*, loc. 1370.

41 Ibid., loc. 1369.

42 *Ibid.*, loc. 1412.

43 *Ibid.*, loc. 1575.

44 Smiley, "Nowhere Man"

45 Musil, *The Man Without Qualities*, loc. 1203.

46 *Ibid.*, loc. 2214.

47 *Ibid.*, loc. 4845.

48 *Ibid.*, loc. 4955.

49 See Jonathan Lethem's "Introduction: Paul Arnheim is a Prussian-Jewish industrialist-scion and bon vivant," whose biting irony matches Ulrich's. *Ibid.*, loc. 50–75.

50 *Ibid.*, loc. 8131.

51 *Ibid.*, loc. 8146.

52 Thomas Pynchon, *Mason & Dixon* (New York: Henry Holt, 1997), 345.

53 Musil, *The Man without Qualities*, loc. 1660.

54 Smiley, "Nowhere Man."

55 Musil, *The Man Without Qualities*, loc. 4940.

56 Kenneth Burke, "The Rhetoric of Hitler's 'Battle'," in Michael J. Shapiro ed. *Language and Politics* (New York: New York University Press, 1984), 61.

57 Johann Gottlieb Fichte, *Addresses to the German Nation*, trans. R. F. Jones and G. H. Turnbull (Chicago: The Open Court, 1922), 68.

58 *Ibid.*, 69.

59 Musil, *The Man Without Qualities*, loc. 1595–1612.

60 *Ibid.*, loc. 1640.

61 Burke, "The Rhetoric of Hitler's 'Battle'," 69.

62 *Ibid.*, 79.

63 See Timothy W. Ryback, "Hitler's Forgotten Library," *The Atlantic*, May 2003, on the web at www.theatlantic.com/magazine/archive/2003/05/hitlers-forgotten-library/302727/.

64 See "Hitler's Philosophical Enablers," *The Catholic Thing*, June 12, 2012, on the web at: www.thecatholicthing.org/2013/06/12/hitlers-philosophical-enablers/.

65 Paul R. Sweet, "Fichte and the Jews: A Case of Tension Between Civil Rights and Human Rights, *German Studies Review* 16: 1 (February, 1993), 44.

66 "Hitler's Philosophical Enablers."

67 Burke, "The Rhetoric of Hitler's 'Battle'," 67.

68 *Ibid.*, 68.

69 *Ibid.*, 78.

70 Carl Hiaasen, *Lucky You* (New York: Alfred A, Knopf, 1991), 2.

71 Jean Paul Sartre, *The family Idiot: Gustave Flaubert 1821–1857* trans. Carol Osman (Chicago: University of Chicago Press, 1989), 127.

72 Burke, "The Rhetoric of Hitler's 'Battle'," 77.

73 See J. L. Austin, *How to Do Things with Words* 2nd edition (Cambridge: Harvard University Press, 1975).

74 I am quoting from an earlier treatment of the event of National Socialism: Michael J. Shapiro, *Politics and Time: Documenting the Event* (Cambridge: Polity, 2016), vi.

75 C. Wright Mills, "Review of Franz Neumann's *Behemoth: The Structure and Function of National Socialism 1933–1944, Partisan Review*, on the web at: http://wbenjamin.org/Behemoth.html.

76 Burke, "The Rhetoric of Hitler's 'Battle'," 77.

77 *Ibid.*, 79.

78 William E. Connolly, *Aspirational Fascism: The Struggle for Multifaceted Democracy under Trumpism* (Minneapolis: University of Minnesota Press, 2017), 11.

79 *Ibid.*, 19.

80 The expression is from Sabine von Dirke's analysis of the contemporary resonances of the Adorno et al work on the authoritarian personality: "Neoliberalism's Reengineering of the Authoritarian Personality," *Colloquia Germanica* 50: ¾ (2017), 334.

81 Max Horkheimer, "Preface" to T. W. Adorno et. al. *The Authoritarian Personality* (New York: W. W. Norton, 1969), ix.

82 See Alfred Hoche's, *Arztliche Bemerkungen* in Karl Binding and Alfred Hoche, *De Freigabe der Vernichtung Lebensunwerten Lebens: Ihr Mass und ihre Form* (Leipzig, 1920), 61–62.

83 The quotations are from Roberto Esposito, *Third Person* trans. Zakiya Hanafi (Cambridge: Polity, 2012), 64.

84 I am quoting from a description of Jaensch's perverse pseudo psychology in Roger Brown's chapter, "The Authoritarian Personality," in his *Social Psychology* (New York: The Free Press, 1965), 477.

85 *Ibid.*

86 *Ibid.*, 478.

87 Adorno et. al. *The Authoritarian Personality*, 1.

88 See Milton Rokeach, *The Open and the Closed* Mind (New York: Basic Books, 1973), and H. J. Eysenck, *The Psychology of Politics* (London: Routledge and Kegan Paul, 1954).

89 Horkheimer, "Preface," ix.

90 This succinct characterization of Ranulf's imitating question is by Harold Lasswell in the "Preface to Sven Ranulf, *Moral Indignation and Middle Class Psychology* (New York, Schocken, 1964; originally published in 1938).

91 *Ibid.*, 8–9.

92 *Ibid.*, 1.

93 See Sarah Lippek, "Disrupted Values, Erupting Culture: Cabaret and Sexual Persona in Weimar Berlin" *SSRN*, on the web at: https://papers.ssrn.com/sol3/papers.cfm?abstract_id=1079945.

94 Andrew Dickson, Culture in Weimar Germany: on the edge of a volcano," *Discovering Literature: Twentieth Century,* on the web at: www.bl.uk/20th-century-literature/articles/on-the-edge-of-the-volcano-culture-in-weimar-germany.

95 V. N. Volosinov, *Freudianism: A Critical Sketch*, trans. I. R. Titunik (Bloomington: Indiana University Press, 1987).

96 Derrida, "Freud and the Scene of writing," 199.

97 Elsewhere, I have analyzed the literary structure of Freud's writing. Treating it as a series of Barthesian codes applied to his case study of "The Wolfman." See Michael J. Shapiro, "Metaphor in the Philosophy of the Social Sciences," In Terrill Carver and Samuel A. Chambers eds. *Michael J. Shapiro: discourse, culture, violence* (London: Routledge, 2012), 19–20.

98 Derrida, "Freud and the Scene of writing," 200.

99 *Ibid.*, 220.

100 *Ibid.*, 199.

101 *Ibid.*, 225.

102 Adorno et. al. *The Authoritarian Personality*, 5.

103 Brown, "The Authoritarian Personality," 479.

104 Jacques Lacan, "Subversion of the Subject and the Dialectic of Desire, in *Ecrits*, trans. Alan Sheridan (New York: W. W. Norton, 1977), 301.

105 Rancière, "Fictions of Time," 26.

106 Gilles Deleuze and Felix Guattari, *Anti-Oedipus*, trans. Robert Hurley, Mark Seem, and Helen R. Lane (New York: Viking, 1977).

107 The quotations are from Michael Rothberg, "Documenting Barbarism: Yourcenar's "Male Fantasies', Theweleit's 'Coup'," *Cultural Critique* 29 (Winter, 1994–1995), 82.

108 Klaus Theweleit, *Male Fantasies Volume 1: women floods bodies history* (Minneapolis: University of Minnesota Press, 1987), 57.

109 *Ibid.*, 211.

110 Elizabeth Schambelan, "Pseudo-Conservatism, The Solider Male, and the Air Horn," *Los Angeles Review of Books*, April 18, 2016, on the web at: https://lareviewofbooks.org/article/pseudo-conservatism-soldier-male-air-horn/.

111 Klaus Theweleit, *Male Fantasies volume 2: Male bodies: psychoanalyzing the white terror* trans. Erica Carter and Chris Turner (Minneapolis: University of Minnesota Press, 1989), 162.

112 *Ibid.*

113 Barbara Ehrenreich, "Foreword" to Theweleit, *Male Fantasies Volume 1*, xix.

114 I am quoting from Jessica Benjamin and Anson Rabinback "Foreward, to Theweleit, *Male Fantasies volume 2*, xix.

115 Russell Banks, *Continental Drift* (New York: Harper, 2007), 101.

116 That Theweleit statement is central to the Schambela's analysis, which she quotes in "Pseudo-Conservatism, The Solider Male, and the Air Horn."

117 Theweleit, *Male Fantasies volume 2*, 185.

118 *Ibid.*, 179.

119 Rothberg, "Documenting Barbarism," 78.

120 Theweleit, *Male Fantasies volume 2*, 348.

121 *Ibid.*, 349.

122 *Ibid.*, 358.

123 I am quoting Rothberg, "Documenting Barbarism," 85.

124 Brian Massumi, "Fear (The Spectrum Said)," *Positions* 13: 1 (2005), 31.

125 *Ibid.*, 33.

126 DeLillo, *White Noise*, 66.

127 Michael J. Shapiro, "The Politics of Fear," in *Reading the Postmodern Polity: Political Theory as Textual Practice* (Minneapolis: University of Minnesota Press, 1992), 133.
128 DeLillo, *White Noise*, 61.
129 Massumi, "Fear (The Spectrum Said)," 47.
130 DeLillo, *White Noise*, 111.
131 Massumi, "Fear (The Spectrum Said)," 32.
132 As is noted in the discussion of Musil's novel, the concept of the conceptual persona is developed in Deleuze and Guattari, *What is Philosophy*, 61–83.
133 DeLillo, *White Noise*, 51.
134 Massumi, "Fear (The Spectrum Said)," 34.
135 DeLillo, *White Noise*, 146.
136 Massumi, "Fear (The Spectrum Said)," 35.
137 *Ibid.*, 36.
138 Gilles Deleuze, *Proust and Signs* trans. Richard Howard (Minneapolis: University of Minnesota Press, 2000), 26.
139 *Ibid.*, 154.
140 Ibid., 287.
141 Massumi, "Fear (The Spectrum Said)," 36,
142 *Ibid.*, 41.
143 *Ibid.*, 42. Massimi is quoting from C. S. Peirce, *The Essential Peirce: Selected Philosophical Writings*, vol 2 (Bloomington: Indiana University Press, 1998), 402.
144 *Ibid.*, 43.
145 *Ibid.*, 44.
146 *Ibid.*, 47.
147 DeLillo, *White Noise*, 325.
148 See Walter Benjamin, "The Work of Art in the Age of Mechanical Reproduction," in Hanah Arendt ed. *Illuminations* (New York: Schocken, 1969), 217–251.
149 The expression belongs to Jacques Rancière, *The Politics of Aesthetics* (London: Continuum, 2004), 65.

Bibliography

Adorno, Theodor et al. (1969) *The Authoritarian Personality*, New York: W.W. Norton,
Austin, J. L. (1975) *How to Do Things with Words* 2nd edition, Cambridge, MA: Harvard University Press.
Banks, Russell (2007) *Continental Drift*, New York: Harper.
Benjamin, Jessica and Rabinback, Anson (1989) 'Foreword,' to Theweleit, *Male Fantasies Volume 2: Male Bodies: Psychoanalyzing the White Terror*, trans. Erica Carter and Chris Turner, Minneapolis: University of Minnesota Press, pp. ix–xxv.
Benjamin, Walter (1969) 'The Work of Art in the Age of Mechanical Reproduction,' in Hannah Arendt ed. *Illuminations*. New York: Schocken, pp. 217–251.
Blanchot, Maurice (2003) *The Book to Come*, trans. Charlotte Mandell, Stanford, CA: Stanford University Press.
Beer, Gillian (2009) *Darwin's Plots: Evolutionary Narrative in Darwin, George Eliot and Nineteenth-Century Fiction*, Cambridge, UK: Cambridge University Press.
Brown, Roger (1965) *Social Psychology*, New York: The Free Press.
Burke, Kenneth (1984) 'The Rhetoric of Hitler's "Battle",' in Michael J. Shapiro ed. *Language and Politics*, New York: NYU Press, pp. 61–80.

Coetzee, J. M. (2001) 'Introduction' to the Penguin edition of *The Confusions of Young Törless*, trans. Shaun Whiteside, New York: Penguin, pp. v–xii.

Connolly, William E. (2017) *Aspirational Fascism: The Struggle for Multifaceted Democracy under Trumpism*, Minneapolis: University of Minnesota Press.

Deleuze, Gilles (1997) 'Literature and Life,' *Critical Inquiry* Vol 23 (2), pp. 225–230.

Deleuze, Gilles (2000) *Proust and Signs*, trans. Richard Howard, Minneapolis: University of Minnesota Press.

Deleuze, Gilles and Guattari, Felix (1977) *Anti-Oedipus*, trans. Robert Hurley, Mark Seem, and Helen R. Lane, New York: Viking.

Deleuze, Gilles and Guattari, Felix (1994) *What is Philosophy?* trans. Hugh Tomlinson and Graham Burchell, New York: Columbia University Press.

DeLillo, Don (1985) *White Noise*, New York: Penguin.

Derrida, Jacques (1978) 'Freud and the Scene of Writing' in *Writing and Difference*, trans. Alan Bass, Chicago: University of Chicago Press, pp. 196–231.

Dickson, Andrew (2016) 'Culture in Weimar Germany: on the edge of a volcano,' *Discovering Literature: Twentieth Century,* on the web at: www.bl.uk/20th-century-literature/articles/on-the-edge-of-the-volcano-culture-in-weimar-germany.

Dirke, Sabine von (2017) 'Neoliberalism's Reengineering of the Authoritarian Personality', *Colloquia Germanica* Vol. 50 (3/4), pp. 327–338.

Ehrenreich, Barbara 'Foreword' to Klaus Theweleit, *Male Fantasies Volume 1: Women Floods Bodies History*, trans. Stephen Conway, Minneapolis: University of Minnesota Press, 1987, pp. ix–xiii.

Esposito, Roberto (2012) *Third Person*, trans. Zakiya Hanafi, Cambridge, UK: Polity.

Eysenck, H. J. (1954) *The Psychology of Politics*, London: Routledge and Kegan Paul.

Fichte, Johann Gottlieb (1922) *Addresses to the German Nation*, trans. R. F. Jones and G. H. Turnbull, Chicago: The Open Court.

Foucault, Michel (1973) *The Birth of the Clinic: An Archaeology of Medical Perception,* trans. A. M. Sheridan Smith, New York: Pantheon.

Foucault, Michel (1978) 'About the Concept of the "Dangerous Individual" in 19th-Century Psychiatry,' *International Journal of Law and Psychiatry,* Vol. 1: 1, on the web at: http://schwarzemilch.files.wordpress.com/2009/02/foucault_dangerous_individual.pdf.

Foucault, Michel (1978) *The History of Sexuality Vol I: An Introduction*, trans. Robert Hurley, New York: Pantheon.

Foucault, Michel (2007) *Security, Territory, Population*, trans. Graham Burchell, New York: Palgrave Macmillan.

Hansen, Mark B. N. (2015) *Feed Forward: On the Future of Twenty-First-Century Media*, Chicago: University of Chicago Press.

Harrison, Thomas (1960) 'The Essayistic Novel and Mode of Life: Robert Musil's The Man without Qualities,' *The Republic of Letters*, on the web at: https://arcade.stanford.edu/rofl/essayistic-novel-and-mode-life-robert-musils-man-without-qualities.

Hiaasen, Carl (1991) *Lucky You*, New York: Alfred A, Knopf.

'Hitler's Philosophical Enablers,' (2012) *The Catholic Thing*, on the web at: www.thecatholicthing.org/2013/06/12/hitlers-philosophical-enablers/

Hoche, Alfred (1920) *Arztliche Bemerkungen* in Karl Binding and Alfred Hoche, *De Freigabe der Vernichtung Lebensunwerten Lebens: Ihr Mass und ihre Form*, Leipzig.

Hoffman, Frederick (1962) 'William James and the Modern Literary Consciousness,' *Criticism* Vol. 4 (1), pp. 1–13.

Horkheimer, Max (1969) 'Preface' to T. W. Adorno et al. *The Authoritarian Personality*, New York: W. W. Norton, pp. v–xii.

James, William (1910) *Pragmatism: A New Name for Some Old Ways of Thinking*, New York: Longmans, Green & Co.

James, William (2017) *Principles of Psychology – Vols 1–2*, Leamington Spa, UK: Pantianos Classics.

Kaag, John (2020) *Sick Souls, Healthy Minds: How William James Can Save Your Life*, Princeton, NJ: Princeton University Press.

Kimball, Roger (1996) 'The Qualities of Robert Musil,' on the web at: https://newcriterion.com/issues/1996/2/the-qualities-of-robert-musil.

Lacan, Jacques (1977) 'Subversion of the Subject and the Dialectic of Desire,' in *Ecrits*, trans. Alan Sheridan, New York: W. W. Norton, pp. 292–325.

Lasswell, Harold (1964) 'Preface' to Sven Ranulf, *Moral Indignation and Middle Class, Psychology*, New York, Schocken, pp. ix–xiii.

Lethem, Jonathan (2018) 'Introduction' in Robert Musil, *The Man Without Qualities* Collingdale, PA: Diana Publisher, loc. 50–75.

Lippek, Sarah (2020) 'Disrupted Values, Erupting Culture: Cabaret and Sexual Persona in Weimar Berlin' *SSRN*, on the web at: https://papers.ssrn.com/sol3/papers.cfm?abstract_id=1079945.

Lukács, Georg (1971) *Theory of the Novel*, trans. Anna Bosock, Cambridge, MA: MIT Press.

Massumi, Brian (2005) 'Fear (The Spectrum Said),' *Positions* Vol. 13 (1), pp. 31–48.

Mills, C. Wright (1944) "Review of Franz Neumann's *Behemoth: The Structure and Function of National Socialism 1933–1944*, *Partisan Review*, on the web at: http://wbenjamin.org/Behemoth.html.

Musil, Robert (2018) *The Man Without Qualities*, Collingdale, PA: Diana Publisher.

Peirce, C. S. (1998) *The Essential Peirce: Selected Philosophical Writings*, vol 2, Bloomington: Indiana University Press.

Pynchon, Thomas (1997) *Mason & Dixon*, New York: Henry Holt.

Rancière, Jacques (2013) *The Politics of Aesthetics,* trans. Gabriel Rockhill, London: Bloomsbury.

Rancière, Jacques (2016) 'Fictions of Time,' in Grace Hellyer and Julian Murphet eds. *Rancière and Literature,* Edinburgh, UK: Edinburgh University Press, pp. 1–19.

Ranulf, Sven (1964) *Moral Indignation and Middle Class Psychology*, New York: Schocken.

Rokeach, Milton (1973) *The Open and the Closed Mind*, New York: Basic Books.

Rothberg, Michael (1994–1995) 'Documenting Barbarism: Yourcenar's "Male Fantasies", Theweleit's Coup,' *Cultural Critique* No. 29, pp. 77–105.

Ryan, Vanessa L. (2009) 'Reading the Mind: From George Eliot's Fiction to James Sully's Psychology,' *Journal of the History of Ideas* Vol. 70 (4), pp. 615–635.

Ryback, Timothy W. (2003) 'Hitler's Forgotten Library,' *The Atlantic*, on the web at: www.theatlantic.com/magazine/archive/2003/05/hitlers-forgotten-library/302727/.

Sartre, Jean Paul (1989) *The Family Idiot: Gustave Flaubert 1821–1857*, trans. Carol Osman, Chicago: University of Chicago Press.

Schambelan, Elizabeth (2016) 'Pseudo-Conservatism, The Solider Male, and the Air Horn,' *Los Angeles Review of Books*, on the web at: https://lareviewofbooks.org/article/pseudo-conservatism-soldier-male-air-horn/.

Shapiro, Michael J. (1992) 'The Politics of Fear,' in *Reading the Postmodern Polity: Political Theory as Textual Practice*, Minneapolis: University of Minnesota Press, pp. 122–139.

Shapiro, Michael J. (2012) 'Metaphor in the Philosophy of the Social Sciences,' In Terrill Carver and Samuel A. Chambers eds. *Michael J. Shapiro: discourse, culture, violence*, London: Routledge, pp. 15–32.

Shapiro, Michael J. (2016) *Politics and Time: Documenting the Event*, Cambridge, UK: Polity.

Smiley, Jane (2006) 'Nowhere man,' a review of *The Man Without Qualities* in *The Guardian*, on the web at: www.theguardian.com/books/2006/jun/17/featuresreviews.guardianreview28.

Sweet, Paul R. (1993) 'Fichte and the Jews: A Case of Tension between Civil Rights and Human Rights,' *German Studies Review* Vol. (1), pp. 37–48.

Theweleit, Klaus (1987) *Male Fantasies Volume 1: women floods bodies history*, trans. Stephen Conway, Minneapolis: University of Minnesota Press.

Theweleit, Klaus (1989) *Male Fantasies Volume 2: Male Bodies: Psychoanalyzing the White Terror*, trans. Erica Carter and Chris Turner, Minneapolis: University of Minnesota Press.

Turner, Norman (1998) 'Cezanne, Wagner, Modulation,' *Journal of Aesthetics and Art Criticism*, Vol. 56 (4), pp. 353–364.

Volosinov, V. N. (1987) *Freudianism: A Critical Sketch*, trans. I. R. Titunik, Bloomington: Indiana University Press.

Wilshire, Bruce (1969) 'Protophenomenology in the Psychology of William James,' *Transactions of the Charles S. Peirce Society*, Vol. 5 (1), pp. 25–43.

3

SCRIPTING "AMERICA"

Malignancies

Carl Safina's rendering of the contemporary relevance of *Moby Dick* provides a bridge from Chapter 2 to this one. His reading of the novel emphasizes Captain Ahab's malignant and dangerous mentality. Reflecting on the roles of the whale and his antagonist, Ahab, he writes,

> Moby Dick…is a white prop contrasting with the demonic Captain Ahab, the tormented tormentor, the malignant abused abuser of authority and of men. Ahab's bias is color based. A white whale becomes a blank pincushion for Ahab's thrusting mania as Melville shades pages with his madness… he flatters his men into allegiance with his maniacal quest…[I]impeccably skillful at manipulating people into abetting him, at making his self-destructive obsession their own…he becomes contagious, truly dangerous.[1]

Safina goes on to note the novel's hospitality to "varied skin shades…[men] breathing one another's sweat in close company [while they] tended whale-boiling caldrons and looked one another in the eye" and surmises, "Melville cast a frigatebird-like perspective on the American character's deepest congenital malignancy, then called Negrophobia."[2] It was a phobia lent a macabre visuality, the scars produced by the whips applied to the backs of plantation slaves, "a kind of hieroglyphics of the flesh" as Hortense Spillers puts it.[3]

As I have note elsewhere, Melville also addressed himself to another "congenital malignancy" in the American character, what he termed. "The Metaphysics of Indian Hating," the title of a chapter in his 1857 novel *The Confidence-Man* in which he registers his "disgust with the pious celebration of America's sense of community.

Where some saw a healthy expanding democracy, Melville saw crass materialism and exploitation, slavery, poverty, and a continuing war of extermination against Native Americans." Form-wise, "the novel did not simply say what was happening; [Melville] mobilized ironic tropes, enigmatic characters, peculiar narrative structures, and disrupting juxtapositions to challenge the Euro-American imaginary – its views of space and stories of settlement and expansion."[4] Roughly a century and a half later, Thomas Pynchon crafted another epic treatment of the aspects of the American character that Melville had impugned. His novel *Mason & Dixon* (the main focus of this chapter) dwells within a subjunctive ethos while it picks up Melville's version of the American story, with Melville-like form, to expose once again those same (and enduring) malignancies. For example, what his protagonists, Mason and Dixon learn in Lancaster Town when they reach the American continent is that it's the place where a vigilante group, the "Paxton Boys"[5] massacred Native Americans and where they witness "Whippings, the open'd flesh, the welling blood."[6]

Melville's epic provides two other bridges to Pynchon's *Mason & Dixon*. From its opening pages, "Melville [through his narrator Ishmael] foregrounds the issue of knowledge and its multiple and contradictory sources" by showing the many different ways that whales have been understood "throughout the ages and in all corners of the globe."[7] Similarly, throughout his *Mason & Dixon*, Pynchon stages epistemological uncertainly, in part through the way his main narrator, the Revered Wick Cherrycoke (sitting in his sister's Philadelphia living room) tells the story of the Mason and Dixon survey to young children 20 years after the event, and in part through the way the novel evokes dissensus by using multiple narrators. The other bridge is provided by the way Pynchon, like Melville, recognizes the Native American cultural markings on the landscape, to which Euro-Americans have failed to accord historical recognition (the evidence of "other civic entities" that Mason and Dixon discover as their survey pushes westward). Similarly, as *Moby Dick*'s Ishmael is observing the "visible surface of the sperm whale…uniquely crossed and re-crossed with numerous straight marks," drawing on his "retentive memory" he discerns another American hieroglyphics, "old Indian characters chiseled on the famous hieroglyphic palisades on the banks of the Mississippi."[8] Much of the coherence of this chapter is lent by the connection between scars and history that Melville was allegorizing. Ultimately, what is pervasively shared in the two epics are their allegorical structures which articulate historical time with adventure time, set in nineteenth-century America.[9]

Mason & Dixon Redux

> Continuity in the presentation of history is unattainable.
>
> *Walter Benjamin*

Pub conversations in Thomas Pynchon's *Mason & Dixon* inspired two of my past writing projects. The first one, which Pynchon locates in an eighteenth-century

English pub, is about an impending calendar reform instituted to rectify English time with global time because a 1582 commission under Pope Gregory XIII had decreed that October 4, 1582 was to be followed by October 15th and England had not followed suit. Much to the disgruntlement of the patrons of the pub, two centuries later the English head astronomer has decreed a similar removal of 11 days from the English calendar so that 2nd September would be followed by 14th September. Charles Mason, who is among patrons, explains to those assembled the kind of people who could be "hired" to accept such a change: "Strangers from far to the east" "The Indies?" "China?" "Stepney!" "His Lordship [the astronomer, Macclesfield]…required

> a people who lived in a different relation to time – one that did not, like our own, hold at its heart the terror of Time's passage, for more preferably, Indifference to it, pure and transparent as possible. The verbs of their language no more possessing tenses, than their Nous Case-Ending, – for these People remain'd as careless of Sequences in Time as disengaged from Subject, objects Possession, or indeed anything which among Englishmen require a Preposition.[10]

Alerted to the relationship between grammar and temporality by that fictional conversation, I pursued an analysis of the complex coexistence among disparate aspects of lived time within national formations, to which I referred as a "disjoint copresence."[11] The second is an encounter Pynchon invents between the Mason/Dixon team and Thomas Jefferson in an eighteenth-century American pub, "Raleigh's Tavern" in Virginia, which is described as a place "congenial to the *newness* [my emphasis] of history a-transpiring."[12] That conversation helped me to inaugurate a critique of Jefferson's foundational influence on the shaping of the US political order.

Because in my initial encounters with Pynchon's novel I was in pursuit of two distinct projects, I failed to appreciate the connection between the two conversations on which I drew. It has now become clear that as is the case with many of the novel's encounters, the Virginia conversation doesn't stand alone. It serves as a contrast with the other pub conversation in England, a venue that features *oldness* rather than newness. It also shares in a historical continuity; for centuries pubs have been alternative public spheres. If we heed the grammatical and temporal tropes in the Mason/Dixon – Jefferson encounter, we can recognize yet another connection with the earlier English conversation. Because the conversation in the English pub is not only about a historical episode, but also (allegorically) about writing – specifically about the role of grammar in the creation of one's experience of time – it prepares the reader to be attentive to the way the temporal aspects of the encounter in Virginia's Raleigh tavern are figured.

Here are the details of the Raleigh tavern scene I summarized in my earlier reading of the novel: Dixon, a *bon vivant* and reveler (in contrast with the austere

Presbyterian Mason), raises his ale-can and offers a toast: "To the pursuit of happiness." An unnamed Jefferson hears the toast: "'Hey sir, – that's excellent' exclaims a tall red-headed youth at the next table. 'Ain't it oh so true…You don't mind if I use the phrase some time?'" The landlord, recognizing that the customer is a surveyor, says, "Tom takes a *relative* interest in West lines….his father having help'd run the one that forms our own southern border."[13] In my original analysis of that conversation I suggested that Jefferson, who inherited a surveying mentality from his surveyor/father, authored a land survey that is a more telling document in the construction of his version of "America" than his other initiatives, (e.g.., *The Declaration of Independence*) and writings (e.g., *Notes on the State of Virginia*) which have received most of the scholarly attention.[14]

In this reading, I am concerned instead with the way the literary structure of Pynchon's novel combines with the novel's narrated metacommentaries to articulate his argument about the political significance of the Mason and Dixon survey. Much of the political sensibility of the novel works through theme- and concept-reversing repetitions in which alternating grammars are crucial. Thus, the above-noted juxtaposition of oldness and newness brings a grammar lesson in the English pub to bear on the "newness transpiring," in the Virginia pub. The Virginia conversation is structured with a grammatical movement from the past perfect tense (the "having help'd") to an infinitive that points to a future "pursuit." It contains the narrative and philosophical threads that are woven together throughout the text. Pynchon's narrative coherence is thus constructed by having one episode set up another. As a whole, they work as a composite to deliver his philosophically shaped and temporally expressed political ethos, a commitment to the subjunctive (the might-have-been). Form-wise, the repetitions shape and deepen the implicit argument and "normative mentality"[15] of the text. To illustrate how the composition of the novel accomplishes Pynchon's ideational positions, all involved in a subjunctive ideology that identifies the alternative possible Americas that the Mason and Dixon survey helped to foreclose, I want to suggest it works very much the way another writer's texts are structured. The legendary Longinus's compositions can be redeemed, even though they also seem to be wandering aimlessly from one aside to another with no overall coherence to connect them. Accordingly, I offer my own discursion, a review of Neil Hertz's defense of Longinus's style, which applies well to Pynchon's.

Hertz points out that Longinus's elliptical style, which does not follow a linear narrative progression, had both admirers who were willing to "release him from the strictures of theoretical discourse and allow him the license of a poet" (appreciating "his transgressions of conventional limits without ever calling them into question"). Although some have criticized Longinus' tendency to slide from one theoretical distinction to another, in defense of Longinus's style, Hertz admits that

> a "slide" is observable again and again in the treatise, and not merely from one theoretical distinction to another [so that one finds] oneself attending to

> a quotation, a fragment of analysis, a metaphor – some interestingly resonant
> bit of language that draws one into quite another system of relationships

but he goes on to rescue the value of Longinus' style.[16] As I've put it elsewhere, what Hertz shows convincingly is that although the "movement" of Longinus' treatise "is clearly not linear; it does not run in tandem with the progress of rhetorical argument from topic to topic but is in some ways cumulative" – that is, at certain points one becomes aware of a "thickening of texture." I am ascribing that "thickening of texture" to the progression in Pynchon's *Mason & Dixon*. However, before elaborating that part of my analysis, I want to theorize the interweaving of plot and essay in the novel because, (as is the case with Robert Musil's novel *The Man without Qualities* analyzed in Chapter 2), the novel's essay-like commentary – its historiographic metafictional form[17] – alerts the reader to its ethico-political mentality.

The Aesthetic and the Conceptual

The ideational contributions of Pynchon's novel are counter-Jeffersonian. As I have suggested, Jefferson's commitment was to turn the contingencies of encounter on the American Continent into certainties. His goal, which was expressed in among other documents his land survey (The Land Ordinance of 1785), was to have the Euro-American assemblage (most of which was temporarily situated in the eastern part of the continent) spread westward in a pattern of small "yeoman" farms. Although industrialization was to alter that aspirational political economy, the ultimate effect of the forceful implementation of Jefferson's impulse was to turn a "frontier" into "region." The frontier, as William Cronon et al. point out, was a space of negotiation at the outset of the Euro American-Native American encounter, a space in which institutionalized regionalization had not yet been installed. How to share a life world was in continual negotiation.[18] Birgit Rasmussen describes an exemplary one, a peace negotiation in 1645 between the French settled in the vicinity of the St, Lawrence River and a group of interconnected nations the French identified as "Iroquois." The negotiation was an encounter of "multiple and distinct literacies, each of which was strange and illegible outside of its own cultural context."[19]

Pynchon's protagonists are not negotiators. They are complicit in the process of "regionalization," which the text construes as a form of violence. A poetic epigraph at the opening of Chapter 26 refers to how Mason and Dixon "mark the Earth with geometrick Scars"[20] and ultimately have to concede that they're trespassing. "Rather than merely helping to consummate the invention of [what Jefferson imagined as a] predestined nation-state, they were involved, as Mason puts it, in 'trespass, each day ever more deeply'."[21] A similar trope is used to treat temporality. Later in the novel The Reverend Cherrycoke refers to the calendar reform that removed 11 days as "a chronologik wound."[22] The pairing of those tropes – spatial and temporal wounds – is one among many instances of the novel's re-inflected repetitions, "a 'parallactic' doubling of views" that deliver much of the novel's ethos.[23] In short, as it thinks about the interrelationship between cartography and historicity, the novel testifies to the "complex temporality that figures alongside spatial concepts [both of which are] multiply layered."[24]

What I want to emphasize is the form with which the novel thinks. With its meta commentaries that are interspersed in the plot, it narrates Mason and Dixon's (as well as other character's) gradual realization of the political implications that accompany the scientific aspect of their boundary-making survey. Tellingly, at one point Dixon perceives "something invisible going on" and Mason chimes in with the suggestion that it's "American politics."[25] On the one hand, the novel's protagonists, Charles Mason and Jeremiah Dixon, are the main "aesthetic subjects," who serve as the primary vehicles for the plot (while much of the commentary belongs to The "Reverend Cherrycoke"). Their roles are represented not only as character types with distinctive personalities, but also as guides and shapers of the eighteenth-century American life world. As such their "movements and actions (both purposive and non-purposive) map and often alter experiential, politically relevant terrains."[26] As aesthetic subjects their actions are more significant for what they reveal about the world within which they move than about their personalities.

On the other hand, Mason and Dixon (along with some other characters) are also "conceptual personae." In that role they serve as vehicles for the "author's concepts," articulated through the novel's essayistic commentary that accompanies its plot.[27] In their conceptual role, rather than mapping the novel's geopolitical terrain, they "show thought's territories."[28] In the moments in which instead of experiencing the world they're engaged in commentary about the implications of their roles, their statements convey the novel's ideational, ontological and political thinking. Although as Deleuze and Guattari observe, "art thinks no less than philosophy, but it thinks through affects and percepts,"[29] reserving concepts for the way which philosophy thinks, I want to suggest that insofar as novel contains an essayistic as well as artistic dimension, it thinks with concepts as well. Mason is explicit about their role as conceptual personae; he figures himself and Dixon as "philosophical frigates."[30] That imagery for their roles is previewed earlier in the novel when the ship they're on (in an astronomical expedition to Sumatra prior to their American survey) is drawn into naval battle, which is referred to with the French euphemism as "*Une Affair des Frégates.*" The two frigate mentions (separated by 230 pages) are yet another example of two seemingly disparate fragments being connected in Pynchon's narrative cartography.[31]

The conceptual and aesthetic roles assigned to characters apply to Pynchon's landscapes as well. In his analysis of cinematic landscapes, Martin Lefebvre supplies a distinction that fits well with the conceptual strategy in *Mason & Dixon*. Noting that landscape can have different connections with setting (where setting is simply the space where a story takes place), Lefebvre points out that while at times landscape plays a "supporting role as background or setting to events and characters," at others is serves as "a completely distinct aesthetic object."[32] There are two notable scenes in which the landscape is a "distinct aesthetic object" (which in both cases pushes back against the assumptions directing the Mason and Dixon surveying task). In one scene, Mason and Dixon find themselves confronting "one of the major High-ways of all inland America," a route that has been a Native American "Warrior Path," which though invisible, is a "Line that *makes itself felt*" (my emphasis); it asserts itself with the "sub-audible Hum of its Traffic."[33] In another scene, the two surveyors encounter "the notorious wedge," shaped to stymie "the Geometrickal Pilgrim." Its boundary line-defying shape disrupts the task of the surveyors whose charge is to settle conflicting proprietorships with a single path. It's a place of "doubtful ownership" that is part of "an unseen world beyond Resolution and of transactions never recorded." The wedge thus holds a space/time archive of historical erasure and manifests at the same time a temporal ambiguity, presenting to the surveying task a legal and geometric challenge.[34] Ultimately, because the content of *Mason & Dixon* cannot be separated from its literary structure, access to its political thinking demands close attention to Pynchon's writing, especially to the way his characters, objects, and scenes disclose the way *what* it thinks is a function of *how* it thinks.

In the Beginning: Hints about the Contingency of Assemblages

As I suggested in my earlier treatment of Jeffersonian America, Jefferson viewed the formation of a Euro-American dominated American nation as predestined. He imagined that nature was issuing a summons for a Euro-American dominated nation-state.[35] In contrast, Pynchon's writing conveys the contingency of assemblages. Conveying that perspective at the very beginning of the (elliptical) plot, the novel opens with a furniture allegory in which a room with a haphazard assemblage of pieces of furniture from earlier times and places is described. The ill-matching collection of pieces furnishes a "comfortable Room" at the rear of the House where children have entered from outdoor play (it's Pynchon's first evocation of the connection between scars and history):

> Here have come to rest a long scarr'd sawbuck table, with two mismatch'd side benches, from the Lancaster County branch of the family, – some Second-Street Chippendale. Including an interpretation of the fam'd Chinese sofa, with a high canopy of yards of purple stuff ..., – a few odd Chairs sent from England before the war...[36]

The scar allegory is thickened a few pages later when the Reverend Cherrycoke is described reading from "a scarr'd old Note-book." Thereafter the scar-history connection isn't repeated until 250 pages later when Mason and Dixon's survey has created the above noted "geometrick Scars" on the landscape. Allegorical throughout, Pynchon's text is structured as a vehicle for critical writing. As Walter Benjamin puts it "the allegorical intention" is one in which consciousness performs creatively as "a kind of writing."[37]

Holding in abeyance for the moment, the scar allegory (to be picked up at the end of the chapter), the haphazard collection of furniture in the living room plays two roles. First, it's likely a parodic reference to one of John Locke's metaphors for the mind; Locke raises the question, "if it is supposed that it ['Mind'] is a white Paper, void of all Characters, without any *ideas*, How comes it to be *furnished* [my emphasis]"[38] Second, it shapes another aspect of Pynchon's historiography. The brief description of the contingency of assemblage, articulated as a furniture allegory on the very first page, is picked up and reiterated as a national story roughly 130 pages later when Pynchon has the English astronomer Maskelyn say, "Ev'ry People have a story of how they were created," and adds that the story could be otherwise: "If one were heretickal enough which I certainly am not, one might begin to entertain some notion of the Garden in Genesis, as an instance of extra-terrestrial Plantation."[39] The suggestion is that every story providing a people's collective coherence could be replaced by another, which would supply a counter-coherence. In accord with that suggestion, I've put it this way:

> Given the complex set of forces that have been responsible…for assembling as a "people" those groupings identified as "nations"…their primary national stories must bear considerable weight. Indeed, there is nothing other than commitment to stories for a national people to give themselves a historical trajectory that testifies to their collective coherence.[40]

Pynchon adds a temporality to the counter-coherence he lends to the American assemblage. Through his primary narrator, the Reverend Wick Cherrycoke, the novel articulates a counter-enlightenment perspective with both retrospective and futuristic grammars. Looking back, Cherrycoke, (in the past tense) describes accompanying Mason and Dixon as they carried out a purportedly scientific project:

> Twas not too many years before the [Revolutionary] War, – what we were doing out in that Country together was brave, scientific beyond my understanding, and ultimately meaningless – we were putting a straight line through the heart of the Wilderness, eight yards wide and due west, in order to Separate two Proprietorships.[41]

Looking forward in a subjunctive grammar, contrived to show that alternatives could have been possible, Cherrycoke delivers a sermon, *Christ and History*, in which he suggests an alternative future for the past, a way to remake history by creating "More than one life-line back into a Past."[42]

Cherrycoke's observations are among the most frequent vehicles for the novel's historiography, driven by a commitment to counter-memory as a critique of institutionalized, rationally delivered linear histories. History needs, he states, "to be tended lovingly and honorably by fabulists and counterfeiters."[43] Another aspect of the novel's thinking, delivered in Cherrycoke's sermons (which punctuate the novel in several places), is a thoroughgoing challenge to the enlightenment narrative within which the Euro-American "ethnogenesis"[44] is legitimated as the spread of a scientific rationality that has displaced cultural impediments to progress. The conceptual basis of that critique is captured in Michel Foucault's critical remarks on enlightenment. Referring to a "movement by which, at the end of the colonial era, people began to ask the West what rights its culture, its science, its social organization and finally its rationality itself could have to laying claim to a universal validity" Foucault asks, "Is it not a mirage tied to an economic domination and a political hegemony?"…insofar as it is a form of "enlightenment reason," it is "reason as despotic enlightenment."[45]

What Foucault provides by way of a politically acute, conceptual intervention, Pynchon provides with the form of his writing. He challenges scientific rationalism with grammars that reorient subjects and history, and with his use of multiple generic threads, he displaces simplistic narratives of scientific discovery with "genre poaching,"[46] a literary approach to a historiography ("historiographic metafiction"[47] as one commentator puts it) in which he enlists a trajectory of genres ranging from classical epics, through sermons, to detective fiction and contemporary product commercials. That writing strategy operates symbiotically. Pynchon's grammatical rhythms are nested within diverse narrative genres to deliver his primary (grammatically figured) commitment to the subjunctive, to the possibilities of what could have been.

That subjunctive grammar is applied to his narrator as well as to the history of the continent. At one point, when Cherrycoke's subject is "Hanging," as he is reading to young twins (a Scheherazadean task that will sustain his welcome only as long as his story entertains), the scene is described as follows: "The Rev, producing [his already noted] scarr'd old Note-book, cover'd in cheap Leather begins to read" [a passage suffused with the subjunctive – emphases mine],

> *had I been* the first Churchman of modern times to be swung from Tyburn Tree, – *had I been* then taken for dead, whilst in fact but spending an Intermission among the eventless corridors of Syncope, due to the final Bowl of Ale, – *had a* riotous throng of medial students taken what they deem'd to be my Cadaver back beneath the somber groins of their College, – *had I then been* taken "resurrected" into an entirely new "Knowledge of the terms of being, in which Our Savior…though present, *would not have* figur'd as pre-eminently as with most Sectarians, – howbeit, – I should closely resemble the nomadic Parson you behold today…"[48]

Pynchon's Cherrycoke elaborates a trans-personal, historical subjunctive as well. The grammatical self he articulates in the subjunctive (occupying a persona at the cost what he could have been alternative versions) parallels the subjunctive grammar through which he sees the American Continent, where Mason and Dixon's survey has imposed a fixed unitary order on a space that *could have* allowed for the persistence of another "civic Entity."[49] As a locus of enunciation, Cherrycoke is a nomad in two senses: He's what Foucault famously attributes to the madman who is forcibly loaded onto a "ship of fools"; he's a traveler *par excellence*, i.e., one with no fixed address. In Cherrycoke's particular case, he's on the move as a fugitive from English justice, having fled imprisonment for the crime of "Anonymity" (he had "printed up" anonymous notices of "Crimes...committed by the Stronger against the Weaker").[50] At the same time he is Pynchon's vehicle for what Deleuze calls "nomad thought," a way of thinking with which one "evade[s] the codes of settled people"[51] He is one of the major vehicles for the way Pynchon unsettles the story of Euro-American settlement.

Although Cherrycoke delivers some of the novels most significant ideational utterances, – for example a sermon providing his heretical, anti-Pauline version of Christianity in which "doubt is the essence of Christ"[52] – there are many other narrators through whom the author's voice (though not necessarily his unambiguous point of view) is ventriloquized. Pynchon lends a degree of stability to the clashing voices by locating them within the historical moments of their utterances. Along with the multiplicity of voices he assigns to the eighteenth century is his own locus of enunciation in the twentieth century, which he conveys by having characters use contemporary products, for example, placing Dixon in a coffee house ordering a "Mount Kenya Double A" coffee drink that's characteristic of the kinds of names affixed to Starbuck selections.

Pynchon's composition of the novel in an eighteenth-century writing style (and spelling), while switching back and forth between eighteenth and twentieth-century scenes and sensibilities, provokes thinking by putting the reader in an unstable set of historical moments and disjunctive spaces. Moreover, she/he is prevented from identifying with a single ideational viewpoint as the novel constantly introduces "rupture[s] of narrativity [that]...bring into relief the non-convergence of discourses."[53] That effect is intensified by the existence of multiple narrators – an implicit Pynchon, a talking dog and a mechanical duck among others – which produce a heteroglossia that resists a single "verbal ideological center."[54]

The Surveyor's Gaze

It is power, not justice, which keeps rearranging the map.

James Baldwin

From the beginning of the novel, when Mason and Dixon team up under the sponsorship of England's Royal society to observe the transit of Venus in the vicinity of Sumatra (a task The Royal Society assigned to Captain James Cook in 1769), their personalities and ways of looking are contrapuntal; one favors grain (Dixon is a beer drinker) and the other the grape (Mason is a wine drinker); one is a nonbeliever and boisterous reveler, having been expelled from his Quaker meeting (Dixon), the other is a staid and pious Christian (Mason); and crucially for purposes of their tasks in the Pacific and on the American Continent, their gazes are aimed differently. Mason, an astronomer looks up, and Dixon, a surveyor looks down and ahead. As it turns out, however, they achieve an "emergent attunement."[55] Their different gazes combine symbiotically because both astronomical guides and landscape maps are required for the Mason and Dixon survey. However, apart from the enabling sciences on which the survey draws are its political implications. Recognizing that the eighteenth-century gaze was more than a mere look – it was the implementation of "an epistemological field [associated with] a new form of governance"[56] – Pynchon figures surveying technologies as governmentally sponsored weapons of ethnocide. Describing the tools involved in the "era of the [white] settlement of this [American] West" with violent metaphors – "An ax-bit blow quench'd in living wood…A percussive 'Sandwich' of hammer, anvil, and the Work between" – his text includes an aggressive, litigiously inclined "Capt. Shelby avid for any occasion to quarrel…with litigations great and petty…with Boundary issues a particular passion" participating in the western portion of the Mason and Dixon survey.[57]

Capt. Shelby, "also a surveyor," explicitly figures the surveyor's visual technology as a weapon; "bearing and wielding his Instrument [his spyglass turned to surveying use] like a weapon," he exults in surveying as a vehicle for the power of possession. "At our pleasure, we may look thro' this brazen Tube, thro' glass mathematickally shap'd and whatsoever describable scene sweeps by as we turn it, – why 'tis ours for writing down the Angle! Good heavens, what Power!" He adds, (mentally erasing the "previous lines" that Mason and Dixon had discovered that "run through the supposedly boundless forest"[58] as their survey began), that the violent possession that his surveying instrument enables is welcomed by the land: "Space awaits the surveyor, – no previous lines, no fences, no streets to constrain the polygony…"[59] Here Shelby is recapitulating Thomas Jefferson's landscape gaze, expressed in his famous *Notes on the State of Virginia,* where while describing a landscape from his location in his Monticello residence, he suggest that it promises "a pacified locus of possession."[60]

Capt. Shelby's view that there were "no previous lines, no fences, no streets" and thus an absence of cultivated landscape in the West is belied by ethnohistorical research. For example, in an investigation of the cultural history of the Iroquois, Matthew Dennis points out, "Many Europeans failed to recognize or acknowledge America as the product of centuries of cultural modification as a

'landscape' shaped by the desires of its denizens to provide themselves with a pros-
perous, secure, and fulfilling existence." Among their other landscaping practices,
they distinguished spaces of game management and zones of protection (with
clearings and cultivate densities). Accordingly, the Euro-American mapping process was experienced by Native Americans as an antagonistic intervention in their
life world. As Alan Trachtenberg puts it (in accord with Mason's remark about
trespassing), "The act of mapping and naming was in the eyes of the Indians, an act
of trespass, not upon property but on religion, upon the sacred itself. The white
man's maps threatened a whole way of life."[61]

Presuming as evident a well-developed Native American cultural as well as
physical presence in the landscape (expressed with Mason and Dixon's constant
discovery of "previous lines"), Pynchon contests the univocity of much of Euro-
America construction of the western landscape as an empty wilderness with a
plurivocity (at this juncture by having Dixon's voice oppose Capt. Shelby's
proprietary usurping of western space). After noting, "He's never regarded his
Occupation in quite this way before," Dixon enjoins an ironic repetition that
undercuts the Captain's weaponized gaze:

> Things to survey your Domain. Even if you don't own it. Here at the
> Allegheny Crest ye may stand and look either way, down mile after mile of
> the Visto ye've cut, and from our Eminence pretend that you own it.[62]

That instance of an encounter of voices operates in Pynchon's distinctive form
of polivocity; his characters constantly re-narrate and thereby re-inflect other's
narrations.[63]

Another aspect of the novel's literary structure emerges right after Dixon parodies Capt. Shelby's ownership pretentions. Interrogating another member of the
party, Capt. Zhang, a practitioner of "Geomancy," Dixon seeks knowledge of the
Luo-Pan, an alternative way of interpreting the "Zenith-Star" a knowledge practice that "has brought me," Dixon says, "to imagine an *Anti-celestial, or backwards
Astrology.*" As in other connections between remote sections of the novel, Pynchon's
Anti-Celestial reference is previewed very early in the novel with a description of
another "anti." There's an "Uncle Lomax's Soap-Works" that produces

> "Philadelphia Soap" …a Byword, throughout the American Provinces, of
> low quality. At the touch of water, nay damp Air, it becomes a vile mucus
> that refuses to be held in any sort of grip, gentle or firm, and often leaves
> things dirtier than they were before its application, – making it, more prop-
> erly, an Anti-Soap.[64]

That seeming aside about Philadelphia soap previews yet another "anti."
Philadelphia, shows again later in the novel, represented as an anti-Philadelphia.

Anti-Philadelphias

Philadelphia moments are frequent in *Mason & Dixon* not only because the "Great Experiment" (as Alexis de Tocqueville famously put it) is inaugurated there, but also because it has been an important nexus in global political economy. It sits in the novel at the origin of two journeys. One involves the story of the survey. Dixon noting where they will first set a post for the survey, refers to "the Zero Point, or Beginning, of the West line [which will start at]…the south Edge of Philadelphia."[65] The other journey is ideational; it's a legitimation of the westward expansion of the "experiment," which migrates from the promulgation of words about freedom spoken in Philadelphia to the implementation of radical unfreedom, the spread of slavery westward along with the process of what is euphemistically called the "Indian removal." As Jamaica Kincaid (from Antigua, one of what the novels calls the "cruel Sugar-Islands," where "sweetness" is "bought…with the lives of African Slaves," beginning in 1674[66]) remarks after observing the image of the signers of the Declaration of Independence in Independence Hall in Philadelphia:

> American begins with the Declaration of Independence…There's a painting in Philadelphia of the men who signed it. These men look relaxed; they are enjoying the activity of thinking…the luxury of it. They have time to examine the thing called their conscience and act upon it…some keep their hair in an unkempt style (Jefferson, Washington), and other keep their hair well groomed (Franklin), their clothes pressed…

She then proceeds to reflect on the people (slaves and servants) who worked to prepare the men for the occasion: "the people who made their beds and made their clothes nicely pressed and their hair well-groomed or in a state of studied dishevelment."[67] The unfreedom of the people to whom she is referring are pointedly noted by Mason, who acknowledges that the task they took on for the proprietors whose dispute they're resolving, resulted in "having drawn a Line between their Slave-Keepers, and their Wage-Payers."[68]

In his novel *Philadelphia Fire*, John Edgar Wideman updates the unfreedom in the freedom-inaugurating Philadelphia. He delivers the Philadelphia that visited lethal fire on some of its residents (the firebombing of the city block occupied by African American members of the MOVE organization). Beginning with an epigraph by the city's founder, William Penn's September 30, 1681's instructions on the positioning of dwellings:

> Let every house be placed, if the Person pleases, in the middle of its plait… so there may be ground on each side, for Gardens or Orchards or fields, that it may be a greene Country Towne, which will never be burnt, and always be wholesome,[69]

the novel repeats the fire imagery as it took lives and property among its poorer residents. The novel parallels that juxtaposition with one between the recreational dining in upscale restaurants by the affluent classes, enjoying Philadelphia's "restaurant renaissance," and a homeless "trash diver" who scavenges among the garage the restaurants discard.[70]

Pynchon's, *Mason & Dixon*, relying on its predominant form, re-inflected repetitions, also constructs a Philadelphia whose reality fails to live up to the founding ideals (but does continue to perpetuate its foundational violence). The "Philadelphia Soap," product described early in the novel as an "Anti-Soap" because of its failures to live up to a soap product ideal (its ability to clean) is an allegory for the city which becomes (more than 700 pages later) an anti-Philadelphia, expressed in the text as "unchosen Philadelphia." That expression surfaces as the room in which the Reverend Cherrycoke's story telling had been going on begins to fill up with

> Black servants, the Indian poor, the Irish runaways, the Chinese sailors, the overflow'd from the mad hospital [all of whom]…bring their Scars, their pox-pitted Cheeks, their Burdens and Losses, their feverish eyes, their proud fellowship in a Mobility that is to be, whose shape none inside this House may know.[71]

Doubtless Pynchon selects the adjective "unchosen" to impugn the story of American exceptionalism presumed by the early New England settlers, who figured themselves as a chosen people entering an America they viewed as a new Jerusalem, "a site specifically favored by God – perhaps the very place that He had chosen to initiate the millennial Kingdom of Christ."[72] That presumption was extended by more secularly oriented American historians who perpetuated a version of American exceptionalism as an invidious comparison, the "assumption that the United States, Unlike European nations, has a covenant that makes Americans a chosen people who have escaped from the terror of historical change to live in timeless harmony with nature."[73] To mount a critique of American exceptionalism, Pynchon resorts to parodies of historical moments and to fictional versions of the characters involved in them, to "reinscribe into the birth of the nation the cultural erasures and the epistemic violence involved in the narration of American exceptionalism."[74]

However, a grasp of Pynchon's critique of exceptionalism requires a treatment of another one of his oppositions, The Reverend Cherrycoke's (and accordingly Pynchon's) anti-Pauline version of Christianity. There is a crucial theological thread running through *Mason & Dixon*, which participates in the construction of the novel's onto-political thinking. Mason seconds Cherrycoke's anti-Pauline sermons. After reading "I Corinthians," in particular Chapter 15 (up to verse 42) in which Paul's case for Resurrection proceeds from Human bodies to Animal Bodies, and thence to Bodies Celestial and Terrestrial, and the Glories proper to each, – "'So also is the resurrection of the Dead', Mason says aloud, 'Excuse me?'. 'So also? I don't see the Connection. I never did'."[75]

Pynchon's Christian Time

To rehearse briefly Paul's version of Christian time: Everything significant for the Christian emerges from "the event." As Paul puts it, "Jews require a sign, and the Greeks seek after wisdom: But we preach Christ crucified" (Corinthians 1: 22–23). For Paul, Christ's crucifixion and resurrection presage the end of historical time, an apocalypse for which Christians must wait with keen anticipation. In Martin Heidegger terms, Paul's version of "Christian time," enjoins an "obstinate waiting."[76] It is a "waiting," according to Paul for the end of biological and historical time, "for the adoption, *to wit*, the redemption of our body [Romans 8: 23]." In contrast, "Christian time" for Cherrycoke (and Pynchon) articulates *with* rather than replacing historical time; it is figured as a prolonged and continuous "hunt." From Reverend Cherrycoke's sermon, "Christ and History" (first inserted early in the novel),

> History is the Dance of our Hunt for Christ, and how we have far'd. If it is undeniable so that he rose from the Dead, then the event is taken into History, and History is redeem'd from the service of Darkness, – with all the secular Consequences, flowing from that one Event, design'd and will'd to occur.[77]

When Cherrycoke's "Christ and History" sermon is revisited hundreds of pages later, it's evident that for Pynchon, rather than "obstinate waiting," Christian time requires an obstinate deferral.

Along with its thematizing of a non-closural duration, the novel stages a multi-genre coalition of imaginative genres with which history, as it is articulated with Christian time, manifests a "Tangle of Lines." That expression impugns the very idea of the single straight line, separating jurisdictions, that Mason and Dixon were hired to draw:

> Facts are but the Play-things of lawyer, – Tops and Hoops, fore-ever a-spin…History is not Chronology, for that is left to Lawyers, – nor is it Remembrance, for remembrance belongs to the people. History can as little pretend to the Veracity of the one, as claim the Power of the other, her Practitioners, to survive, must soon learn the arts of the quidnunc, spy, and Taproom Wit – that there may ever continue more than one life-line back into a Past [it's a] "Tangle of Lines, long and short, weak and strong, vanishing into the Mnemonick Deep, with only their Destination in common.[78]

That passage harbors several significant effects and implications. First by inter-articulating a spatial and temporal figuration, it provides a way to thicken the suggestion stated early in the novel that time is "the space that may not be seen."[79] In addition, when considered along with a line later in the text from one of the Reverend Cherrycoke's "*Undelivered Sermons*, "The final pure Christ is pure uncertainty. He is become the central subjunctive fact of Faith,"[80] it becomes evident that the way the novel's literary structure articulates its temporal ideology and (heretical) theological positioning is considerably influenced by Kierkegaard, whose anti-Pauline view of Christianity is articulated as his attachment to dance as a crucial metaphor for thought.

Pynchon and Kierkegaard

> I have trained myself…always to be able to dance in the Service of thought. [81]
>
> *Kierkegaard*

Kierkegaard, whose writings range over a variety of literary forms, provides several connections to Pynchon's styles and thinking. As is the case in Pynchon's *Mason & Dixon* (among other works), Kierkegaard, throughout his writings – both his treatises and fictional texts – uses many voices. In his case they are the alternative pseudonyms with which his texts are narrated, none of which constitutes a singular subject position with which Kierkegaard identifies. (He explicitly denied the writings of the pseudonymous authors as accurate representations of himself.[82]) Although the pseudonym count adds up to 19 (not counting the unused ones he prepared for texts he didn't publish) rather than enumerating them, I want to identify those that compare with the way Pynchon's characters operate as thought vehicles.

In his novelistic *Repetition*, which developed the repetition temporal trope in a way that accords with how repetition works as a temporal operator structuring Pynchon' style, Kierkegaard uses two contrapuntal characters, not in his case to enact a plot that reveals and extols the subjunctive but to distinguish good from bad repetition, where the former is an aesthetic and disinterested view of life and the latter an ethical committed one. The bad repetition is represented by the character Constantine Constantius who views life from an abstract disinterested stance; he reflects eloquently on ideas but doesn't live them. The latter is represented by an anti-Constantius, a young unnamed advice-seeking fiancé who ultimately rejects Constantius's aesthetic distancing advice and *moves* to actualize his ideals. As Kierkegaard's allegorical novel thematizes and extols movement, Pynchon follows suit. Mason and Dixon's movement toward the West is accompanied by a movement in their thinking, a realization of the epistemic violence of their task. They are European "Mobility," as Mason puts it, engaged in "Acts that in Whitehall would merit hanging."[83]

Along with the legacy that Kierkegaard's literary structure provides for Pynchon, is the inspiration in his anti-Pauline theology. In his *Journals* Kierkegaard laments the way Paul turned Christianity into his own religion. Whereas Paul's Christian time is apocalyptic, a waiting for the end of time, Kierkegaard (like Pynchon's Reverend Cherrycoke) relocates Christianity in the present:

> In the teachings of Christ, religion is completely present tense: Jesus is the prototype and our task is to imitate him, become a disciple. But then through Paul came a basic alteration. Paul draws attention away from imitating Christ and fixes attention on the death of Christ The Atoner. What Martin Luther in his reformation failed to realize is that even before Catholicism, Christianity had become degenerate at the hands of Paul. Paul made **Christianity the religion of Paul, not of Christ**. Paul threw the Christianity of Christ away, completely turning it upside down, making it just the opposite of the original proclamation of Christ.[84]

As Deleuze suggests, Pauline Christianity is "a mortuary enterprise... Paul ... keeps Christ on the cross, ceaselessly leading him back to it, making him rise from the dead, displacing the center of gravity toward eternal life."[85] As Paul conceded, an anticipation of "eternal life" renders the present life world inconsequential. He abjures those "caught up in what life offers," for those "remain stuck in the worldly" (Thessalonians 5: 5).

Contrary to Paul's rejection of locating life in the "worldly" domain, favoring instead a transcendent eternity, Machiavelli opted for the opposite. Challenging the Pauline emphasis on eternal time, Machiavelli famously insisted that citizens should see themselves in historical time, i.e., as beings situated in a present life world rather than as eternal beings. If located in the city rather than the cosmos, he argued, they can recognize their civic obligations. That temporal commitment is what constitutes the "Machiavellian moment," as J. G. A. Pocock puts it. It is the displacement of a heaven-centered cosmology with earth-centered obligations.[86] Kierkegaard argued in behalf of a similar temporal commitment; in his case the aim was to direct people's attention to Christ's lessons on how to live in the life world rather than to the implication of his crucifixion, the promise of eternal life. Instead of placing one's faith in externally promised hope, Kierkegaard counselled living an ethical life by drawing spiritual strength from within. That ethical pedagogy, which is developed in the interactions of his conceptual personae in *Repetition*, has had an undeniable impact on Pynchon's version of the ethical life. In his novel *The Crying of Lot 49*, for example, Pynchon draws on Kierkegaard's use of the "post horn," a symbol of repetition that keeps announcing itself with a "different squawk,"[87] to structure the novels interpersonal relationships and to thematize an "epistemological uncertainty."[88] And in *Mason & Dixon,* in accord with Kierkegaard's privileging of forward-looking repetition over backward-looking recollection, Pynchon has the Reverend Cherrycoke voice Kierkegaard's anti-Pauline version of Christianity in which (to repeat quotations from his sermons) to search for Christ is to dance: "History is the Dance of our Hunt for Christ,"[89] (which Kierkegaard expresses as the turning of the "the leap of life into a gait"[90]). And Kierkegaard anticipates another Pynchon commitment. His call to heed Christ's message as an embrace of epistemological uncertainty comports with Pynchon/Cherrycoke's view, "Doubt is the essence of Christ...The final pure Christ is pure uncertainty."[91] Nevertheless, it's likely that Pynchon's politically attuned onto-theology is influenced, at least obliquely, by the crucifixion, evident in the many references throughout the novel to scars and wounds. Before returning to the importance of those tropes, I want to consider one more "anti" in *Mason & Dixon*, an anti-James Fenimore Cooper in order to draw out more elaborately the novel's political resonances.

"The Novel and the Nation-State"

In his *Atlas of the European Novel*, Franco Moretti refers to the historical novel as "the most successful full form of the [nineteenth] century" and adds that while the novels are "historical" in terms of "their peculiar relationship to time...their spatial component is just as striking as their temporal one."[92] Treating Sir Walter Scott's Waverley novels as exemplary of the genre, Moretti refers to Scott's ability "to read time in space" in novels that take the shape of what Bakhtin famously designates as *Bildungsromans* – novels that combine the adventure time of protagonists with historical time – (noted above as applied to both Melville's *Moby Dick* and Pynchon's *Mason & Dixon*).[93] In an analysis that applies well to Pynchon's *Mason & Dixon*, Moretti identifies the intertwined "space-tropes" that shape the journeys of Scotts protagonists.[94] Attentive to the way "geography acts upon style,"[95] Moretti describes the way Scott figures borders – anthropological borders (e.g., one that show up when the character, Waverley visits the Scottish Highlands) as well as politico-military ones – all involved in the geopolitical dynamic featured in Scott's time, the process through which England became Britain as internal borders were being effaced. Identifying "Geography as the foundation of narrative form," Moretti analyzes Scott's Waverley novels to demonstrate how space becomes time in historical novels in general:

> Not obvious...is the fact that space does not become time just anywhere, in historical novels, but *only in the proximity of the internal border*. Only there it becomes possible to "see" a journey into the past – *and thus to imagine the very form of the historical novel, which is itself a journey into the past*.[96]

Inasmuch as Scott's Waverley novels articulate history with romance – with novels that combine adventure time with historical time – he needed an aesthetic subject to accomplish the genre's way of thinking. Accordingly, he "sends his young man [Waverley] to the Highlands – and invents the key genre of the century."[97]

One of the most notable of the century's practitioners of the genre was James Fenimore Cooper, whose novels mimicked Scott's literary form as well as the political ideology it delivered – legitimation for the consolidation of diverse peoples into a (mythic) national people, what is euphemistically called "nation-building" in political science texts. However, there's a radical difference in the nation-building appreciations of the two writers. While Scott was erasing anthropological borders, Cooper was erasing an ethnos. His elegiac Leatherstocking novels participated in what Patrick Brantlinger calls a "dark vanishing." "Cooper, like Scott," he writes, "offers a future-oriented history or prophecy by hindsight, according to which the past of the new nation-state of American lies all in the future – in contrast to the Mohicans who have no history."[98]

Cooper repeated his view that the "Indians" are outside of history in a chapter he contributed to a coffee table book featuring "picturesque" landscapes. Saying that his contribution is meant to "serve those who, unable to travel in the American continent, must depend on the pen, the pencil, and the graver"[99] for their information, he contrasts the "American landscape," which has "an air of freshness, youthfulness, and in many instanced...rawness,"[100] with the landscapes of Europe "on which are impressed the teeming history of the past."[101] His evacuation of the national and cultural Native American presence from the landscape in his contribution to an American scenery anthology follows his novelistic evacuation of them from America's future. By the time he published his scenery reflections he had already helped to legitimate the disqualification of Native American entitlement to their lands. His novel *The Pioneers* addresses and endorses an answer to the question, "Who has the right to own and govern the land originally possessed by the Indians and inherited through the revolution."[102] It's the Euro conquerors.

While the visual technologies in Cooper's evocation of the picturesque in his American scenery essay serve to evacuate Native American presence, in *The Pioneers* the narrative extinguishes their presence in the land with a turn to a different technology, the legal instrument. Because an assertion of Euro-American sovereignty "rested upon the rights of conquest" and the "Doctrine of Discovery," evidence of "direct ties of political kinship and inheritance between the United States and England" was required to assert those rights.[103] Accordingly, Chief Justice John Marshall, in his opinion in *Johnson v. McIntosh* (1763) (though conflicted because of misgiving about what natural law would indicate as an injustice) used the principle of conquest and the continuity of the Euro-community to assert civil law, which allowed him to turn "the Indian inhabitants" from owners into "occupants to be protected."[104]

Cooper's *The Pioneers* is complicit with Marshall's tortured reasoning. His aesthetic subject/protagonist, Natty Bumppo, who, because of his commitment to natural law challenges the legal weapons used against Indians, becomes inadvertently one who "fulfills a strategic function of Cooper's management of the conflict between natural and civil law as it intersects with the problem of race."[105] By assembling a hybrid "family" residing in Natty's hut, one of whom is an adopted son of the "Indian" Chingachgook, Cooper has invented an "inheritance through an unbroken family lineage," that enacts the same justification for seizing native American land as the one to which Marshall turned.[106] As is well-known, the legal erasure of Native America's legitimate rights to space was followed by more violent forms of erasure, direct military assaults aided by weapons technologies, and the encroachments of predatory commercial enterprises, aided by the steel manufacturing that provided the tracks and trains enabling the establishment of markets and thus the movement of capital and settlers westward.

A contemporary technology is associated with another more recent erasure of Native American (historical) presence, robotic-created semiconductor circuits. "The Fairchild Corporation…the largest private employer of indigenous workers in the US," once manufactured the circuits in their semiconductor divisions using (from 1965–1975) "almost entirely…female Navajo workers [whose]… weaving skill (part of the 'traditional' Navajo arts'[led to the assumption that they are] 'naturally' suited to the detailed labor involved in building the circuits." Having been replaced by circuit printing technology, "Native American women have been all but erased from official histories of the microchip…"[107] While large corporations don't write romantic elegies about the people erased from their milieu, Cooper did. His novel *The Last of the Mohicans*, although a bloody account of genocidal battles, which constructs Indians as vicious killers decimating each other as well as threatening settlers, is also a romantically inclined elegy for their disappearance. Noting that, "the Mohicans were the possessors of the country first occupied by the Europeans in this [the eastern] portion of the continent [and that] they were, consequently, the first dispossessed," rather than wondering would might have been had the "continent" been shared in the form of a negotiated structure of co-governance – the subjunctive rarely entered Cooper's literary musings – he begins the novel with a eulogy to "the seemingly inevitable fate of all these people who disappear before the advances…of civilization, as the verdure of their naïve forests falls before the nipping frost."[108]

Cooper's Natty Bumppo, whom he sends into the midst of "Indian country," expresses that view, a combination of sympathy and a sense of civilizational superiority, of admiration on the one hand and contempt on the other. However, while symbolically evacuating the landscape of an "Indian" presence, Cooper, unlike Jefferson, envisioned the Euro-American dominance as maritime rather than agricultural:

> the tide of emigration, which has long been flowing westward, must have its reflux…the great outlet to the rest of the world, the path of adventure, and the only, at least the principle, theater for military achievements open to the people of this country, is on the ocean.[109]

Nevertheless, Cooper shared a patrimony with Thomas Jefferson. In the "Introduction" to *The Pioneers*, he identifies his father's real estate accumulation and the surveying vocation with which it was abetted: "In 1785 the author' father, who had an interest in extensive tracts of land in the wilderness, arrived with a party of surveyors" and has his character, Judge Temple experience what he imagines his father experienced when "the scene [of that 'wilderness'] met his eye,"[110] the same opportunity for possessing the emptiness that Jefferson presumed as he gazed outward from his estate. As the literary geography of his Leatherstocking novels attests, among what Cooper inherited from his father was a commitment to what Joseph Conrad called "imperial geography." More attuned than Cooper to "the representational violence intrinsic to geographic imaginaries," Conrad

> proposed a chronology of geographic perspectives that accompanied and legitimated various stages in the process of European colonization... [running from] "geography fabulous" based on myths of the new world, through "geography militant" coinciding with "invasions", to "geography triumphant", expressed in the subsequent representations of the European settlements.[111]

Cooper's geographic imaginary and narrative legitimation of the law of conquest is a literary historiographic realization of what Foucault mapped out elaborately in his 1975–1976 lectures at the Collège de France, a history of invasion that supplants the mythic contract history model attributed to the origin of the state. State building, he shows, is owed to a "war-repression" rather than a "contract-oppression" model of power.[112] Cooper Leatherstocking novels are a post hoc legitimation of the result on the American continent. In addition to articulating natural law through his protagonist, Natty Bumppo, he turned to a classical defense of natural law to justify turning land, which in its pristine state (what he called "wilderness") is unowned by anyone, into property. To do so he adopted John Locke's labor theory of value in which mixing one's labor with land (e.g., by farming) translates as ownership.[113] He accomplishes that Lockean justification for possession with his usual literary form, using a protagonist as his aesthetic vehicle. It is with his "Indian" protagonist Chingachgook that Cooper references a Lockean labor theory of value. Early in *The Pioneers*, he describes Chingachgook's frail arms:

> His shoulders, and body to his waist, were entirely bare, with the exception of a silver medallion of Washington, that was suspended from his neck by a thong of buckskin, and rested on his high chest, amid many scars. His shoulders were rather broad and full; but the arms, though straight and graceful, wanted the muscular appearance *that labor gives to a race of men* [my emphasis].[114]

Through the invention of a disability in Chingachgook's body, Cooper disqualifies Native Americans as property holders because of their inability to engage in "labor."

Just as I've suggested, Pynchon's *Mason & Dixon* is an anti-Jeffersonian text, it is also an anti Fenimore Cooper text. While Cooper's elegy for the Continent's Indians is located in a romantic adventure novel in which, without irony, his protagonist affirms his political affirmation of an inevitable Euro-American dominance, Pynchon's novel is a parody rather than an elegy. While the aesthetic ideology in Cooper's elegy celebrates conquest, even as it delivers some sympathy for the conquered, Pynchon's "counter-song" (the Greek meaning of parody), sung in the subjunctive, constructs Mason and Dixon's westward movement, while representing the "European Mobility," as an historic *mis*adventure that turned "Possibilities into Simplicities that serve the ends of Government."[115] Nevertheless, although Cooper's legitimation of Euro-American imperialism in his Leatherstocking novels contrasts with the anti-imperial force of Melville's and Pynchon's epics, there is a significant figurative convergence among their works. For both Cooper and Pynchon, the land speaks, albeit with different resonances. While Cooper invents a Gothic mood in *The Last of the* Mohicans where he has the landscape mimic an Indian menace – "When the [Euro-American] characters approach Glen Falls to secrete themselves for the night in its caves, the ominous landscape [casting up shadows that appear like hidden enemies] adds to the Gothic mood"[116] – Pynchon's "Warrior Path" with a "sub-audible hum" testifies to the "Indians" unheeded civic life.

Continental Wounds: The Historiography of Scars

Cooper's description of the bare-chested Chingachcook, which refers to his "many scars," evokes the relationship between scars and history elaborated in both Melville's and Pynchon's epics. Doubtless while Cooper's description was meant to identify Chingachgook as a battle tested warrior who wears his fighting history on his body, Melville's and Pynchon's turn to scars to reference a different historical dynamic. While Cooper's Leatherstocking novels collaborate with the erasure of subordinated population's ability to gain a recognizable place within national history and space, leaving them "invisible to geography,"[117] Melville's *Moby Dick* and Pynchon's *Mason & Dixon* testify to the violence and injustices associated with what has been erased from historical visibility. Thus, the scars on Melville's Moby Dick constitute the body of the whale as an allegory that connects the whale's markings with Native American markings. Seeing the bio-history of the whale inscribed on his skin turns Ishmael's attention to the bio-history of Native America inscribed in the landscape. As it is put is at the beginning of the chapter, Ishmael's look at the "visible surface of the sperm whale…uniquely crossed and re-crossed with numerous straight marks," is followed in the text by his reference to his "retentive memory" of "old Indian characters chiseled on the famous hieroglyphic palisades on the banks of the Mississippi." Like Melville, Pynchon "anatomizes the nation,"[118] locating scars on things, on spaces and on bodies, in his case to elaborate his subjunctive ethos. His references to scars participate in a historiography that discloses alternative possible Americas under erasure.

Scar references show up five times in *Mason & Dixon*. As already noted, they appear as the Revered Cherrycoke begins his account of the Mason and Dixon survey, seated among scarred furniture in the living room where he is narrating the tale while holding a scarred notebook from which he speaks. At that point, the scarred furniture reflects an eclectic assemblage – an allegory for the contingencies of the national assemblage (as already noted) – and the scarred notebook references old recollections that situate the story teller's participation in the events he's narrating: history-as-story. Both scars set the iconoclastic mood of Pynchon's novel. Subsequently, the reference to the "geometrick scars," indicates that rather than engaged in a mere scientific activity, the surveyors are perpetrating violence. That figuration is reinforced a few hundred pages later, when a Chinese interlocutor to whom Mason recounts the object of his survey as "a boundary, nothing more," responds (within the idiom of an alternative cosmology),

> Boundary!...Ev'rywhere else on earth, Boundaries follow nature, – coast-lines, ridge-tops, river-banks, -so honoring the Dragon of *shan* within, from which Land-Scape ever takes its form. To mark a right Line upon the Earth is to inflict upon the Dragon's very Flesh, a sword-slash, a long perfect scar, impossible for any who live out here the year 'round to see as other than hateful assault. How can it pass unanswer'd?[119]

Finally, as the last chapter of *Mason & Dixon* unfolds, the scar allegory is applied to immigrant bodies. Chinese sailors are described seeking refuge in Cherrycoke's sister's house in (unchosen) Philadelphia: "They bring their Scars, their Pox-pitted Cheeks, their Burdens and Losses, their feverish Eyes, their proud fellowship in a Mobility that is to be, whose shape none inside the House may know."[120] Ultimately, Pynchon's novel provides an answer to the Chinese character's question, "How can it [the survey-as-sword-slash] go unanswer'd." *Mason & Dixon* offers a version of history that "none inside the House" (as an allegory for the nation) have wanted to know." To borrow an apt phrase from Arundhati Roy, it serves to "nudge [America's] hidden morality from its resting place and make it bubble to the service and float for a while. In clear view, for everyone to see."[121]

Notes

1 Carl Safina, "Melville's Whale Was a Warning We Failed to Heed," *The New York Times*, May 2, 2020, on the web at: www.nytimes.com/2020/05/02/books/review/herman-melville-moby-dick.html.

2 *Ibid.*

3 Hortense Spillers, "Mama's Baby, Papa's Maybe: An American Grammar Book," *Diacritics* 17: 2 (1987), 67.

4 Michael J. Shapiro, *Violent Cartographies: Mapping Cultures of War* (Minneapolis: University of Minnesota Press, 1997), 38.

5 Thomas Pynchon, *Mason & Dixon* (New York: Henry Holt, 1997), 341.

6 *Ibid.*, 347.

7 The quotation is from Birgit Brander Rasmussen, *Queequeg's Coffin: Indigenous Literacies and Early American Literature* (Durham, NC: Duke University Press, 2012), 112.

8 Herman Melville, *Moby Dick: or The Whale* (Evanston, IL: Northwestern University Press, 201), 305–306.

9 As genres, both novels are what M. M. Bakhtin refers to as a *Bildungsroman* (a novel that combines the adventure time of protagonists with historical time). See M. M. Bakhtin, "Forms of Time and the Chronotope of the Novel," in *The Dialogic Imagination* trans. Caryl Emerson and Michael Holquist (Austin: University of Texas Press, 1981), 84–258.

10 Pynchon, *Mason & Dixon*, 195.

11 See Michael J. "National Times and Other Times: Rethinking Citizenship," in *For Moral Ambiguity: National Culture and the Politics of the Family* (Minneapolis: University of Minnesota Press, 2001), 112–138.

12 Michael J. Shapiro, *Deforming American Political Thought: Challenging the Jeffersonian Legacy* (London: Routledge, 2016), 9.

13 Pynchon, *Mason & Dixon*, 395.

14 Shapiro, *Deforming American Political Thought*, 10. The inner quotations are from *Ibid.*, 608.

15 The expression belongs to Georg Lukács, *Theory of the Novel* trans. Anna Bosock (Cambridge, MA: MIT Press, 1971), 84.

16 Neil Hertz, "A Reading of Longinus," in *The End of the Line: Essays in Psychoanalysis and the Sublime* (New York: Columbia University Press, 1985), 1–2.

17 The genre designation, "historiographic metafiction," belongs to by Linda Hutcheon, "Historiographic Metafiction: Parody and the Intertextuality of History," on the web at: http://yunus.hacettepe.edu.tr/~jason.ward/ied485britnovel4/LindHutchHistiogra phicMetafiction.pdf.

18 See William Cronon, George Miles, and Jay Gitlin, "Becoming West," In Cronon et. al. *Under an Open Sky: Re-thinking America's Western Past* (New York: W. W. Norton, 1992), 3–27.

19 Rasmussen, *Queequeg's Coffin*, 53.

20 Pynchon, *Mason & Dixon*, 257.

21 *Ibid.*, 608.

22 *Ibid.*, 555.

23 Elizabeth Jane Wall Hinds, "Introduction: The Times of *Mason & Dixon*," in Elizabeth Jane Wall Hinds ed. *The Multiple Worlds of Pynchon's Mason & Dixon* (Rochester, NY: Camden House, 2005), 18.

24 *Ibid.*, 4.

25 Pynchon, *Mason & Dixon*, 478.

26 Michael J. Shapiro, *Studies in Trans-Disciplinary Method: After the Aesthetic Turn* (London: Routledger, 2012), xiv.

27 Gilles Deleuze and Felix Guattari, *What is Philosophy?* trans. Hugh Tomlinson and Graham Burchell (New York: Columbia University Press, 1994), 63.

28 *Ibid.*, 69.

29 *Ibid.*, 66.

30 Pynchon, *Mason & Dixon*, 283.

31 *Ibid.*, 44.

32 Martin Lefebvre, "Between Landscape and Setting in Cinema," in Martin Lefebvre ed. *Landscape and Film* (London: Routledge, 2006), 23.

33 Pynchon, *Mason & Dixon*, 650.

34 *Ibid.*, 469–470.

35 See Shapiro, *Deforming American Political Thought*, 7 and 124.

36 Pynchon, *Mason & Dixon*, 5.

37 For Benjamin's perspective on allegory see Walter Benjamin, *The Origins of German Tragic Drama*, trans. John Osborne (London: Verso, 1998). The quotations are from a commentary on Benjamin's treatment of allegory in his *Origin*. See Bainard Cowan, "Walter Benjamin's Theory of Allegory," *New German Critique* No. 22 (Winter, 1981), 112.

38 John Locke, *An Essay Concerning Human Understanding* (Oxford, UK: Clarendon Press, 1982), 104.

39 Pynchon, *Mason & Dixon* 133–134.

40 Michael J. Shapiro, "Narrating the Nation, Unwelcoming the Stranger," in *Cinematic Political Thought* (Edinburgh, UK: Edinburgh University Press, 1999), 47.

41 Pynchon, *Mason & Dixon*, 8.

42 *Ibid.*, 349.

43 *Ibid.*, 350.

44 The expression belongs to William Boelhower, "Stories of Foundation, Scenes of Origin," *American Literary History* 3: 5 (1993), 389–401.

45 The quotations are from Michel Foucault's "Preface" to Georges Canguilhem, *The Normal and the Pathological* trans. Carolyn R. Fawcett (New York: Zone Books, 1989), 12.

46 See Brian McHale, "Genre as History: Pynchon's Genre-Poaching," in Jeffrey Severs and Christopher Leise eds. *Pynchon's Against the Day: A Corrupted Pilgrim's Guide* (Newark: University of Delaware Press, 2011).

47 See Paul Hutchinson, "Discursive Life in Thomas Pynchon's *Mason & Dixon* Honors Thesis at The Ohio State University," on the web at: https://kb.osu.edu/bitstream/handle/1811/6492/Mason_Dixon_Thesis.pdf.

48 Pynchon, *Mason & Dixon*, 8–9.

49 *Ibid.*, 650.

50 *Ibid.*, 9.

51 Gilles Deleuze, "Nomad Thought," in David B. Allison ed. *The New Nietzsche* (New York: Delta, 1977), 149.

52 Pynchon, *Mason & Dixon*, 511.

53 I am quoting Judith Butler, "Restaging the Universal," in Judith Butler, Ernesto Laclau, and Slavoj Zizek, *Contingency, Hegemony, Universality* (New York: Verso, 2000), 37.

54 See M. M. Bakhtin, "Discourse and the Novel," in *The Dialogic Imagination*, trans. Michael Holqvist (Austin: University of Texas Press, 1981), 259–422.

55 I am quoting from Erin Manning and Brian Massumi, *Thought in the Act: Passages in the Ecology of Experience* (Minneapolis: University of Minnesota Press, 2014), ebook, loc, 2133. The concept, which they borrow from Daniel Stern, conceives relationships as polyrhythmic rather than harmonious. It fits the way Pynchon constructs the Mason-Dixon relationship.

56 I am quoting my explication of Foucault's concept of the gaze in Michael J. Shapiro, "What Does a Weapon See," in *War Crimes, Atrocity, and Justice* (Cambridge, UK: Polity, 2015), 85.

57 Pynchon, *Mason & Dixon*, 585.

58 *Ibid.*, 80.

59 *Ibid.*, 586.

60 The quotation is from my earlier reading of Jefferson's text: Shapiro, *Deforming American Political Thought*, 4.

61 Alan Trachtenberg, "Naming the View," in *Reading American Photographs* (New York: Hill and Wang, 1989), 125.

62 Pynchon, *Mason & Dixon*, 587.

63 For a reading of *Mason & Dixon* that emphasizes that aspect of Pynchon's style, see Mitchum Huehls, "The Form of Historicity in *Mason & Dixon*," in Hinds ed. *The Multiple Worlds of Mason & Dixon*, 25–46.

64 Pynchon, *Mason & Dixon*, 47.

65 *Ibid.*, 331.

66 Antigua's sugar production began near the end of the seventeenth century, inaugurated by the entrepreneurial Sir Christopher Coddington, who made his initial visit in 1684. "By the middle of the 18th century the island was dotted with more than 150 cane-producing windmills." As a result of the Coddington-initiated enterprise, "[m]ost Antiguans are of African lineage, descendants of slaves brought to the island…to labor in the sugarcane fields." Information and quotations on the web at: www.geographia.com/antigua-barbuda/aghis01.htm.

67 Jamaica Kincaid, "The little Revenge from the Periphery," *Transition* 73 (1997), 70.

68 Pynchon, *Mason & Dixon*, 692.

69 John Edgard Wideman, *Philadelphia Fire* (New York: Mariner, 2005).

70 *Ibid.*, 176.

71 *Ibid.*, 759.

72 The quotation is from Michael Kammen, *In the Fast Lane: Historical Perspectives on American Culture* (New York: Oxford University Press, 1997), 175.

73 I am quoting David Noble, *The Eternal Adam and The New World Garden* (New York: George Braziller, 1968), ix

74 Quoting Pedro Garcia-Caro, "'America was the only place…':American Exceptionalism and the Geographic Politics of Pynchon's *Mason & Dixon*," in Hind ed. *The Multiple Worlds od Pynchon's Mason & Dixon*,103.

75 Pynchon, *Mason & Dixon*, 409.

76 Martin Heidegger, *The Phenomenology of Religious Life* trans. Matthias Fritsch and Jennifer Anna Gosetti-Ferencei (Bloomington: Indiana University Press, 2010), 66. Heidegger uses the verb, *Erharren* for that kind of waiting. See the untranslated version of the text: *Phänomenologie des religiösen Lebens, Gesamtausgabe* Volume 60 (Vittorio Klostermann, 2011).

77 Pynchon, *Mason & Dixon*, 75–76.

78 *Ibid.*, 349.

79 That line shapes already cited the chapter by Hinds, "Introduction: The Times of Mason and Dixon," 3–24

80 Pynchon, *Mason & Dixon*, 511.

81 Kierkegaard, quoted in Karl Jaspers, *Reason and Existenz* trans. William Earle (New York: Noonday, 1955), 43.

82 Michael Edwin Seehorn Glass, "The Many Styles of Søren Kierkegaard, 'Digital Textual Analysis'," on the web at: https://sites.temple.edu/tudsc/2016/10/25/the-many-styles-of-soren-kierkegaard/.

83 Pynchon, *Mason & Dixon*, 478.

84 Kierkegaard, *The Journals*, quoted in www.jesuswordsonly.com/recommendedreading/83-kierkegaard.html.

85 Gilles Deleuze, "Nietzsche and Paul, Lawrence and John of Padmos," in *Essays Critical and Clinical* trans Daniel W. Smith and Michel A. Greco (Minneapolis: University of Minnesota Press, 1997), 37.

86 See J. G. A. Pocock, *The Machiavellian Moment: Florentine Political Thought and the Atlantic Republican Tradition* (Princeton, NJ: Princeton University Press, 2003).

87 Quoting Scott Dill, "Pynchon's Repetition of Kierkegaard's Post Horn: Theology, Communication Theory, and *The Crying of Lot 49*," *Literature and Theology* 32: 1 (March, 2018), 44.

88 That expression is attributed to Kierkegaard's *Repetition* by Brian McHale, *Postmodern Fiction* (New York: Methuen, 1987), 72.

89 Pynchon, *Mason & Dixon*, 75–76.

90 Soren Kierkegaard, *Fear & Trembling*, trans. C. Stephen Evans, Sylvia Walsh (Cambridge, UK: Ambridge University Press, 2006), 34.

91 Pynchon, *Mason & Dixon*, 511.

92 Franco Moretti, "The Novel and the Nation-State," in *The Atlas of the European Novel: 1800–1900* (London: Verso, 1998), 33.

93 *Ibid.*, 38; and see Bakhtin, "Forms of Time and the Chronotope of the Novel," 84–258.

94 Moretti, *Atlas of the European Novel*, 43.

95 *Ibid.*, 45.

96 *Ibid.*, 38.

97 *Ibid.*

98 Patrick Brantlinger, *Dark Vanishings: Discourse on the Extinction of Primitive Races: 1800–1930* (Ithica, NY: Cornell University Press, 2003).

99 James Fenimore Cooper, "American and European Scenery Compared," in Motley E. Deakins facsimile reproduction of *The Home Book of the Picturesque: Or American Scenery, Art, and Literature* (Gainesville, FL: Scholars Facsimiles and Reprints, 1952), 51.

100 *Ibid.*, 68.

101 *Ibid.*, 52.

102 Susan Scheckel, The *Insistence of the Indian: Race and Nationalism in Nineteenth-Century American Culture* (Princeton, NJ: Princeton University Press, 1998), 17.

103 *Ibid.*, 17–18.

104 *Ibid.*, 18.

105 *Ibid.*, 30–31.

106 *Ibid.* 34.

107 Neda Atanasoski and Kalindi Vora, *Surrogate Humanity: Race, Robots, and the Politics of Technological Fuures* (Durham, NC: Duke University Press, 2019), 92–93.

108 James Fenimore Cooper, *The Last of the Mohicans* (Oxford, UK: Oxford World's Classics, 1990), 6–7.

109 James Fenimore Cooper, *Notions of the Americans* (New York: 1828), quoted in Thomas Filbrick, *James Fenimore Cooper and the Development of American Sea Fiction* (Cambridge, MA: Harvard University Press, 1961), 49.

110 James Fenimore Cooper, *The Pioneers Or, The Sources of the Susquehanna* (London: Heritage Illustrated, 2014), 4.

111 I am quoting one of my earlier analyses of cartographic ethics: Michael J. Shapiro, "The Events of Discourse and the Ethics of Global Hospitality," in Hakan Seckinelgin and Hideaki Shinoda eds. *Ethics and International Relations* (London: Palgrave, 2001), 112.

112 See Michel Foucault, *Society Must be Defended* trans. David Macey (New York: Picador, 2003), 17.

113 See John Locke's *Second treatise of Government*, II section 6, in *Two Treatises of Government* (Cambridge, UK: Cambridge University Press, 1988).

114 Cooper, *The Pioneers*, 59.

115 Pynchon, *Mason & Dixon*, 345.

116 The quotation is from Donald A. Ringe, "Mode and Meaning in *The Last of the Mohicans*," in W. M. Verhoeven ed. *James Fenimore Cooper: New Historical and Literary Contexts* (Atlanta, GA: Amsterdam, 1993), 111.

117 The expression is from Emmanuel Désveaux, "Lévi-Strauss and the Diffusionist Moment," in Claude Lévi-Strauss, *From Montaigne to Montaigne* trans. Robert Bonoono (Minneapolis: University of Minnesota Press, 2019), 13.

118 The expression belongs to David Cowart, "he Luddite Vision," in *Thomas Pynchon and the Dark passages of History* (Athens: University of Georgia Press, 2012), 137.

119 Pynchon, *Mason & Dixon*, 542.

120 *Ibid.*, 759.

121 I am borrowing that apt sentence from Arundhati Roy's novel *The God of Small Things* (New York: Random House, 1997), 35.

Bibliography

Atanasoski, Neda and Vora, Kalindi (2019) *Surrogate Humanity: Race, Robots, and the Politics of Technological Futures,* Durham, NC: Duke University Press, 92–93.

Bakhtin, M. M. (1981) 'Forms of Time and the Chronotope of the Novel,' in *The Dialogic Imagination* trans. Caryl Emerson and Michael Holquist, Austin: University of Texas Press, pp. 84–258.

Bakhtin, M. M. (1981) 'Discourse and the Novel,' in *The Dialogic Imagination,* trans. Michael Holqvist, Austin: University of Texas Press, pp. 259–422.

Benjamin, Walter (1998) *The Origins of German Tragic Drama*, trans. John Osborne, London: Verso.

Boelhower, William (1993) 'Stories of Foundation, Scenes of Origin,' *American Literary History* Vol. 3 (5), pp. 391–428.

Brantlinger, Patrick (2003) *Dark Vanishings: Discourse On the Extinction of Primitive Races: 1800–1930*, Ithaca, NY: Cornell University Press.

Butler, Judith (2000) 'Restaging the Universal,' in Judith Butler, Ernesto Laclau, and Slavoj Zizek, *Contingency, Hegemony, Universality*, New York: Verso, pp. 11–43.

Cooper, James Fenimore (1952) 'American and European Scenery Compared,' in Motley E. Deakins facsimile reproduction of *The Home Book of the Picturesque: Or American Scenery, Art, and Literature,* Gainesville, FL: Scholars Facsimiles and Reprints.

Cooper, James Fenimore (1990) *The Last of the Mohicans*, Oxford, UK: Oxford World's Classics.

Cooper, James Fenimore (2014) *The Pioneers Or, The Sources of the Susquehanna*, London: Heritage Illustrated.

Cowan, Bainard (1981) 'Walter Benjamin'Theory of Allegory,' *New German Critique* No. 22, pp. 109–122.

Cowart, David (2012) *Thomas Pynchon and the Dark passages of History*, Athens: University of Georgia Press.

Cronon, William, Miles, George and Gitlin, Jay (1992) 'Becoming West,' In Cronon et al. *Under an Open Sky: Re-thinking America's Western Past*, New York: W. W. Norton, pp. 3–27.

Deleuze, Gilles (1977) 'Nomad Thought,' in David B. Allison ed. *The New Nietzsche*, New York: Delta, pp. 148–161.

Deleuze, Gilles (1997) 'Nietzsche and Paul, Lawrence and John of Padmos,' in *Essays Critical and Clinical*, trans. Daniel W. Smith and Michel A. Greco, Minneapolis: University of Minnesota Press, pp. 36–52.

Deleuze, Gilles and Guattari, Felix (1994) *What is Philosophy?* trans. Hugh Tomlinson and Graham Burchell, New York: Columbia University Press.

Dill, Scott (2018) 'Pynchon's Repetition of Kierkegaard's Post Horn: Theology, Communication Theory, and *The Crying of Lot 49*,' *Literature and Theology* Vol. 32 (1), pp. 39–52.

Filbrick, Thomas (1961) *James Fenimore Cooper and the Development of American Sea Fiction*, Cambridge, MA: Harvard University Press.

Foucault, Michel (1989) 'Preface' to Georges Canguilhem, *The Normal and the Pathological*, trans. Carolyn R, Fawcett, New York: Zone Books, pp. 7–24.

Foucault, Michel (2003) *Society Must be Defended*, trans. David Macey, New York: Picador.

Garcia-Caro, Pedro (2005) '"America was the only place"…: American Exceptionalism and the Geographic Politics of Pynchon's *Mason & Dixon*,' in Hind ed. *The Multiple Worlds of Pynchon's Mason & Dixon*, Rochester, NY: Camden House, pp. 101–124.

Glass, Michael Edwin Seehorn (2016) 'The Many Styles of Søren Kierkegaard, "Digital Textual Analysis,' on the web at: https://sites.temple.edu/tudsc/2016/10/25/the-many-styles-of-soren-kierkegaard/.

Heidegger, Martin (2010) *The Phenomenology of Religious Life*, trans. Matthias Fritsch and Jennifer Anna Gosetti-Ferencei, Bloomington: Indiana University Press.

Hertz, Neil (1985) 'A Reading of Longinus,' in *The End of the Line: Essays in Psychoanalysis and the Sublime*, New York: Columbia University Press, pp. 1–20.

Hinds, Elizabeth Jane Wall (2005) 'Introduction: The Times of *Mason & Dixon*,' in Elizabeth Jane Wall Hinds ed. *The Multiple Worlds of Pynchon's Mason & Dixon*, Rochester, NY: Camden House, pp. 3–24.

Huehls, Mitchum (2005) 'The Form of Historicity in *Mason & Dixon*,' in Elizabeth Jane Wall Hinds ed. *The Multiple Worlds of Mason & Dixon*, Rochester, NY: Camden House, pp. 25–46.

Hutcheon, Linda (1988) *A Poetics of Postmodernism: History, Theory, Fiction*, New York: Routledge.

Hutchinson, Paul (2006) 'Discursive Life in Thomas Pynchon's *Mason & Dixon*' Honors Thesis at The Ohio State University, on the web at: https://kb.osu.edu/bitstream/handle/1811/6492/Mason_Dixon_Thesis.pdf.

Jaspers, Karl (1955) *Reason and Existenz*, trans. William Earle, New York: Noonday.

Kammen, Michael (1997) *In the Fast Lane: Historical Perspectives on American Culture*, New York: Oxford University Press.

Kierkegaard, Søren (2006) *Fear & Trembling*, trans. C. Stephen Evans, Sylvia Walsh, Cambridge, UK: Cambridge University Press.

Kierkegaard, Søren (2007) *The Journals,* quoted in: www.jesuswordsonly.com/ recommendedreading/83-kierkegaard.html.

Kincaid, Jamaica (1997) 'The Little Revenge from the Periphery,' *Transition* 73 (1997), pp. 68–73.

Lefebvre, Martin (2006) 'Between Landscape and Setting in Cinema,' in Martin Lefebvre ed. *Landscape and Film,* London: Routledge, pp. 19–60.

Lévi-Strauss, Claude (2019) *From Montaigne to Montaigne,* trans. Robert Bonoono, Minneapolis: University of Minnesota Press.

Locke, John (1982) *An Essay Concerning Human Understanding,* Oxford, UK: Clarendon Press.

Locke, John (1988) *Second Treatise of Government,* in *Two treatises of Government,* Cambridge, UK: Cambridge University Press.

Lukács, Georg (1971) *Theory of the Novel,* trans. Anna Bosock. Cambridge, MA: MIT Press.

Manning, Erin and Massumi, Brian (2014) *Thought in the Act: Passages in the Ecology of Experience,* Minneapolis: University of Minnesota Press.

McHale, Brian (1987) *Postmodern Fiction,* New York: Methuen.

McHale, Brian (2011) 'Genre as History: Pynchon's Genre-Poaching,' in Jeffrey Severs and Christopher Leise eds. *Pynchon's Against the Day: A Corrupted Pilgrim's Guide,* Newark: University of Delaware Press, pp. 15–28.

Melville, Herman (2001) *Moby Dick; or The* Whale, Evanston, IL: Northwestern University Press.

Moretti, Franco (1998) 'The Novel and the Nation-State,' in *The Atlas of the European Novel: 1800–1900,* London: Verso.

Noble, David (1968) *The Eternal Adam and The New World Garden,* New York: George Braziller.

Pocock, J. G. A. (2003) *The Machiavellian Moment: Florentine Political Thought and the Atlantic Republican Tradition,* Princeton, NJ: Princeton University Press.

Pynchon, Thomas (1997) *Mason & Dixon,* New York: Henry Holt.

Rasmussen, Birgit Brander (2012) *Queequeg's Coffin: Indigenous Literacies and Early American Literature,* Durham, NC: Duke University Press.

Ringe, Donald A. (1993) 'Mode and Meaning in *The Last of the Mohicans*', in W. M. Verhoeven ed. *James Fenimore Cooper: New Historical and Literary Contexts,* Amsterdam: Rodopi, pp. 109–124.

Roy, Arundhati (1997) *The God of Small* Things, New York: Random House.

Safina, Carl (2020) 'Melville's Whale Was a Warning We Failed to Heed,' *The New York Times,* on the web at: www.nytimes.com/2020/05/02/books/review/herman-melville-moby-dick.html.

Scheckel, Susan (1998) The *Insistence of the Indian: Race and Nationalism in Nineteenth-Century American* Culture, Princeton, NJ: Princeton University Press.

Shapiro, Michael J. (1997) *Violent Cartographies: Mapping Cultures of War,* Minneapolis: University of Minnesota Press.

Shapiro, Michael J. (1999) 'Narrating the Nation, Unwelcoming the Stranger,' in *Cinematic Political Thought* Edinburgh, UK: Edinburgh University Press, 1999, pp. 39–81.

Shapiro, Michael J. (2001) 'The Events of Discourse and the Ethics of Global Hospitality,' in Hakan Seckinelgin and Hideaki Shinoda eds. *Ethics and International* Relations, London: Palgrave, pp. 110–131.

Shapiro, Michael J. (2001) 'National Times and Other Times: Rethinking Citizenship,' in *For Moral Ambiguity: National Culture and the Politics of the Family,* Minneapolis: University of Minnesota Press, pp. 112–138.

Shapiro, Michael J. (2012) *Studies in Trans-Disciplinary Method: After the Aesthetic Turn*, London: Routledge.

Shapiro, Michael J. (2015) *War Crimes, Atrocity, and Justice*, Cambridge, UK: Polity.

Shapiro, Michael J. (2016) *Deforming American Political Thought; Challenging the Jeffersonian Legacy* 2nd edition, London: Routledge.

Spillers, Hortense (1987) 'Mama's Baby, Papa's Maybe: An American Grammar Book,' *Diacritics* Vol. 17 (2), pp. 64–18.

Trachtenberg, Alan (1989) 'Naming the View', in *Reading American Photographs*, New York: Hill and Wang, pp. 119–163.

Wideman, John Edgard (2005) *Philadelphia Fire*, New York: Mariner.

4

CZECH CONNECTIONS

Scripting the Epicenter of the Holocaust

> In this worldly lager that is called life...I believe in writing – nothing else...
> the world is composed of disintegrating fragments, an incoherent dark
> chaos, sustained by writing alone.
>
> *Imre Kertész, Liquidation*

Prelude: "Hurbinek"

Imre Kertész testified that he wrote in order to recover his selfhood and "trust in the world."[1] That trust had failed for his fellow Holocaust survivor, Primo Levi, who did not survive his survival. However, Levi left an important legacy, inscribed among other places in his memoir, *The Reawakening* in which he narrates a "micro event within the larger event of the Holocaust."[2] Entering the utterance of a child in his barracks in the Auschwitz *Lager* into history, he writes:

> Hurbinek was the smallest and most harmless among us...the most inno-
> cent...Hurbinek was a nobody, no one knew anything of him, he could not
> speak and he had no name...During the night we listened carefully ...from
> Hurbinek's corner there occasionally came a sound, a word...It sounded
> something like "mass-klo" or "matisklo".....that curious name Hurbinek
> had been given to him by us, perhaps by one of the women who had
> interpreted with those syllables one of the inarticulate sounds that the baby
> let out now and again.[3]

Levi is explicit that his motivation for reporting those sounds was to give "Hurbinek" a historical presence: "Nothing remains of him; he bears witness through these words of mine."[4]

FIGURE 4.1 The Hurvinek character from the Czech puppet theater.

Unbeknownst to Levi (who was not privy to Czech culture and language), the name Hurbinek was likely adapted from a Czech character, "Hurvinek," a popular figure from Czech puppet theater (see Figure 4.1), and the sound he reports was likely the child calling out to his mother (The Czech word for mother is *matka,* pronounced mashka). I was also unaware of the Czech connection when I quoted Levi's brief narration of the short life of Hurbinek in a chapter draft of earlier work. I was apprised of it while delivering the draft in Prague at Charles University. My commentator, Petr Kouba of the Department of Contemporary Continental Philosophy in the Czech Academy of Sciences recognized and identified for me the likely national provenance of the name and utterance.

Because the Czech experience of the Holocaust is among the most variously and creatively scripted (and because having it continually retold in as many ways as possible is owed to the victims), in this chapter I pursue a politics of writing by drawing on diverse Czech connections to the Holocaust. I begin with an analysis of an extraordinary writing performance, Laurent Binet's novelistic biography of Reinhard Heydrich, the main architect of the Holocaust. After orchestrating *Kristallnacht* and shaping the infamous SD, Heydrich managed the beginning stages of the "final solution" from his post in Czechoslovakia as Hitler's Governor, the *Reichsprotektor* of Bohemia and Moravia, where he was installed after the German annexation of the Sudetenland in 1938.[5]

Authoring *HHhH*

> Even the most nonsensical crime stories and the wildest science fiction/
> fantasies are permeated with the germs of reality which were part of their
> author's life.
>
> *Josef Škvorecký, When Eve Walked Naked*

Like Thomas Pynchon's *Mason & Dixon*, Binet's alliteratively titled novel *Himmler's Hern Heist Heydrich* (Himmler's Brain is named Heydrich) has attracted the genre designation "historiographic metafiction."[6] And there is yet another connection with the texts treated in Chapter 3. In a review of *HHhH*, James Wood has an oblique reference to Melville's *Moby Dick*. Beginning his review of *HHhH* with a reflection on the Petschek family villa where the Nazis installed their governing staff after the annexation, Wood (who had visited the villa) likens it to Melville's description of Moby Dick's scarred hide: "As with many buildings in Europe, the Petschek villa is scored and crossed, like the hide of a whale, with the history of its accidents."[7] I want to note as well a connection with Chapter 1's various textual treatments of Radovan Karadžić, who earned the title, "the butcher of Bosnia." The Karadžić featured in Edna O'Brien's novel *The Little Red Chairs* (and in some of the chapter's other texts) shares his violent metaphor with Binet's Reinhard Heydrich, who was known as "the butcher of Prague."

However, those comparisons require qualification. Binet's novel, the assiduous historical work on which it rests notwithstanding, doesn't approach the level of the epic qualities of Melville's *Moby Dick* or Pynchon's *Mason & Dixon*; its motivation is less ambitious. Although Binet situates his plot within an extensive mapping of the historical terrain of Heydrich's violent career, it's more of an assassination thriller than an expansive treatment of a life world unfolding at a key historical moment. And as regards a comparison between O'Brien's and Binet's protagonists, the organization and scope of the atrocities Karadžić orchestrated pale in comparison with Heydrich's management of the Holocaust. Karadžić's main genocidal event, the Srebrenica Massacre, killed 8000, while Heydrich is implicated in at least 11,000,000. However, observing together the processes through which Karadžić and Heydrich ascended to positions from which genocides could be launched yields an important insight. The perpetration of large-scale violence involves career choices at various levels of "security" hierarchies. Some like Karadžić and Heydrich end up in the roles of atrocity CEO's, while many others end up in more minor parts of the necropolitical apparatuses.

Don DeLillo succinctly captures the need for the minor roles with a mere phrase. In a brief throwaway line in the midst of his 1985 novel *White Noise* (in which as noted in Chapter 3 he invents a college with a Department of Hitler Studies), a voice describes a new security agency-related vocation, "food stylists for NASA."[8] In contrast, in his study of the orchestration of the Holocaust, *The Destruction of the European Jews*, it took Raul Hilberg 1388 pages to elaborate that point (He conducted a meticulous investigation of all the vocations involved in the genocide).[9] In any case, the career choices of atrocity perpetrators constitute much of the contribution of novelistic biographies. In Karadžić's case, a political career opened for a man who might have continued with his medical career (having been employed as a psychiatrist after earning a medical degree), or a literary career (having been part of a Belgrade literary circle), or a career in private business (having bought and sold housing in the village of Pale). However, according to testimony from literary colleagues, he was a bad poet; testimony from medical colleagues suggests that he was a lazy and indifferent doctor (a "restive psychiatrist" as it's put in a biography[10]); and his business endeavors were cut short when he was arrested and imprisoned briefly for fraud.[11]

Just as one can wonder what might have been had Karadžić been more successful and content with his pre-political endeavors, Binet wonders about what might have been for Heydrich and his victims had earlier options not been foreclosed before his political career was launched, when Heinrich Himmler made him second in command of the SD (*Sicherheitdienst*), an apparatus that incorporated the Gestapo, Kripo and other implementing departments involved in the Nazi eugenic fantasies. Prior to his political appointment on "April 30, 1931 Heydrich is ignominiously dumped from the navy"; "is this the day that seals the fate of Heydrich and his future victims?" Binet wonders. Can we "suppose that even if he'd remained a navy officer, he would have ended up making a good career with the Nazis. Only perhaps not quite so monstrous." The other contingency Binet brings up is the role of Heydrich's fiancée/wife, Lina, "who hasn't dropped him" after his navy fiasco. She's "a rabid anti-Semite [who] pushes him to get in touch with a Nazi who is highly placed in the new elite organization with a growing reputation: the SS."[12]

Binet, who is both author and narrator of *HHhH*, frequently turns to the subjunctive to tell the story, not only to situate the contingencies in the careers and fates of Heydrich and others involved in the assassination drama, but also to situate his own choices in the fashioning of the novel's coverage. He imagines, for example, that Heydrich's wife Lina's post war memoire, "*Leben mit einem Kriegsverbrecher* ('Living with a War Criminal')…would be a mine of information," but then frets about the price of a rare copy that's available and about his rudimentary German reading ability, "no better than the average French Twelve-year old's." He concludes, "So I should do without this book," even as he continues to worry,

> But I've reached the point in the story where I have to recount Heydrich's first meeting with his wife. Here more than for any other section, that extremely rare and costly tome would undoubtedly have been a great help…if I am to portray Heydrich's character, which I would very much like to do, it's difficult to ignore the role played by his wife in his ascent within Nazi Germany.[13]

As I noted in Chapter 3, Pynchon's uses the subjunctive to reflect on the historical contingencies shaping the terrain his novel is addressing, *his* might-have-beens are alternative Americas. In contrast, Binet's uses of the subjunctive are in the form of should haves and would haves associated Heydrich's career and with his decisions as a writer deciding how to tell the story of Heydrich's career ascent – its decision points and consequences – and his assassination. While Pynchon is asking the more epic question, what kind of world might have been, Binet is asking the smaller question, what kind of Heydrich might have been; he might, for example, have been a more benign version as a navy officer. Moreover, while for Pynchon history and fiction and indistinguishable – "History," his narrator the reverent Cherrycoke, states, needs "to be tended lovingly and honorably by fabulists and counterfeiters."[14] – for Binet invented facts and characters don't belong in historical fiction: "'This is what I think', he writes, 'Inventing a character in order to understand facts is like fabricating evidence'."[15] Early in his narrative he insists that his writing will have very little shaping effect on the history he's telling. He says, "all the dialogues I invent (there won't be many) will be written like scenes from a play. A stylistic drop in an ocean of reality."[16]

I want to suggest, however, that Binet's style shapes the contours of the ocean rather than being a mere drop in it. His placement of himself in the story, although not a unique way of writing fiction, is nevertheless a writing style-contrived challenge to typical ways doing a history of the Holocaust. James Wood, rightly skeptical of Binet's insistence on a radical separation of fact and fiction, points to "telling details" strewn throughout the novel, e.g., a moment when Binet projects himself into a scene that unites the past and present. While looking at the underside of a piece of ambassadorial furniture he spots next to the "naked wood [with a] faded Nazi stamp…a bar code strip proclaiming the American government's present ownership." Wood asks, "To what extent is the useful vitality of that detail inseparable from its historical reality?" and goes on to suggest, "Binet's novel has a vitality very different from that of most historical fiction. He has threaded his novel with a contemporary story, which is the drama of the book's own making."[17]

The Annexation

Early in the novel, Binet refers to the cartographic imaginary that the Nazis use to legitimate Germany's violent expansion, which began with the annexation of Bohemia and Moravia and the turning of Slovakia into a satellite:

> Imagine a map of the world, with concentric circles closing in around Germany. This afternoon, November 5, 1937, Hitler reveals his plans to the army high command…The objective of German politics, he reminds them…is to ensure the safety of Germany's racial identity, to guarantee its existence, and to aid its development…For reasons he never bothers to

explain, Hitler decrees that the Germans have the right to bigger living space than other races.[18]

The novel's other relevant spaces are spatio-temporal; they are the trajectories of movement that comprise its mobile literary geography: the movement of Germany's army and attending security agencies into Czechoslovakia during the annexation; the entry of the two assassins involved in "Operation Anthropoid," Jozef Gabčík (a Slovak), and Jan Kubiš (a Moravian), parachuting into the Czech protectorate after training for the mission in England; the forced movement of the Jewish population to the *Theresienstadt* concentration camp; and finally the movements involved in the assassination drama: Heydrich's daily travel route in an open car which left him vulnerable to the attack, the move by the assassins to a favorable spot on Heydrich's route (where they almost botched the assassination when Gabčík's Sten gun jammed) and their retreat to their hiding place in a church where they died after their location was betrayed (the Saints Cyril and Methodius Cathedral, where bullet holes remain as a memorial to their heroics).

The novel's opening sections inaugurate its historiographic metafictional orientation, its mixture of historical fact and imagination. After signaling the factual basis of his investigation: "Gabčík – that's his name – really did exist," Binet adds his imagination (explicitly identified as such) of what Gabčík was experiencing while in hiding:

> Lying alone on a little iron bed, did he hear, from outside, beyond the shutters of a darkened apartment, the unmistakable creaking the Prague tramways? I want to believe so, I know Prague well, so I can imagine the tram's number…its route, and the place where Gabčík waits, thinking and listening.[19]

Dedicated to the facticity of his characters' roles in the story of the assassination, constantly intruding in the narrative to explain his choices of coverage, and at the same time inventing dialogues as well as impressions for his protagonists, Binet is more focused on telling the reader what happened than with the aesthetics of writing. To the extent that the account narrates the writing process along with the story, what Binet wants to convey is the difficulty of making the composition adequate to the events. Figuring out the genre of his story as the plot unfolds, at one point he writes, "I think I'm beginning to understand. What I'm writing is an *infranovel*."[20]

Despite what Binet may have wanted to "understand" about what he was doing, the textual community within which his novel was to be inevitably located by critics – Holocaust writing in general and Holocaust fiction in particular – is extraordinarily crotchety. As one commentator observes, the Holocaust fiction writer has to "negotiate a very thin ethical demarcation line between inventing a narrative and creating fictional characters while, simultaneously, being true to the historical facts and the 'real' people involved in the Shoah, in particular its victims."[21] Some critics adhere to what Jacques Rancière identifies as the "ethical regime" of the arts in which texts and/or images are judged on the basis of their "truthfulness" (their conformity to the ideal hierarchical form of human existence). Translated into Holocaust texts, fictional elements have to be excluded because they compromise the ontological veracity of the Holocaust.[22]

The fictional element in *HHhH* is thus clearly anathema to the moralistic, ethical regime of the arts which Rancière attributes to the Platonic hierarchy-enfranchising aesthetic. However, Rancière identifies two other aesthetic regimes which Binet's text stands athwart. On the one hand, there a "representational regime" of the arts within which the aim is to achieve sufficiency of representation, governed by what Rancière calls the proper "ways of doing, making, seeing."[23] That Binet aspires to fulfill that regime is evident especially in his insistence that the persons in his story "are not characters" and that he has tried not to turn his story into "literature."[24] Ironically, however, he derives legitimation from a literary source. He cites Flaubert approvingly, quoting his remark, "Our worth should be measured by our aspirations more than our works."[25]

On the other hand, there is *HHhH's* aesthetic sensibility. Inasmuch as Rancière posits the aesthetic regime of the arts as a regime that "strictly identifies art in the singular and frees it from any specific rule, from any hierarchy of the arts, subject matter, and genre,"[26] there are aspects of *HHhH* that adhere to that regime. In addition to his jumping in and out of the narrative with metatextual reflections on his writing choices, Binet admits to "fighting a losing battle." Despite his best intentions, he's unable to

> tell the story the way it should be told. This whole hotchpotch of characters, events, dates, and infinite branching of cause and effect – and these people, these real people who actually existed, I'm barely able to mention a tiny fragment of their lives, their actions, their thoughts.[27]

With his "leap outside of mimesis,"[28] the poesis of Binet's writing shares the space of the text with what he had intended faithfully to represent. *HHhH*, as a historiographic metafiction, is indeed literature.

As a result, the "real people," whose observations and words are invented serve the structural composition of Binet's story as much as they disclose the forces shaping the events to which the novel refers. Although Binet would have liked to be able ascribe unadulterated realism to his novel – "The good thing about writing a true story," he claims, "is that you don't have to worry about giving the impression of realism"[29] – what he creates is both what Roland Barthes famously calls "the effect of the real," reinforced with resort to an epistemic code (frequently punctuating his account with "I know"[30]) and at the same time what Hayden White calls "metahistory," which relies on the way it is plotted.[31] Although Binet carefully scoured the historical archives related to Heydrich's career, to the assassination plan and to the circumstances of the assassination, much of the inspiration for the shaping of the text comes from literary models. For example, in addition to expressing his identification with Flaubert's struggle to capture history adequately with his writing style, he mentions being "transfixed" by William T. Vollman's *Europe Central*, a book, he says, "I would have loved to have written." What he especially admires is "this style, this incredible tone…This is perhaps the first time history has resounded so perfectly"; it's "a novel that is 'more fantastical than historical'."[32]

The "tone" Binet achieves is obsessive rather than fantastical, as he punctuates the novel with reflections about his responsibility to history. Although much admired as an extraordinary writing performance, *HHhH* is controversial within the historical, ongoing, heavily policed, textual community – Holocaust literature – within which it has been located. That critical climate extends to the venue Binet was writing about. Within the Czech Holocaust writing culture, stylistic departures from moralistic and/or strictly representational accounts have been extensively condemned. As one writer points out, "Holocaust fiction has had to establish its legitimacy against the charge that a fictional text is either inadequate, inappropriate, or even endangering to the task of representing the Nazi genocide of the Second World War."[33] The three texts to which I now turn have been subjected to that charge. However, they are not mere fictions; they are laughter-inducing stories that render the atrocities visited on Czechoslovakia by the German annexation with irony and humor.

Holocaust Laughter

> The heaviness of thinking finds its counterpoise in the levity of writing.
>
> *Anthony Curtis Adler*

> Laughter is hostile to the world it depicts and subverts the respect on which representation depends.
>
> *Terrence Des Pres*

Put in terms of the development of an ethos, Holocaust laughter is "Life reclaiming."[34] "Laughter and humor" can be critical vehicles for the "transformative forces that not only challenge dominant assumptions about the Holocaust and is representational limits, but also reclaim humanity, ethics, and difference from new angles and juxtapositions."[35] Alternatively, put in terms of a politics of history, the inclusion of laughter-inducing Czech Holocaust fiction alters the event's will-have-been. As I have argued elsewhere, a critical historical purchase on events must locate them in a future anterior grammar, i.e., in a temporal perspective from which events are perpetually open to being repeatedly reconfigured.[36] Consequently, as I summon and analyze three Czechoslovakian Holocaust fictions, I am allowing those texts to participate once again in the meaning the event *will have had*.

Yellow Stars

> The shade of these stars was harrowing in its undeniability, its ugliness and intensity…On September 1, 1941, all Jews in the Protectorate of Bohemia and Moravia were compelled to identify themselves with such stars.
>
> *Ariana Neumann, When Time Stopped*

> They gave me a star. It's not at all nice and there's something special about it. It doesn't shine at night, only in daytime. No helmsman could steer a ship by it, because he'd lose his way.
>
> *Jiří Weil, Life with a Star*

> What little health [artists] possess is often too fragile, not because of their illnesses or neuroses but because they have seen too much for anyone…
> And that has put on them the quiet mark of death.
>
> *Gilles Deleuze and Felix Guattari, What is Philosophy?*

Early in his first Holocaust novel *Fatelessness*, Imre Kertész's makes a joke of the situation in which the Jews of Budapest have been forced to wear yellow stars in public. His protagonist 14-year-old Gyorgy Köves calmly reports his growing libidinal interest in a girl his age who, he says, "has a long neck and is already starting to round out under her yellow star."[37] The humorous matter-of-fact mood of Kertész's protagonist in the face of the horrific situation in Budapest matches that of the yellow star-wearing protagonist Josef Roubicek (known by the nick-name Pepik) in Prague in Jiří Weil's novel *Life with a Star*. Styled the way Kertész's Köves tells his story, Roubicek a former bank clerk, "tells the story so matter-of-factly that he might be describing a trip to the grocery store." He, like the rest of the city's Jewish population, has become *"persona non grata* as a result of abstract and frequently senseless laws affecting his everyday life, restricting the restaurants he is allowed to visit, the food he is allowed to eat, and is ability to own a pet."[38] He is not allowed "to buy meat…own a musical instrument, or eat asparagus, or shoot partridges or travel by steamer."[39]

Apart from the Weil's representation of the identity-confiscation and social obloquy a star-wearing Jew faces – "I was no longer one of them…I had become a special person whom everyone looked at and made way for"[40] – is the change in the urban cartography that star-wearing entails. As I noted, much of the cartographic emphasis of Binet's *HHhH* is geopolitical; it's focused on the Nazi justification for annexing Czechoslovakian national space. Insofar as Prague's urban space is part of the novel's literary geography, the referents include Heydrich's habitual route, which created the opportunity for his assassins, and the assassins' subsequent escape route and hiding place in the cathedral where they were killed after their hiding place was betrayed, In contrast, Weil's literary geography is a more extensive map of Prague, emphasizing the incessantly expanding prohibitions constraining the Jewish population's uses of space, both outside throughout the city and in their own private dwellings. In Weil's novel, rather than a mere background, Prague's architecture and urban map are narrative elements. To situate the effects of the changes to Prague wrought by the Protectorate one has to appreciate the way the organization of urban space affects everyday life. As I have put it elsewhere, "[T]o locate the way in which the design of urban space is actualized in everyday life in the cities of the world…Three functions stand out; the first involves dwelling, the second seeing, and the third moving."[41] When I made that observation (in 2013), while trying to navigate Prague, a city with which I was unfamiliar, my intent was trans-personal, an attempt to situate the topological implications of public protest. "It follows," I wrote, "that to violate the everyday phenomenology in which these three functions are being rearticulated is to engage in an exemplary act of politicization,"; it is to create what "Jacques Rancière refers to as a 'repartitioning', or a change in the way that political is portioned-off from the non-political."[42]

In the case of Prague under the Nazi Protectorate, the topological changes – which included the removal of certain iconic statues, e. g, the (allegedly) Jewish composer, "Felix Mendelssohn that stood on the roof of the Rudolphinum concert hall"[43] and the imposition of a juridical repartitioning – had an opposite intention. Instead of enabling an expanded political life for previously uninvolved subjects, the aim was the disqualification of the presence of Prague's Jewish population (e.g., Jews were barred from most bars and restaurants). The novel registers the changes by narrating the protagonist' Josef Roubicek's experiences (from his first-person point of view) of a loss of control of his own living quarters and an increasingly curtailed ability to move about the city and use public accommodations. Consequently, whereas the emphasis in Binet's *HHhH* is on what happened in Prague, Weil's novel emphasizes "how what happened affected the people it happened to."[44] By the end of the novel, when all of Roubicek's attachments have been violently taken from him – not only all his possessions, but also his human connections: his girlfriend Ruzena, his aunt and uncle who had raised him, his old school friend Pavel, and even his last emotional attachment, a stray cat he's named Tomas who has shared his apartment and meager food – he is able to dismiss a concern with possessions and cling to life fearlessly, in contrast the Nazi's occupiers, who "were afraid of the city…which they had not succeeded in subjugating,"[45] and whom he regarded as dead: "They're scarecrows who love death and objects. They're as dead as those objects of theirs."[46]

Weil's novel uses humor and irony not to lighten the mood of the situation but to stress its absurdities. For example, when the Jewish actor Ludvik Porges is caught violating the 8:00 PM curfew imposed on the Jewish population, after a visit to a family where he was served tea and played Hamlet, a "former owner of a clothing store," says (in an unintentionally clever quip), "Hamlet isn't worth dying for."[47] And much of the humor and irony in the novel is conducted through plays on the words lucky/unlucky (a binary with a long tradition in Jewish literature, rendered in Yiddish as mazel versus schlimazel). For example, at a crisis moment when Jews are being rounded up for transport in alphabetical order, he's told that he's "lucky" because he's "pretty far along in the alphabet."[48] That moment is followed by one in which Roubicek imitates the novel's delivery of an anti-Nazi lexicon: "They don't care too much about the alphabet. They have their own alphabet."[49] The most humorous irony is played out when Roubicek's alter-ego, Robitschek, tries to commit suicide by gassing himself. Having failed in the attempt he says to Roubicek, "I'm damn unlucky. I shouldn't have tried gas. I should have known what would happen with those economy measures" (gas was supposed to be on "full blast at lunch time" but wasn't).[50]

Along with its irony and humor, the novel is structured by the mordant use of a circus metaphor. One of Roubicek's paradigmatic experiences is a childhood visit to the circus where his uncaring aunt and uncle take him because, he says, "They probably thought that it was the right thing to do or that it was their obligation."[51] However, rather than enjoying the spectacle of the acts, Roubichek experiences the circus as a series of atrocities. He sees captive animals being forced to perform and says that he would not want "to enter the circus with a shaved head of a clown [Jews' heads are shaved before they're herded onto transports] and let myself be kicked in the behind."[52] Thereafter, "circus" is a metaphor throughout the rest of the novel to figure the choreography imposed on Prague's Jews. That figuration culminates in a passage in which Roubicek describes the Nazi accounting system that allocates forced labor:

> People who were pronounced strong built roads, dug holes, quarried stone, mixed concrete and carried bricks. Yet they were still called up for transports; their hard labour didn't save them and their places were taken by weaker people. Anything could be done with numbers; a person could be transformed from someone weak into someone strong, a person could be changed into a circus animal.[53]

In Weil's *Life with a Star*, the protagonist, the innocent Jewish bank clerk, Josef Roubicek, is a Kafkaesque character, whose experience of the Nazi occupation is reminiscent of *The Trial*'s Joseph K, another "martyr to senselessness" (as Milan Kundera describes him).[54] The novel to which I now turn has a different kind of protagonist, another innocent, which in this case is a non-Jewish character coerced into complicity with the Nazi genocide. Forced to play a role in the Nazi expropriation of Jewish property Ladslav Grosman's, Tono Brtko is structured as a camera rather than, like Roubicek, as a first-person voice. The reader sees the action through Brtko's eyes while his voice is mediated through a free indirect discourse narration. A critical consciousness of the historical moment is thereby rendered with the intelligibility-challenge afforded by an ambiguous gap between third and first-person perspectives. Grosman looks at and narrates the Nazi atrocities carried out by Slovak collaborators through the perspective of a naïve protagonist.

The Shop on Main Street

The "reality effect" featured in much of the Holocaust literature exhibits that effect with "authentic details and resources (e.g., diaries, newspaper articles, photographic interviews)" and contrasts with an "estrangement effect" featured in works that focus on the mundane everyday aspects of the life world rather than on "dramatic" events. As is the case with Weil's *Life with a Star*, these latter works are often characterized by laughter-inducing "black humor,"[55] a main feature of Grosman's *The Shop on Main Street*. I saw the award-winning film version (1965), directed by Ján Kadár and Elmar Klos when it first came out and don't recall appreciating the humor. What sticks in my memory is a slow-motion dream sequence as the two main protagonists, the elderly Jewish shop owner, Rozalia Lautmannova (Ida Kaminska) and the "Aryanizer" selected to take over her shop, Tono Brtko (Jozef Kroner), emerge from the shop dressed as if headed to a ball. The sequence is in Brtko's dream, described in the novel at a moment in which he has passed out drunk, having rushed back to the shop to warn Rozalia that Jews are being rounded up for transport to a concentration camp: "Rosalie stepped right out of the mirror into the square, calling Brtko with a coquettish wave of the hand to follow her through the door."[56]

Because reading the novel version (based on the screenplay) years later allows for slower consumption, the humor becomes immediately evident. Despite the horrific historical moment in which the story is located, I found myself laughing. Slovakia had become a German satellite and had been obliged to begin the process of expropriating Jewish property. The first step involved assigning non-Jewish "Aryanizers" to take over and manage all Jewish owned businesses. In an "Afterword," Benjamin Frommer describes the novel's historical moment (1942).

> Ladislav Grosman returns the reader to the period before the deportation of Slovakia's Jews to their deaths in Auschwitz and other killing centers and explores the motivations and dilemmas inherent in what was known throughout Nazi Europe as "Aryanization," the seizure and reallocation of the property and valuables of the continent's Jews.[57]

The plot of the novel takes off when, against his proclivities, Tono Brtko, a carpenter with no ethnic enmities or ideological sensibilities, is the Aryanizer assigned to the Rosalie Lautman's shop, which bears the sign, "ROSALIE LAUTMAN, WIDOW – BUTTONS, LACES, RIBBONS."[58] Upon entering, Brtko tries to explain his assignment to Mrs. Lautman, who is elderly, rheumatic, and virtually deaf. Feeling diffident about the assignment (unlike the more predatory types taking over Jewish businesses), he says, "'I...er...I've been made your Aryanizer, as they say...' and he thrust his hand deep into his pocket to fish out the license." Having heard nothing but unintelligible sounds, "The old lady moved her head forward a little and watched his lips closely; there seemed to be something she had missed. 'I beg your pardon?' She cupped her ear in her hand."[59]

Rosalie Lautman continues to miss that "something." Partly due to her optimistic outlook on human nature and largely due to her bad hearing, Brtko is never able to make the situation understandable to her. Throughout the time he inhabits her shop, Rosalie assumes that he's come to help her as an assistant. As a result of her egregious misunderstanding of what has happened – to her shop and the life world outside of it – she remains oblivious throughout the story. Near the end of the novel, as Jews are being rounded up for deportation, Brtko makes one last effort to explain what's happening: "Mrs. Lautman! The world is run this way now…there are special laws for Jews…you'd better look out there, Mrs. Lautman, can you see your people out there in the square?"[60] As has been the case all along, Brtko cannot get her to grasp the reality of the situation. As he becomes increasingly agitated, all he is able to affect is her mood: "She half opened her mouth in horrified incomprehension. Had her friendly assistant gone mad?"[61]

> "Friendly assistant" is Rosalie's consistent mis-interpellation of Brtko (once she realizes he has not entered the shop as a customer), while he, out of kindness and growing affection for "the old woman," gives up trying to disabuse her of her assumption. The initial conversation is hilarious: "'I've been given the job of Aryanizing this blasted – er, blessed, business', he declared heavily, thinking it would be child's play to come to an agreement with the talkative old lady…The old lady's eyes were on her customer's lips and her heart was warmed by such a succession of b's. 'Buttons' she cried joyfully, and started bustling about, pulling out boxes and spilling their contents on the counter.[62]

As Brtko tries to get accustomed to the rhythms of the shop's opening and closing, *his* misunderstanding becomes apparent as well. Wholly ignorant of the other relevant temporal rhythms – the traditional sundown Friday to sunset Saturday observance of the Jewish Sabbath – he is confused when he arrives on a Saturday morning and the shop is closed. Rosalie assumes he has just "dropped in." When finally, in agitation, Brtko asks for the keys to open the shop's shutters, she says, "the shop? Whatever are you thinking of, on the Sabbath. I've never opened on the Sabbath in my life."[63] At that moment, *he* becomes the obtuse conversation partner as Rosalie has to explain the situation. Finally understanding, "Brtko held his peace like a true assistant,"[64]

The pressures Brtko experiences inside the shop pale in comparison to what he endures outside. A nationalist fervor prevails, symbolized by the construction of a War Memorial pyramid that celebrates the nation. His brother-in-law Marcus Kolkochy leads the town's fascist Hlinka Guard. He and other Guard members threaten Brtko because of his failure to assert his ownership of the shop; he's called a "white Jew," one whose sympathy for the old shopkeeper is regarded as collaboration with an enemy. His home is no haven. He is harassed by his wife, Eveline who represents the predatory, wealth-seeking portion of the town's gentile population. They hope to get rich on expropriated Jewish possessions. Calling Rosalie "your Jewess," Eveline reprimands Brtko for not bringing home "the takings," the valuables he is supposed to take from the shop.

As the novel concludes, Brtko is in a conflicted and agitated state. As the town's Jewish population is gathering in the town square for deportation, he's in the shop trying to get Rosalie to go out and join the parade to the railway station, as the towns Jews are being "marched away from the overturned War Memorial in rows of six." Unable to understand his wild gestures and pleading, she assumes he's taken to the bottle because of a fight with his wife: "Why, oh why, did you start drinking."[65] "Mrs. Lautman," he shouts, "can't you hear me. It's either you or me. There's nothing else I can do."[66] However, as the Czech writer Josef Škvorecký puts it, there are moments when "human sympathy…is…deeper than the Java Trench of our hatred."[67] Brtko looks out at the street and is powerfully affected by the scene:

> The sight of the crowds with their yellow mark, the weary feet, and the children trotting along filled him with horror. He felt as though he was caught up in the maze of silent marchers himself. Elbowing his way through the cloud of dust and despair and knowing from the start that there was no escape.[68]

Observing that scene is enough to change Brtko's mind. With a single leap he was at the old woman's side. "Hurry up!" he hissed. "Kolkocky's on his way here, he mustn't see you."[69] It's at that point that the novel reveals itself as a *tragi*comedy. To hide the old woman, Brtko drags her through the shop, pushes her inside a "cubby hole" and slams the door. There's a telltale "crack of the skull against the wall"; while trying to save her, he's killed her. Ironically at that very moment, "An enormous shadow passed indifferently by the shop door. Marcus, his brother-in-law, had not had the slightest intention of coming inside."[70]

As Milan Kundera suggests, "When you reach the end of the book, you should still find it possible to remember the beginning."[71] Grosman has enabled that. Jumping back to the beginning of the novel, it becomes clear that there was a hint about tragic outcomes as the story began:

> There was something up, although nobody else in the street seemed to notice it…Brtko checked on the time, in case he had made a mistake, and shook his head uncomprehendingly. All the years he had lived near the station he had never known them to close the level crossing at this hour of the day. It was a train – a special train, not in the timetable, and it roared past

as though the engine driver were afraid, he'd be in for it if he didn't reach the end of the world before sunset.[72]

Trains and train stations! They're pervasive in Holocaust literature and are the main feature in the text to which I now turn, Bohumil Hrabal's *Closely Observed Trains*.

A "Small but Strategic Railway Station in Bohemia in 1945"[73]

[I]n Zeitz…the feeling I had was that the train had come to a standstill.

Gyorgy Köves / Imre Kertész, Fatelessness

I start inhaling the images that are impelling me to write and then, through the typewriter, I exhale them at great length.

Bohumil Hrabal, Why I Write

Hrabal's story begins three years after Grosman's. It's 1945 and the German air force has lost control of the air space over Czechoslovakia. Having already deported the Jewish population the Nazis are using the railway system to transport troops and munitions. Apart from the novel's drama, a narrative that culminates when Miloš Hrma, a young traffic apprentice and the novel's main protagonist and narrator, throws a bomb that blows up a train carrying German munitions, is the setting, a small railway station and the Czech characters who run it, which are realizations of the ethos that shapes Hrabal's writing. Using a camera metaphor, he "refers to his style as the "Leica style," with which he "captured reality at peak moments of people talking and then composed a text out of it all."[74] Because he believed "that it is only within the 'low' world of the plebeian, the world of the 'little Czech' that real beauty or nobility emerge,"[75] he decided that he had to dwell within that reality and patiently wait for "images to accumulate and then for the command to sit down at the typewriter." For that to happen, he had to work along with those who peopled his stories. He testifies, for example,

> I spent four years commuting to Kladno and the open-hearth furnaces of the Poldi iron and steel works and that gradually made a difference to the way I played with sentences… Lyricism became slowly regurgitated as total realism, which I barely even noticed because, working as I was next to fires and the milieu of the steelworks and the rugged steelworkers and the way they spoke, it all struck me as super-beautiful, as if I were working and living at the very heart of pictures by Hieronymus Bosch.[76]

Hrabal's visually attuned, experiential approach to the venues he writes about results in an attention to detail and a sensitivity to human foibles that the literary critic, James Wood refers to as in his diverse critical pieces as "serious noticing." Like other fiction writers capable of such noticing, Hrabal does it through the perspectives of his characters: "Detail is always *someone's* detail," as Woods puts it.[77] For example, as the novel opens Miloš is observing the aftermath of the downing of a German plane whose wing had landed in a "deanery garden."

> And within five minutes our townspeople had made a clean sweep of all the plates and sheet-metal from this wing, and the pieces reappeared the very next day as little roofs for rabbit-hutches and hen houses: in fact one man spent that same afternoon cutting out patterns from this plundered sheet metal, and in the evening made them into beautiful, leg-guards for motor-bikes.[78]

To read Hrabal's *Closely Observed Trains* after reading Grosman's *The Shop on Main Street* is to enter a very different life world. His novel acquaints us with a dimension of Czechoslovakian mentality that resides at the opposite end of the continuum from Grosman's head of the Hlinka Guards, Marcus Kolkochy, and Brtko's acquisitive wife, Eveline (the one seeking to destroy the Jewish population and the other to acquire its valuables). Barring a couple of calcitrant types – stiff bureaucratically inclined collaborators with the Nazi occupation – Hrabal's protagonists are thoroughly resistant to Nazism as much in spirit as in deed. The novel is at once a playful and humorous Bildungsroman and a paean to the Czechoslovakian mentality at its best. It embraces the spirit of life-as-shared-pleasure in each other, maintained while living during the last days of the Nazi orchestration of death.

The novel has two interwoven narrative threads following the endeavors of young Miloš. One treats the situation on the ground, a growing Czech resistance to the last stages of the German occupation to which Miloš ultimately contributes. The other chronicles Miloš's attempt to overcome a sexual malfunction, premature ejaculation (*Ejaculata Praecox*), which he deems essential to achieving manhood (so much so that in despair he attempts suicide after being unsuccessful at having sex with his girlfriend Masha). However, both endeavors are successfully accomplished by the end of the novel. Before the dual "climax" – the "little death" (*petite mort*) associated with an orgasm and the big death, Miloš's demise after being shot as he sabotages a German munitions train – the novel proceeds with a mixture of two genres. One is a coming of age story, the Bildungsroman, which is frequently constructed as a "novel of ordeal," effectuated as "a series of tests."[79] The other is the Rabelaisian folk humor novel that participates in what Bakhtin calls "the history of laugher"[80] in which playful forms of sensuality parody and unsettle the seriousness of those who occupy positions of authority.[81]

The successful accomplishment of Miloš's two endeavors are enabled by accomplices. The main one is the irreverent and incessant womanizer, train dispatcher Ladislav Hubička, who, Miloš says, "had always been my ideal."[82]

Early in the novel, much to the consternation of stationmaster Lánský, Hubička and a "certain lady tore the station-master's couch," while having rambunctious sex on it.[83] Inasmuch as the structure of the station building interpolates its employees, Hubička's refunctioning of the couch constitutes resistance to the identity-shaping force of the building's architecture. The stationmaster, the puritanical Lánský, wholly committed to the station's organization, is thrown into a rage. He rolls out a series of angry vituperations, referring to Hubička as a "swinish, rooting pig" and a "spotted hyena." With the latter imagery, Hrabal has evoked Hitler's reference to Jews as "Laughing Hyenas" (at the 1938 Nuremberg Rally). However, Hubička's most famous performance, described by Miloš, is an affront not only to the station's management, but also to the German orderliness and decorum (that the novel's Nazi collaborator, Councilor Zedníček had been trying to impose on the station). Approaching his station co-worker, Hubička "bowled Virginia over, and then turned up her skirt and printed all over our station stamps, one after another, all over the telegraphist's backside."[84]

Rather than mere humorous asides, Hubička's antics are quintessentially anti-Nazi gestures. His Rabelaisian behavior – "anarchic" and "lackadaisical," and "committed" to "embodied enjoyments" – challenges the Nazi passion for order, and his undisguised lustful attitude toward women – e.g., upon seeing the Countess Kinská visiting the station astride a black stallion, he confides to Miloš that he wishes he could be part of her horse's saddle – contrasts dramatically with the way the exemplary Nazi "soldier male" regards women. As Klaus Theweleit points out, the fascist soldier male – those who were part of the *Freikorps*, the ultra-right-wing militias from which the Nazi Party drew its initial followers (treated in Chapter 2) – had a dread of sensuality in general and womanhood in particular. In addition to his female-welcoming anti-Nazi sensualism, Hubička is a political activist. He recruits Miloš to help sabotage a German munitions trains:

> Miloš, we're on night duty again tomorrow, you and I together…There'll be a goods train passing through our station, twenty-eight wagons of ammunition, they're carrying it in open trucks, and it will go through here two hours after midnight…that whole train would blow up, and no damage to anything but the open air….[85]

Before joining Hubička in the attack on the train, Miloš accomplishes the other endeavor he regards essential to achieving manhood. He first reveals his sexual malfunction to the stationmaster's wife, Mrs. Lánský, and asks her to teach him how to overcome it. She demurs, pleading old age: " But Miloš, I'm in the change already, I don't want to have anything to do with that any more…."[86] However, Miloš's next such request is decisively fulfilled by the character who becomes his second accomplice, ironically a young Austro-German woman (Tyrolean shoes and all),

Viktoria Freie, who is at the station between trains. After having shared with her a building-shaking, window-rattling orgasm (on the stationmaster's much-abused couch), by the time Miloš joins Hubička in the plan to hurl a bomb onto the munitions train, he is able to tell him he's now wholly prepared: "I'm a man, I'm a man just like you Mr. Hubička, a man and that's wonderful, everything's fallen off my shoulders."[87] He has finally lived up to his erotically symbolic name (his surname Hrma translates as *mons pubis* and Miloš is close to milostný meaning amorous).[88]

As for the other accomplishment: At the decisive moment, as Miloš plays his part, he and a German soldier on the train exchange shots. Although both are mortally wounded, Miloš has accomplished his mission, having successfully hurled the explosive into one of the open trucks. Before he dies, he hears the explosion and says into the "unhearing ears" of the "dead man" lying next to him in the ditch beside the tracks where they had both fallen, "You should have sat at home on your arse...."[89] As Miloš accomplishes his two missions, Hrabal accomplishes his. The literary structure of his *Closely Observed Trains*, an inter-articulation of Miloš's two quests, erotic and political, constitutes a dual rejoinder to the Nazis. The former is an attack on their mentality, the later on their war effort.

Trains and train stations also play a central role in the next literary text to which I turn, W. G. Sebald's *Austerlitz*, a "unique style of prose fiction," as one commentator puts it:

> the inclusion of photographs, stubbornly antiquated sentences that stretches for pages, a narrator who closely resembles the writer in both biography and melancholy temperament, the blending of multiple literary genres, a fascin- ation with walking, and obsession with the past, a playful intertextuality.[90]

With his complex interweavings of literary genres, photos, architecture, film analysis, botanical and entomological reflections, historical references, and a fic- tional biography, *Austerlitz* is a writing performance that distinguishes Sebald's approach to the Czech experience of the Holocaust from all others. There is, however, what James Wood surmises as "an illuminating comparison" between Binet's *HHhH* and Sebald's *Austerlitz* because Sebald's "novel is quite as self-aware as Binet's...[and] produce[s] something akin to Binet's meditation on fiction and the difficulty of writing history."[91]

Austerlitz

The genre multiplicity characterizing Sebald's *Austerlitz* is resident in its title. "Austerlitz" is a family name, the name of a famous battle, the name of a Paris train station, and a word that resounds with a tonality similar to the name of the exter- mination camp at Auschwitz. As for its relationship with the chapter title, *Austerlitz* is among other things, a drama of discovery in which a Czech connection is the telos of the plot. Briefly, during a period of many years, the protagonist, Jacques Austerlitz, journeys often from London to continental Europe for an academic research project. During one such trip he meets the unnamed narrator. Their subsequent off and on dialogue over the years reveals his interrupted history. It discloses his identity as a Czech survivor, having been saved from the Holocaust and raised in Wales under a different name after being sent to the UK as part of the *kindertransport* of Central European Jewish children. He had lost his birth name and learned nothing of his origins from the austere Calvinist Welsh couple that adopted him. After leaving home, "he attends Oxford, where he studies to become an architectural historian and doesn't begin facing the way the Holocaust had claimed his parent's lives and his search to learn the details of their fates until he is middle aged."[92]

Elsewhere, addressing the political sense of the novel, I referred to its rescue dimension. Pointing out that Imre Kertesz explicitly aimed to "rescue himself through writing…[by] taking control over naming himself," after having been given a disqualifying identity by the Nazis, I suggested that Sebald's "…*Austerlitz*," which conducts a variety of rescues, has a similar intention, "to restore to Jacques Austerlitz the individuality of his name and experience, to rescue the living privacy of his surname."[93] While the rescue in *Austerlitz* animates the temporal structure of the plot, it is only one of the novel's disjunctive temporal threads. Its nonlinear structure is articulated by Austerlitz himself in meta-commentaries on time, which locate the novel's genre as historiographic metafictional. For example, in a conversation with the narrator in Europe's time capital, Greenwich, England, he remarks, "time itself has been nonconcurrent over the centuries"[94] and proceeds to personalize his relationship to it, an aspiration to control it (doubtless because until his adulthood, events had controlled him and impeded his recovery of is origins):

> I have always resisted the power of time out of some internal compulsion which I myself have never understood, keeping myself apart from the so-called current events in the hope, as I now think…that time will not pass away, has not passed away, that I can turn back and go behind it, and there I shall find everything as it once was…[95]

Constructing a novel whose rhythms constitute a "poesis of time," Sebald inter-articulates a literary geography with temporal reflections belonging to the narrator as well as his protagonist. Many of them emerge from an object-oriented phenomenology. Rather than intrinsic to mentality, time in *Austerlitz* is sedimented in objects and buildings, most notably railway stations. They are architectural objects which become temporalized as historical event spaces in the narrative, e.g., their role as sites of transfer in the history of Holocaust atrocities, referenced as Austerlitz's search for his origins unfolds). The first such station is Antwerp's Centraal Station, where the narrator and Austerlitz first meet. The station building constitutes one of many of the architectural sites that contribute to Sebald's reflections on history and memory as the text weaves historical time with Austerlitz's personal story. Dwelling on details of the Centraal Station the narrator looks up "at the façade of that fantastical building"[96] and then proceeds to report on the station's origin, "constructed under the patronage of King Leopold II." He observes "a vertiginous Negro boy" seated upon "his dromedary in an oriel turret to the left of the station façade, a monument to the world of animals and naïve peoples of the African continent" and then turns to an account of the station's expression of a darker part of what Belgium extracted from the Congo.

Exemplifying a writing strategy in which "inanimate objects greatly overwhelm the animate ones,"[97] Sebald temporalizes the station by turning its silent materiality into a testimony to the history of Belgium's colonial atrocities. His narrator describes the *Salles des pas perdus*," the station's waiting room, which evokes "the passing thought" of "the last members of a diminutive race which had perished or been expelled from its homeland."[98] That reflection in Sebald's text has had a futurity. It has provoked a commentary by another genocide survivor, Clemantine Wamariya, who fled the Rwanda massacre, was adopted in the US, and was enrolled as a student at Yale University after an arduous journey through Africa. Reflecting on the diverse survival literatures she read in one of her Yale courses – which helped her to develop one of narrative threads in her story – she notes that she has been affected by W. G. Sebald's *Austerlitz,* especially the novel's description of Belgium as "a little patch of yellowish gray barely visible on the map of the world." She notes her surprise – quoting *Austerlitz* – that "Belgium: *a little patch, barely visible.* Belgium, the country that colonized and brutalized Rwanda, Belgium, the country that changed everything, that ruined everything" could seem so visually insignificant.[99]

Apart from its impact on a later survivor, the temporality that Sebald extracts from the Centraal Station's *Salles des pas perdus* references the experiences of both its protagonist, Austerlitz and the writing of the novel. As a "waiting room" it functions as an allegory for the two inter-articulated aspects of the text. It associates the waiting with the fact that Austerlitz's life is on hold, suspended between the present and past as he seeks to recover the story of his name and the fates of his mother and father, and it reflects the way Sebald's text is composed, with its continual deferrals and suspensions of the narrative, referred to as "the stylistics of stasis"[100] in one commentary and a "poetics of suspension"[101] in another.

From the perspective of his vocation as an architectural historian, Austerlitz lends another temporality to the Centraal station; he refers to its *post*colonial essence as a nexus of commerce, describing it to the narrator as a "cathedral consecrated to international traffic and trade." He says that despite its "Byzantine and Moorish" architectural details, whose purpose is to "arouse medieval associations in the minds of railway passengers," its "eclecticism" unites the past and future with "a logical and stylistic approach to the new epoch."[102] The architectural narrative in Austerlitz, which discloses Belgium's rapacious colonial practices (as the map of its violence greatly exceeded the map of its sovereign territory) and refers as well to Belgium's post war commercial aspirations, is initially interwoven with another narrative thread, Sebald's, mimicking of a Kafka literary strategy, the use of bestiaries as allegories. That strategy first emerges when his narrator's visit to Antwerp's Centraal Station is preceded by his visit to Antwerp's zoo, the "Nocturama." He states that the zoo's animals, its "denizens" and its interior, have become confused in his mind with his "memories of the *Salles des pas perdus.*"

Thereafter, animals become some of the allegorical vehicles through which Sebald's story figures Austerlitz hidden biography. For example, to model Austerlitz's mobile tracing of a complex map in his search for his origins – a trail taking him back and forth from London to several other cities; Antwerp, Paris, Prague (among others) – Sebald constructs a moth allegory, which begins in a conversation in which Austerlitz has referred to his Great Uncle Alphonso's practice of observing moths for hours. He tells the narrator – who in an earlier moment has already linked "looking and thinking"[103] – that Alphonso has observed "how each of these extravagant creatures had its own character."[104] He adds that his uncle is fascinated with the way their appearances challenge human perception. That observation translates for Sebald as a lesson in the fragility of the relationship between looking and knowing, i.e., on the uncertainty of one's grasp of reality:

> The trails of light which they seem to leave behind them in all kinds of curlicues and streamers and spirals…were merely phantom traces created by the sluggish reaction of the human eye, appearing to see a certain afterglow in the place from which the insect itself, shining for only the fraction of a second in the lamplight, had really gone. It was such unreal phenomena… the sudden incursion of unreality into the real world, certain effects of light in the landscape spread out before us, or in the eye of a beloved person, that kindled the deepest feelings…[105]

The moth allegory mimics Austerlitz's search map, the difficult-to-discern "trails," which also exist as "merely phantom traces" he has been trying to recover, map not only an individual biography, but also a collective experience common to many that were affected by the Holocaust.

The vagaries of the relationship between seeing and knowing implied in the moth allegory is initiated earlier when the narrator refers to his "confusion" as he contemplates the Station's *Salles des pas perdus* right after visiting the zoo. That confusion is stated in the text right after two sets of uncaptioned photographs punctuate the narrative – first some animal eyes (belonging to an owl and a monkey) and then human eyes. What is Sebald implying there? An allegedly wise animal and one mythically associated with seeing no evil (or alternatively with merely mimicking rather than thinking) are shown together, followed by a pair of human eyes. Do they reflect wisdom, moral obtuseness, or a tension between the two modalities? The reader is left with the task of making sense of the image interruption. Referring to the paradoxical status of the photographic images in *Austerlitz*, a commentator suggests that the photographs defy "legibility."[106] They do; I think that's Sebald's intent. Among other things, he has explicitly resisted locating legibility *in* his images (or text as a whole for that matter). In an interview, he testifies, "Photography is the authentic document *par excellence*. People find photographs convincing," but then adds, "I have no desire to include images of high photographic quality," implying that "photography's referentiality is not inherent in the medium itself."[107]

With that aspect of Sebald's style in view – his "poetics of suspension"[108] – I want to suggest that the way the text crafts its politics of history and memory is best understood if we regard Sebald as a curator who, as he opens Austerlitz story to readers, solicits their active participation in sense making. Given the deferrals and suspensions throughout the text, Sebald's curatorial approach aligns the textual Holocaust experience he invents with the way Daniel Libeskind has curated the Holocaust in the design of his Berlin Jewish Museum. Likening his museum to a Talmudic text that has been open a plurality of readings, Libeskind writes,

> The museum is open to many interpretations and many routes, just like the pages of the Talmud where the margins are often as important as what is being commented on in the center of the text. This experience is dependent on the engagement of the visitors with the implication of an ongoing history.[109]

The museum is without a prescribed route. Instead, it's designed as an event space in which the historical experience of the Holocaust remains inert until activated by visitors who are invited to manage the building's maze of oblique axes to invent an ambulatory narrative of their experience of Holocaust history. The museum-as-text is in effect what Roland Barthes's terms, a "methodological field," a text whose meanings emerge through the interpretive trajectories of visitor/readers. Libeskind designed a space that imposes the kind of temporal suspension that Sebald's text exhibits, an "infinite deferment of the signified." Like Sebald's Austerlitz, Libeskind's building-as-text stage-manages history in process as "*deferred action*"[110] through the visitor choreography his building invites, the challenge of negotiating a "series of complex trajectories, irregular linear structures, fragments and displacements."[111] His visitor therefore bears comparison with both Sebald's Austerlitz and his readers. The building's design deferrals create a space for what Libeskind terms an experience of "unmeaning and a search for meaning."[112]

As curators of their readers' experiences both Libeskind and Sebald seek to unsettle rather than guide. That aim becomes especially apparent in Libeskind's case if we heed a seemingly unintegrated space within his museum. There's an exit from one of the obliques axes to a walled in outdoor square in which the floor is tilted and is made of uneven paving stones. On entering that space (as I did when I visited the museum more than two decades ago) one is at risk of losing one's balance. It's one of the more settling parts of Libeskind's maze. Sebald creates a similar moment for Austerlitz. While in Nuremberg he has to carefully negotiate the "pavement under [his] feet [which] sloped slightly downhill."[113] It's a moment in which Austerlitz' precarious movements mimic the various ways in which Sebald's writing creates unsettling effects. As Austerlitz's movement choreography co-occurs with Sebald writing choreography, the effect is what Erin Manning (in a different context) calls a "co-composition between coincident manners of occurring."[114] As for Sebald's curating of Austerlitz progression toward the recovery of his origins, it is well captured in James Wood's observation that he "contrives not to offer an ordinary, straightforward recital."[115] Instead I suggest that he achieves what Maurice Blanchot identifies as the purpose of literature, "to interrupt the purposeful steps we are always taking toward a deeper understanding and a surer grasp of things."[116] Sebald's interruptions – his many instances of "suspenseful stasis" – work through three stylistic effects: "byzantine structures for his characters to explore as well as mazes…repetition to draw out the moment in which one is 'on the brink'…[and] virtually imperceptible transitions into essayistic digressions."[117]

Like many Holocaust stories, *Austerlitz* finds its way to the Czech fortress/concentration camp Theresienstadt, the place in the novel where Austerlitz's most significant temporal drama takes place. There, the slowness that Sebald enacts stylistically throughout the novel is recreated as interventionist film editing by Austerlitz. He watches the famous Nazi propaganda film, entitled *Die Fuhrer schenkt den Juden eine Stadt* (The Führer gifts the Jews a city).[118] Filmed in Theresienstadt, it was a duplicitous Nazi project aimed at representing the concentration camp as a pleasurable working city. The viewing takes place at a point in the novel where memory and history meet. It's where Austerlitz, having overcome the psychological inhibitions which, he said, "protected me from anything that could be connected…with my early history,"[119] has discovered his personal history and has decided to watch the film to see if he can find his mother, whom he has learned had been sent to the camp.

On his initial viewing of the 14-minute video the Nazis made, he strains to catch a glimpse of his mother as he observes a rapid concatenation of images of "various tasks being carried out.…an unbroken succession of strangers' faces," and a variety of leisure scenes: concert-going, gardening, playing, and reading, all of which merely "flickered" before his eyes."[120] Unable to see his mother's face "among those fleeting faces," he got "the idea of having a slow motion copy of the fourteen minute fragment from Theresienstadt made, one which would last a whole hour."[121]

After Austerlitz has slowed down the Nazi propaganda film so that it runs four times longer, what emerges is a demoralized world of the Theresienstadt inmates among whom is his mother. At its altered pace, the film discloses

> previously hidden objects and people…The men and women employed in the workshops now looked as if they were toiling in their sleep…[and those moving about] seemed to be hovering rather than walking, as if their feet

no longer touched the ground…[and] strangest of all, said Austerlitz was the transformation of sounds in this slow-motion version [for example]…the merry polka of some Austrian operetta composer …had become a funeral march dragging along at a grotesquely… sluggish pace.[122]

As he turns Austerlitz into a film editor, Sebald provides an insight about the value of slowness. The way he casts Austerlitz's film work, has him achieving an attunement to the Czech experience of the Holocaust that accords the way his text as a whole enacts it: slowly, painstakingly, and with an innovative approach to visuality. The look afforded to Austerlitz in the slowed-down version of the film resonates well beyond his catching a glimpse of his mother. He has projected himself experientially into the camp. His slow looking accords with what Grosman's *The Shop on Main Street* shows, as it narrates the moment when the agitated Tono Brtko, who is about to force Rosalie Lautman from her shop to join the deportation queue in the town square, has stopped for a moment from his frantic rushing around and has paused to grasp the scene of Jews mobilized in a march toward their deportation. Brtko does what film directors refer to as a long take, which as the Russian filmmaker Andrei Tarkovsky (famous for his long take style) points out, gives the viewer "an opportunity to live through what is on screen as if it were his own life, to take over the experience imprinted in time on the screen,"[123] Thus as Brtko peers for an extended moment through the window at the scene, he is powerfully affected; as noted, "He felt as though he were caught up in the maze of silent marchers himself."

Coda

Throughout the interactions he stages between his narrator and Austerlitz, Sebald brings the Czech experience of the Holocaust into the present, temporalizing much of the Europe's architecture as sedimented Holocaust history. He also stages an important spatial intervention, incorporating much of Europe's landscape into a Holocaust cartography. Although many places in Europe are implicated in the fictional process of discovery Sebald invents for his aesthetic subject, Austerlitz, as is the case with the other texts I treat in this chapter, Czechoslovakia sits at what I have called the epicenter of his rendering of how the Holocaust was experienced. However, in reaction to what I have narrated thus far, I want to return reflectively to the chapter's title and put quotation marks around "Epicenter" by summoning a novel, Jáchym Topol's *The Devil's Workshop*, which begins with the narrator's account of a survivor-led group seeking to monumentalize Theresienstadt as the Holocaust's exemplary center and proceeds in the second half of the novel to deconstruct that project. The novel serves, as one commentator puts it, as "an intriguing counterpart" to W. G. Sebald's *Austerlitz*. However, I hasten to add that Topol's novel challenges Sebald's literary geography by decentering the Czech experience of the Holocaust and Sebald's style by unsettling the reader with black humor rather than with a poetics of suspension. Taking the reader from the familiar Holocaust site, Terezin – "death's antechamber," as Kundera puts it[124] – to one that has received less publicity, Katyn in Belarus, the novel creates "a reading position through which readers [myself in particular] experience the need and desire to make space for what is missing from particular historical accounts."[125]

Topol's narrator, a former goatherd who was raised in Terezin because his mother was imprisoned there is reminiscent of Grosman's Tono Brtko. As a camera watching the dynamic and a reporter supplying accounts of the main protagonists, he like Grosman's Brtko, is not ideationally wedded to either history or current issues. Having served prison time and functioned as a Kapo while there – selected for his ability to keep condemned men calm as they headed for executions, – his role in the novel's early dynamic, the museumization of Terezin as a Holocaust tourist destination, is pragmatic. He desires only to stay out of prison and have a place to eat and sleep: "I didn't care about memory…I just needed a place to live" he says.[126]

The novel has a Hurbinek counterpart, who, unlike Primo Levi's version (described in the chapter's prelude), has survived. Lebo, who was born in Terezin when it was a concentration camp and was hidden in a shoebox under his mother's bunk, "safely off in a corner room for condemned women and girls," is the novel's main protagonist.[127] He grows up to take on the role of "Guardian of Terezin," dedicated to maintaining it as a monument to those who died there. Zealously involved in the restoration project, he insists that "every splinter of every bunk should be preserved, every battered brick, every corner of the old fortress. Every inch of Terezin should exist always and forever…to feed the memory of the world."[128] Optimism reigns as the project gets underway attracting two streams of visitors, ordinary tourists and memory tourists (called "bunk seekers" in the novel). Thanks to a savvy promoter with a Holocaust legacy, a young woman named Sara whose father (like Austerlitz) had survived the Holocaust thanks to the *kindertransport* that took him to Sweden as a child, the project is sustained by donations and entrepreneurial initiatives. She arranges to have t-shirts printed and sold with the slogan "Theresienstadt: If Kafka hadn't died, they would have killed him here," and gathers the women who set up tents to sell a Terezin signature food, "Ghetto Pizza." Nevertheless, Kafka is alive stylistically as part of Topol's "writerly patrimony"[129] (as is the case with many Czech writers). Even though "in all his works, [Kafka] had his back turned to the problems and crises of the historical environment…he captured the opacity, the uncertainty, the cruelty of this [twentieth] century with decisive clarity,"[130] inspiring other writers to deploy his attunement to the senselessness of those in charge of the social/political order (as Topol does).

While the project is well underway with the stream of donations and visitors peaking, thanks in part to the work of the group's publicist, Rolf, two young visitors, Alex and Maruska from Belarus show up and initiate thinking about the Czech versus Belarus atrocities that occurred during the Holocaust.[131] Shortly thereafter, "something changed." Despite Rolf's best efforts, a hostile press disparages the Terezin project, and before long bulldozers arrive and Lebo and his followers decide to leave Terezin and follow Alex and Maruska back to Belarus to carry on their work with entrepreneurs who want to do there what had been going on at Terezin. The plan is to market Katyn as a site of horror but with a new twist. They plan an exhibition in a basement room where survivors are to willingly allow themselves to be stuffed and turned into robots who broadcast their experiences in a "devil's workshop, which is going to mean work for a lot of people. Maintenance men, technicians. Security guards, guides, all of that."[132]

Quite apart from the dark humor involved in Topol's critique of the commercialization of horror is his assault on the tradition map of the Holocaust. He extends the Holocaust cartography eastward to include the extermination of millions of Slavs along with Jews and gypsies. It's a novelistic counterpart to Timothy Snyder's *Bloodlands*, which exposes the Nazi and Soviet combined extermination of Slavs during the war, accounting for 14 million deaths from "central Poland to western Russia, covering Ukraine, Belarus and the Baltic states."[133] Topol also extends the horror downward to the mass graves of those exterminated; he "makes you feel," as one commentator puts it, "how everywhere you press on the earth, blood wells up out of the ground." The "nightmare basement" he invents is "the closest thing to horror," as he mobilizes a Czech connection with a novel that blurs the line between fact and fiction and decenters the geography of Holocaust atrocities.[134]

Notes

1   Imre Kertész, *The Holocaust as Culture Literature* trans. Thomas Cooper (Calcutta: Seagull Books, 2011), 61.

2   I am quoting from my earlier analysis of Levi's memoir, Michael J. Shapiro, *Politics and Time: Documenting the Event* (Cambridge, UK: Polity, 2016), viii.

3   Primo Levi, *The Reawakening* trans. Stuart Woolf (New York: Collier, 1987), 11.

4   *Ibid.*, 11.

5   Laurent Binet, *HHhH* trans. Sam Taylor (New York: Farrar, Straus, Giroux, 2012).

6   See Cailee S. Davis's honor's thesis, "Laurent Binet's *HHhH*: Historiographic Metafiction in Contemporary French Literature About World War II," on the web at: https://csuepress.columbusstate.edu/theses_dissertations/284/.

7   James Wood, "Broken Record: A historical novel at war with itself," *The New Yorker Magazine*, on the web at: www.newyorker.com/magazine/2012/05/21/broken-record.

8   Don DeLillo, *White Noise* (New York: Viking, 1985), 143.

9   See Raul Hilberg, *The Destruction of the European Jews* (New Haven, CT: Yale University Press, 1961).

10 Robert J. Donia, *Radovan Karadzic: Architect of the Bosnian Genocide* (Cambridge, UK: Cambridge University Press, 2015), 34.

11 *Ibid.*, 40.

12 Binet, *HHhH*, ebook loc. 633.

13 *Ibid.*, loc. 568.

14 Thomas Pynchon, *Mason & Dixon* (New York: Henry Holt, 1997), 350.

15 Binet quoted in Wood, "Broken Record."

16 Binet, *HHhH*, loc. 471.

17 Wood, "Broken Record."

18 Binet, *HHhH*, Loc. 985.

19 *Ibid.*, loc. 206.

20 *Ibid.*, loc. 3861.

21 Christine Berberich, "I Think I'm Beginning to Understand. What I'm Writing is an *Infranovel*: Laurent Binet, *HHhH* and the Problem of Writing History," *Portsmouth Research Portal*, on the web at: https://researchportal.port.ac.uk/portal/en/publications/i-think-im-beginning-to-understand-what-im-writing-is-an-infranovel(0d17446f-c2ec-4672-8b2d-5daafdb3fa6e).html.

22 See Jacques Rancière, *The Politics of Aesthetics* trans. Gabriel Rockhill (London: Continuum, 2004), 20–21. Among the adherents to that aesthetic regime is Berel Lang, "Is it Possible to Misrepresent the Holocaust," *History and Theory* 34: 1 (February, 1995), 84–89.

23 Rancière, *The Politics of Aesthetics*, 22.

24 Binet, *HHhH*, loc. 5095.

25 *Ibid.*, loc. 2972.

26 Rancière, *The Politics of Aesthetics*, 23.

27 Binet, *HHhH*, loc. 2879.

28 Rancière, *The Politics of Aesthetics*, 24.

29 Binet, *HHhH*, loc. 527.

30 Berberich's observation is in "I Think I'm Beginning to Understand. What I'm Writing is an *Infranovel*."

31 See Hayden White, *Metahistory* (Baltimore: Johns Hopkins University Press, 1986).

32 Binet, *HHhH*, loc. 4097. One can see the inspiration. Vollman's novel features stunning figuration, for example early on when "Europe Central Europe," is described, "not a nest of countries at all, but a blank zone of black icons and gold-rimmed clocks whose accidental, endlessly contested territorial divisions...can be overwritten as wel like..." William T. Vollman, *Europe Central* (New York: Viking, 2005), ebook, loc. 111.

33 Emily Miller Burdick, *The Subject of Holocaust Fiction* (Bloomington: Indiana University Press, 2015), 1.

34 Terrence Des Pres, "Holocaust Laughter," in *Writing into the World: Essays, 1973–1987* (New York: Viking, 1991), 278.

35 The quotations are from Michalinos Zembylas, "Holocaust Laughter and Edgar Hilsenrath's *The Last Nazi and the Barber.* Toward a Critical Pedagogy of Laughter and Humor in Holocaust Education," *Studies in the Philosophy of Education* 37 (2018), 302.

36 See Michael J. Shapiro, *Politics and Time: Documenting the Event* (Cambridge, UK: Polity, 2016).

37 Imre Kertész, *Fatelessness* trans. Tim Wilkinson (New York: Vintage, 2004), 13.

38 Mirna Solic, "Narrating and negotiating the repressed city: representations of Prague in Jiří Weil's work," *Bohemia Olomucensiai* 7: 1 (2015), 71.

39 This convenient summary of restrictions is in a review of *Life with a Star* by Anne Tyler in *The New York Times* "Book Review," June 18, 1989, on the web at: http://movies2.nytimes.com/books/99/02/28/nnp/weil-star.html.

40 Weil, *Life with a Star*, 84.

41 Michael J. Shapiro, "Street Politics," *Journal of Critical Globalisation Studies* 5 (2012), 127.
42 *Ibid.*
43 Solic, "Narrating and Negotiating the Repressed City: Representations of Prague in Jiří Weil's work," 69.
44 I am quoting Arundhati Roy's remark about her novel *The God of Small Things* in an interview: Taisha Abraham, "An Interview with Arundhati Roy," *Ariel* 29: 1 (January, 1998), 90.
45 Weil, *Life with a Star*, 214.
46 *Ibid.*, 245.
47 *Ibid.*, 99.
48 *Ibid.*, 129.
49 *Ibid.*, 130.
50 *Ibid.*, 171–172.
51 *Ibid.*, 131.
52 *Ibid.*, 132.
53 *Ibid.*, 252.
54 Milan Kundera. *The Art of the Novel* trans. Linda Asher (New York: Harper, 2000), 48.
55 The quotations are from Lucia Mihálová and Marek Urban, "The Holocaust May Be Important, But It's No Longer Original: Representations of the Holocaust in Slovak Theater Reviews from 2000–2017," *KOME* X:Y 2019), 2
56 Ladislav Grosman, *The Shop on Main Street* trans. Iris Urwin Lewitová (Prague: Karolinum Press, 2019), 101.
57 *Ibid.*, 117.
58 *Ibid.*, 37.
59 *Ibid.*, 39.
60 *Ibid.*, 111.
61 *Ibid.*
62 *Ibid.*, 39–40.
63 *Ibid.*, 52.
64 *Ibid.*, 53.
65 *Ibid.*, 110.
66 *Ibid.*, 111.
67 Škvorecký, *When Eve Was Naked: Stories of a Life's Journey*, 68.
68 Grosman, *The Shop on Main Street*, 113.
69 *Ibid.*
70 *Ibid.*, 114.
71 Kundera, *The Art of the Novel*, 71–72.
72 *Ibid.*, 7–8.
73 The quoted phrase is on the back cover of Bohumil Hrabal, *Closely Observed Trains* trans. Edith Pargeter (London: Jonathan Cape, 1968).
74 *Ibid.*, loc. 14.
75 The quotation is from Jonathan L. Owen, "Closely Observed Bodies: Corporeality, Totalitarianism and Subversion in Jiří Menzels 1960s Adaptations of Bohumil Hrabal," *Canadian Slavonic Papers* 51: 4 (2009), 498.
76 Hrabal, *Why I Write?* 11–14.
77 James Wood, *Serious Noticing: Selected Essays 1997–2019* (New York: Farrar, Straus and Giroux, 2020), 55.
78 Hrabal, *Closely Observed Trains*, 8.

79 The expressions belong to M. M. Bakhtin; see his chapter, "The *Bildungsroman* and Its Significance in the History of Realism," in *Speech Genres and Other Essays* trans. Vern W. McGee (Austin: University of Texas Press, 1986), 11.

80 See M. M. Bakhtin, *Rabelais and His World* trans. Hélène Iswolsky (Bloomington: Indiana University Press, 1984).

81 Hrabal testifies to the influence of Rabelais on his writing style. He says (in *Why I Write*, 9), "I know by heart François Rabelais' *Gargantua and Pantagruel*."

82 Hrabal, *Closely Observed Trains*, 55.

83 *Ibid.*, 22.

84 *Ibid.*, 25.

85 Hrabal, *Closely Observed Trains*, 59.

86 *Ibid.*, 70.

87 *Ibid.*, 79.

88 See the explication of the name in Emmanuel Klimt-Gassner, "The Resilient Czech Spirit on Display in Bohumil Hrabal's "Closely Observed Trains" and "I Served the King of England," *Inquiry* 2: 3 (2010), on the web at: www.inquiriesjournal.com/articles/198/the-resilient-czech-spirit-on-display-in-bhumil-hrabal-closely-observes-trains-and-i-served-the-king-of-england.

89 *Ibid.*, 91.

90 I am quoting Terry Pitts, "Writing After Sebald," *Sebaldiana*, on the web at: http://kosmopolis.cccb.org/en/sebaldiana/post/escriure-despres-de-sebald/.

91 Wood, "Broken Record."

92 I am quoting from my earlier reading of the novel: Michael J. Shapiro, "Holocaust Punctuations," in *Punctuations: How the Arts Think the Political*, (Durham, NC: Duke University Press, 2019), 167.

93 *Ibid.*, 164. The inner quotation is from James Wood, "Introduction" to Sebald, *Austerlitz* (New York: Modern Library, 2001), xviii.

94 Sebald, *Austerlitz*, 100.

95 *Ibid.*, 101.

96 Sebald, *Austerlitz*, 5.

97 The expression belongs to Wood, "Introduction" to *Austerlitz*, xi.

98 Sebald, *Austerlitz*, 7.

99 Clemantine Wamariya (with Elizabeth Weil), *The Girl Who Smiled Beads* (New York: Crown, 2018), 224.

100 See Mark R. McCulloh, "The Stylistics of Stasis: Paradoxical Effects in W. G. Sebald," *Style* 38: 1 (Spring 2004), 38–48.

101 See Amir Eshel, "Against the Power of Time: The Poetics of Suspension in W. G. Sebald's Austerlitz," *New German Critique* No. 88 (Winter, 2003), 71–96.

102 Sebald, *Austerlitz*, 10.

103 Ibid., 5.

104 *Ibid.*, 91.

105 *Ibid.*, 92–93.

106 Samuel Pane, "*Trauma Obscura:* Photographic Media in W. G. Sebald's *Austerlitz*," *Mosaic* 38: 1 (2005), 40.

107 Sebald is quoted in J. J. Long *W. G. Sebald: Image, Archive, Modernity* (Edinburgh, UK: Edinburght University Press, 2007), 48. The follow-up quote is Long's interpretation of John Tagg's position in *The Burden of Representation*.

108 Eshel, "Against the Power of Time, The Poetics of Suspension in W. G. Sebald's Austerlitz."

109 Daniel Libeskind, "Between the Lines," in *Daniel Libeskind: The Space of Encounter* (London: Thames & Hudson), 28.

110 Roland Barthes, "From Work to Text," in *Image Music Text* trans. Stephen Heath (New York: Hill and Wang, 1977), 158.

111 Libeskind, "Between the Lines," 28.

112 Daniel Libeskind, quoted in James E. Young, *At Memory's Edge: Afterimages of the Holocaust in Contemporary Art and Architecture* (New Haven, CT: Yale University Press, 2002), 163.

113 Sebald, *Austerlitz*, 223.

114 Erin Manning, *Always More Than One: Individuation's Dance* (Durham, NC: Duke University Press). 74.

115 That apt phrase belongs to Wood, "Introduction" to *Austerlitz*, vii.

116 I am quoting Ann Smocks characterization of Blanchot's position, her "Translator's Introduction" to Maurice Blanchot, *The Space of Literature* (Lincoln: University of Nebraska Press, 1982), 3.

117 McCulloh, "The Stylistics of Stasis: Paradoxical Effects in W. G. Sebald," 42.

118 *Ibid.*, 246.

119 Sebald, *Austerlitz*, 140.

120 *Ibid.*, 245–246.

121 *Ibid.*, 246–247.

122 Sebald, *Austerlitz*, 147.

123 Andrei Tarkovsky, *Sculpting in Time* trans. Kitty Hunter Blair (Austin: University of Texas Press, 2012), 183.

124 Milan Kundera, *Encounter*, trans. Linda Asher (New York: HarperCollins, 2009). 151.

125 The quotation is from R. J. Keijser, "Oscillations in a Developing Discourse: History, Truth and Cliches Seven Decades after the Holocaust in Laurent Binet's *HHhH* and Jáchym Topol's *The Devil's Workshop*, BA Thesis in Literary Studies, Utrecht University 8 July 2013, 18–19. The inner quotations are from Dorothea Wiese, *The Powers of the False: Reading, Writing, Thinking beyond Truth and Fiction* (PhD dissertation, Utrecht University, 2011), 257.

126 Jáchym Topol, *The Devil's Workshop* trans. Alex Zucker (London: Portobello, 2013), 29.

127 *Ibid.*, 4.

128 *Ibid.*, 29.

129 The expression belongs to Michelle Woods, "Translating Topol: Kafkam the Holocaust Humor," on the web at: www.scribd.com/document/360251173/Translating-Topol-Kafka-the-Holocaust-and-humor, 95.

130 I am quoting Jorge Semprún, *Literature or Life* trans. Linda Coverdale (New York: Penguin, 1997), 264–265.

131 *Ibid.*, 60.

132 *Ibid.*, 142.

133 See Menachim Kaiser, "Unshared Histories: Timothy, Snyder's 'Bloodlands..'" *Los Angles Review of Books*, October 16, 2012. On the web at: https://lareviewofbooks.org/article/unshared-histories-timothy-snyders-bloodlands/.

134 The quotations are from Eve Tushnet's review of *The Devil's Workshop*, on the web at: http://farefwd.com/2018/01/devils-workshop/.

Bibliography

Abraham, Taisha (1998) 'An Interview with Arundhati Roy,' *Ariel* Vol. 29 (1), pp. 88–92.

Bakhtin, M. M. (1984) *Rabelais and His World*, trans. Hélène Iswolsky, Bloomington: Indiana University Press.

Bakhtin, M. M. (1986) 'The *Bildungsroman* and Its Significance in the History of Realism,' in *Speech Genres and Other Essays*, trans. Vern W. McGee, Austin: University of Texas Press, pp. 10–59.

Barthes, Roland (1977) 'From Work to Text,' in *Image Music Text*, trans. Stephen Heath, New York: Hill and Wang, pp. 155–164.

Binet, Laurent (2012) *HHhH*, trans. Sam Taylor, New York: Farrar, Straus, Giroux.

Blanchot, Maurice (1982) *The Space of* Literature, trans. Ann Smock, Lincoln: University of Nebraska Press.

Burdick, Emily Miller (2015) *The Subject of Holocaust Fiction*, Bloomington: Indiana University Press.

Davis, Cailee S. (2018) 'Laurent Binet's *HHhH:* Historiographic Metafiction in Contemporary French Literature About World War II,' on the web at: https://csuepress. columbusstate.edu/theses_dissertations/284/.

DeLillo, Don (1985) *White Noise*, New York: Viking.

Des Pres, Terrence (1991) *Writing into the World: Essays, 1973–1987*, New York: Viking.

Donia, Robert J. (2015) *Radovan Karadzic: Architect of the Bosnian Genocide*, Cambridge, UK: Cambridge University Press.

Eshel, Amir (2003) 'Against the Power of Time: The Poetics of Suspension in W. G. Sebald's *Austerlitz*,' *New German Critique* No. 88, pp. 71–96.

Grosman, Ladislav (2019) *The Shop on Main Street*, trans. Iris Urwin Lewitová, Prague: Karolinum Press.

Hilberg, Raul (1961) *The Destruction of the European Jews*, New Haven, CT: Yale University Press.

Hrabal, Bohumil (1968) *Closely Observed Trains*, trans. Edith Pargeter, London: Jonathan Cape.

Hrabal, Bohumil (2019) *Why I Write?* trans. David Short, Prague: Karolinum Press.

Kaiser, Menachem (2012) 'Unshared Histories: Timothy, Snyder's *Bloodlands*,' *Los Angeles Review of Books*, October 16, 2012. On the web at: https://lareviewofbooks.org/article/unshared-histories-timothy-snyders-bloodlands/.

Keijser, R. J. (2013) 'Oscillations in a Developing Discourse: History, Truth and Clichés Seven Decades after the Holocaust in Laurent Binet's *HHhH* and Jáchym Topol's *The Devil's Workshop*', BA Thesis in Literary Studies, Utrecht University.

Kertész, Imre (2004) *Fatelessness*, trans. Tim Wilkinson, New York: Vintage.

Kertész, Imre (2011) *The Holocaust as Culture Literature*, trans. Thomas Cooper, Calcutta: Seagull Books, (2011), 61.

Klimt-Gassner, Emmanuel (2010) 'The Resilient Czech Spirit on Display in Bohumil Hrabal's "Closely Observed Trains" and "I Served the King of England",' *Inquiry* Vol. 2: (3) on the web at: www.inquiriesjournal.com/articles/198/the-resilient-czech-spirit-on-display-in-bhumil-hrabal-closely-observes-trains-and-i-served-the-king-of-england.

Kundera, Milan (2000) *The Art of the Novel*, trans. Linda Asher, New York: Harper.

Kundera, Milan (2009) *Encounter*, trans. Linda Asher, New York: HarperCollins.

Levi, Primo (1987) *The Reawakening*, trans. Stuart Woolf, New York: Collier.

Libeskind, Daniel (2000) *The Space of* Encounter, London: Thames & Hudson.

Long, J. J. (2007) *W, G, Sebald: Image, Archive, Modernity*, Edinburgh, UK: Edinburgh University Press.

Manning, Erin (2013) *Always More Than One: Individuation's Dance*, Durham, NC: Duke University Press.

McCulloh, Mark R. (2004) 'The Stylistics of Stasis: Paradoxical Effects in W. G. Sebald,' *Style* Vol. 38 (1), pp. 38–48.

Owen, Jonathan L. (2009) 'Closely Observed Bodies: Corporeality, Totalitarianism and Subversion in Jiří Menzel's 1960s Adaptations of Bohumil Hrabal,' *Canadian Slavonic Papers* Vol. 51 (4), pp. 495–511.

Pane, Samuel (2005) '*Trauma Obscura:* Photographic Media in W. G. Sebald's *Austerlitz*,' *Mosaic* Vol. 38 (1), pp. 37–54.

Pitts, Terry (2015) 'Writing After Sebald,' *Sebaldiana*, on the web at: http://kosmopolis. cccb.org/en/sebaldiana/post/escriure-despres-de-sebald/.

Rancière, Jacques (2004) *The Politics of Aesthetics* trans. Gabriel Rockhill, London: Continuum.

Sebald, W. G. (2001) *Austerlitz*, trans. Anthea Bell, New York: Modern Library.

Semprún, Jorge (1997) *Literature or Life*, trans. Linda Coverdale, New York: Penguin.

Shapiro, Michael J. (2012) 'Street Politics,' *Journal of Critical Globalisation Studies*, No. 5, pp. 127–128.

Shapiro, Michael J. (2016) *Politics and Time: Documenting the* Event, Cambridge, UK: Polity.

Shapiro, Michael J. (2019) *Punctuations: How the Arts Think the Political*, Durham, NC: Duke University Press.

Škvorecký, Josef (2003) *When Eve Was Naked: Stories of a Life's Journey*, New York: Picador.

Solic, Mirna (2015) 'Narrating and Negotiating the Repressed City: Representations of Prague in Jiří Weil's work', *Bohemia Olomucensia* Vol. 7 (1), pp. 71–83.

Tarkovsky, Andrei (2012) *Sculpting in Time*, trans. Kitty Hunter Blair, Austin: University of Texas Press.

Topol, Jáchym (2013) *The Devil's Workshop*, trans. Alex Zucker, London: Portobello.

Tushnet, Eve (2018) review of *The Devil's Workshop*, on the web at: http://farefwd.com/2018/01/devils-workshop/.

Tyler, Anne (1989) review of *Life with a Star*, *The New York Times Book Review* on the web at: http://movies2.nytimes.com/books/99/02/28/nnp/weil-star.html.

Vollman, William T. (2005) *Europe Central*, New York: Viking.

Wamariya, Clemantine (2018) *The Girl Who Smiled Beads*, New York: Crown.

Weil, Jiří (2012) *Life with a Star*, trans. Rita Klimova, London: Daunt.

White, Hayden (1986) *Metahistory*, Baltimore: Johns Hopkins University Press.

Wood, James, (2001) 'Introduction' to W. G. Sebald, *Austerlitz*, trans. Anthea Bell, New York: Modern Library, pp. v–xix.

Wood, James (2012) 'Broken Record: A Historical Novel at War with Itself,' *The New Yorker Magazine* May 14, 2012, on the web at: www.newyorker.com/magazine/2012/05/21/broken-record.

Wood, James (2020) *Serious Noticing: Selected Essays 1997–2019*, New York: Farrar, Straus and Giroux.

Woods, Michelle (2017) 'Translating Topol: Kafka, the Holocaust Humor,' on the web at: www.scribd.com/document/360251173/Translating-Topol-Kafka-the-Holocaust-and-humor.

Zembylas, Michalinos (2018) 'Holocaust Laughter and Edgar Hilsenrath's *The Last Nazi and the Barber*. Toward a Critical Pedagogy of Laughter and Humor in Holocaust Education,' *Studies in the Philosophy of Education* No. 37, pp. 301–313.

5

INVENTING ASSASSINS

Some stories never end even in our time, in the sightlines of history, in the retrieved instancy of film and videotape, there are stories waiting to be finished, opened to the thrust of reasoned analysis and haunted speculation. These stories…undergo a kind of condensation, seeping into the texture of everyday life, barely separable from the ten thousand little excitations that define a routine day of visual and aural static processed by the case-hardened consumer brain.

'Lee Harvey Oswald' often seems a secret design worked out by men who will never surface…a procedural diagram, a course in fabricated biography. Who put him together? He is not an actor so much as he is a character, a fictional character who first emerges in the year 1957…Oswald seems scripted out of doctored photos, tourist cards, change-of-address cards, mail-order forms, visa applications, altered signatures, pseudonyms.

Don DeLillo, "American Blood" [1]

The Cinematic Narrative

The three primary texts in focus in this chapter are further examples of the historiographic metafiction genre analyzed in earlier chapters. All three – Justin Cartwright's *The Song Before It Is Sung*, Leonardo Padura's, *The Man Who Loved Dogs*, and Don DeLillo's *Libra* – are novels with assassination plots. With productive tensions between their aesthetic and thematic dimensions, they maintain coherence in each case with an emphasis on the agency through which assassins are constructed. Reading them together, it becomes evident that assassins emerge through a combination of their own self-fashioning and the shaping efforts of others. In the case of the Heydrich assassination – treated in the analysis of Laurent Binet's novel *HHhH* in Chapter 4 – circumstances had yielded a large pool of potential assassins. The head of Czech intelligence services, František Moravic, who orchestrated the assassination plan, was in exile in London along with the president of the Czechoslovakian government, Edvard Beneš, who authorized it, and roughly 2000 exiled Czech soldiers. Starting with two dozen recruits from the pool, Moravic ultimately selected the Slovak Jozef Gabčík and the Moravian Jan Kubiš for Operation Android. Seemingly nothing in their two lives prepared them for their entry into history except whatever was involved in encouraging their loyalty to their country. The Czech government in exile contemplated but never initiated an assassination plan for Hitler. However, others tried and failed. The text to which I turn first, Cartwright's novel, features a fictionalized version of a character who participated in an unsuccessful attempt on Hitler's life on July 20, 1944. A review of the novel provides a brief summary of relevant aspects of the historical event:

> On the outbreak of war [Adam] von Trott tried to gather support against the Nazis in Britain and America, but in vain. Returning to Germany in 1940 against the advice of his friends, one of whom was the Russian-born Jewish Fellow of All Souls, Isaiah Berlin, he was involved in the unsuccessful 20th July plot to assassinate Hitler. He was arrested, tortured and hanged with great cruelty in August 1944, a couple of weeks after his 35th birthday. The hanging was filmed on Hitler's orders, and von Trott's three young children were taken by the Gestapo in accordance with Hitler's policy of Sippenhaft, or kindred seizure.[2]

The opening of Cartwright's novel (hereafter *Song*) is pervasively cinematic. From the outset the reader sees the world through the eyes of the character, Conrad Senior, who serves as the plot's main camera. His wide angle, depth of focus, and *mise en scène* observations conduct the reader through the narrative. As the novel opens, he's a camera filtering what another camera shows. He's recalling a film he's watched of the trial of the would-be Hitler assassin, Axel von Gottberg (the historical Adam von Trott) 60 years after it took place. Reexperiencing his viewing as a series of Bergsonian moments – He's afflicted by memories which, "unsolicited by the needs of perception," can come "washing over us *for their own reasons*"[3] – Conrad explicitly registers "the difference between the thoughts you bid come to you and the ones that come anyway"[4] and figures the latter as unsolicited or "involuntary memory."[5]: "For nearly three years [he] has been thinking about Axel von Gottberg [who] was garroted on the orders of Hitler in August 1944. Thoughts of von Gottberg visit him at any hour of the day, without warning … Conrad is aware that he is not thinking full-blown thoughts, but highlights, like the trailers at his local cinema complex; these thoughts are presenting themselves to him in a chaotic pageant."[6] Conrad is also afflicted by a sense of obligation as a witness to the historical significance of von Gottberg and his (Conrad's) former mentor, E. A. Mendel (a fictional Isaiah Berlin): "He struggles sometimes with the fear that in the process of writing about them he is trivializing their story or introducing new falsehoods into it … he has to decide what material to ignore and what to include."[7]

The haunting images from the trial are of Axel "standing in a capacious suit before the People's Court with his hands folded in front of him," in a film meant to show "what a fine National Socialist the judge, Roland Freisler was, and what wretched traitors the accused were." However, because aesthetic form contradicts directorial intent, Conrad sees it differently. Conjuring Dutch paintings, he sees a courtroom

> beautifully lit…as though the windows of the court are admitting a soft, warm light, a Dutch light, containing the texture of paint, to coat the defendant, the judge himself, and the upstanding members of the public, who, in contrast to the decadents on trial, are mostly uniformed. The unintended effect of this is to make von Gottberg look heroic.[8]

Despite being edited to show Freisler as "the true voice of Nazism," his theatrical rages and facial contortions are such that "even some Nazis are embarrassed by his behavior."

> He says the word Schweinehund at one stage which, until he heard it in Freisler's mouth, Conrad thought was an invention of British and American war-films. It adds to the unreality; Freisler looks as though he has been pulled in by a desperate casting director.[9]

Conrad's cinematic reflections take a more purposive turn as the narrative proceeds. He heads to Berlin to meet an informant claiming to know the whereabouts of a film rumored to be of von Gottberg's execution. He wants to obtain it for use in a play and/or documentary he has been planning. It would be based on aspects of von Gottberg's life as well as on E. A. Mendel's, who had been Conrad's mentor at Oxford and von Gottberg's friend in earlier years. The search for the film is both a drama of detection and a reflection on cinema's effect on consciousness. With respect to the latter, Conrad keeps replaying the courtroom film inside his head:

> Sometimes at night Conrad finds that his picture of the People's Court… [is] played endlessly, as von Gottberg stands with his hands crossed speaking calmly and quietly…[the images] are unbearable because Conrad knows that if the film stops he will be slowly hanged from a meat-hook.[10]

The von Gottberg images are frequently entangled with his images of Mendel. At one point, for example, "he sees von Gottberg in front of Roland Freisler at the People's Court" at the same time he is entertaining images of "Mendel in his rooms at All Souls" College, because it is Mendel's ideas through which Conrad filters his view of von Gottberg's mentality.[11]

With respect to the search for the execution film, the detective narrative thread bears comparison with the plot in Don DeLillo' novel *Running Dog*, a parody of a detective thriller whose main drama is the pursuit of an alleged pornographic film rumored to have footage of a sex romp in Hitler's bunker during the climatic days of the fall of Berlin. At the end of the novel irony prevails. The discovered film turns out to be one of Hitler imitating Charlie Chaplin for a group of children. DeLillo renders that surprising moment as a lyrical film commentary:

> The figure shuffles toward the camera, his cane swinging. Behind him, in a corner of the screen, one of the girls earnestly looks on. Briefly the man is flooded in light – the bleached timeless effect of overexposure, With the return of minimal detail and contrast, he is very close to the camera, and his lifeless eyes acquire a trace of flame, the smallest luster…He produces an expression, finally – a sweet, epicene, guilty little smile, Charlie's smile. An Accurate reproduction.[12]

In creating a moment in which Hitler imitates Chaplin imitating Hitler, DeLillo is using a dark parody to critique the fascist aesthetic while at the same time using Hitler as a prop to expose the vagaries of the intelligence agency mentalities and practices that prompted the search.

In contrast, Cartwright's *Song* is an essayistic novel of ideas. When finally found, the film of von Gottberg's execution shows what it has been expected to show. Upon watching it a sickened Conrad throws it from Westminster Bridge into the Thames. Less important than what the film shows are the circumstances of its context and subsequent fate. Because Hitler is also a prop for Cartwright, what is important about the found film are the clashing history-memory-ontology perspectives that are exposed when Conrad meets the man who has been fearfully in possession of it. Ernest Frisch, who has been holding it, had faced a situation in which "nobody in Berlin," he says, wanted to remember the Nazi atrocities. As he tells his story to Conrad, the "gist" of it becomes "overwhelmingly clear [to Conrad and the reader]: an ordinary man, a film technician, has had his life utterly destroyed by people who believed that spirit operated in the world."[13] Ironically, the same Hegelian notion of a transhuman spirit, which helped fuel Hitler's version of German's historical destiny, also inspired von Gottberg's assassination plot. Much of the novel rehearses the alternative ontologies of history that distinguish von Gottberg and his friend, Mendel. It pits Mendel's Nietzschean view that history has no opinion of us against von Gottberg's Hegelianism in which history has a strong progressive opinion. Mendel at one point refers to "Axel's man, Hegel" whom he sees as responsible for the "state of mind" through which Axel saw a "sacred Germany."[14] Mendel's reflection occurs while he's listening to Beethoven's Ninth Symphony, which he regards as the "touchstone" of German civilization. He proceeds to distinguish Nietzschean and Hegelian musical aesthetics: "Nietzsche believed that music reflected the pain and suffering at the root of human existence…[while] Axel's man Hegel, says that art contributes to the synthesis we require between the personal and external worlds."[15] Much of how the novel thinks is filtered through that polarity.

The Consequences of Ideas

> They – the Arabs of Algeria, the coolies of India, and the blacks of Africa – were the fact, they did not pretend to be the idea.
>
> *Aimé Césaire, Discourse on Colonialism*

Conrad, through whom Axel and Mendel are represented to the reader, spends much of the novel thinking about ideas. The novel's very first sentence, which has Conrad flying to Berlin, also has him "thinking about thoughts."[16] Thereafter he's represented as one continually afflicted by thoughts about thoughts, e.g.

> I am troubled by the accumulation of thoughts, particularly the half-dead aspect of them, like leaves in autumn, still here in outline but lacking life, Conrad thinks. In my thirty-sixth year they seem already to keep piling up and I see no way of disposing of them.[17]

Conrad's idea-contemplating disposition contributes to the disintegration of his marriage. However, rather than a mere event of separation, the sundering process generates telling conversations about the value of ideas. Conrad's wife, Francine sees no value in the task Conrad had agreed to, collecting and organizing Mendel's papers. Skeptical of those interested in the history of ideas, she chides him for picking up ideas rightfully belonging to other people and having no ideas of his own. She says, "no one is interested in E. A. Mendel. He had an idea in 1953 but nobody can remember what it was."[18] Conrad's response, "To understand ideas, to be interested in ideas, you have to have ideas," has failed to impress.[19]

As their conversation proceeds it brings out one of the main questions the novel explores, the nature and consequences of alternative mentalities. Conrad sees Francine as one with a "desire for certainty, for the incorrigible proposition." Her day is taken up as a medical researcher and MD, working from seven to seven, "peering at samples and slides" and seeing "a few patients."[20] She claims tiredness and an absolute lack of good will for philosophical speculation. In an I'm ending our marriage speech she refers to being more content with her new partner, John, "an utterly unremarkable English professional man…known and admired for his pioneering work on the incontinence in women caused by childbirth." She is clear that she values definitive accomplishments over contemplating possibilities and uncertainties. As Conrad infers, she has a desire to "tidy things up mentally, as if by naming them they were settled…a scientific habit: taxonomy applied to emotional life."[21]

Shortly after that encounter, Conrad travels to Israel to follow the path of Mendel and von Gottberg's visit there (then Palestine) together in the winter of 1933. In Palestine/Israel he is able to see that "you can hold at the same time different landscapes in your head – or in your fibers – for instance, the broad openness of Africa and the distilled beauty of Oxford." At the same time, he "finds himself seeing John and Francine conversing about bladders and urine samples."[22] Rather than spiraling into a fit of jealousy, Conrad, after some initial feelings of hurt, has become edified by contemplating the ontological polarity that has disrupted his marriage, just as he is edified by contemplating a parallel one between Mendel and von Gottberg, who react very differently to historical crises. That extended contemplation is the novel's vehicle for thinking about the relationship between individuals and history. Through Conrad's observations and reflections, the reader is introduced to a clash of perspectives between a zealous von Gottberg, a man of "deep belief,"[23] and the philosophically dispassionate Mendel, whose response to Europe's "growing tensions" is "to look more closely at ideas"[24]

The novel also implies – through correspondence between women who have been involved with von Gottberg and Mendel – that the divide between von Gottberg's and Mendel's ontologies is also owed to their very different territorial biographies. In a letter to "Elizabeth," to whom von Gottberg had earlier proposed marriage, "Rosamund" (formerly romantically involved with Mendel and now yet another to whom von Gottberg has proposed marriage), describes her visit to von Gottberg's home in "Pleskow." Noting the extent to which Axel is "rooted," she refers to the family home and area of Germany as his "Heimat," where the von Gottberg family has lived "for six hundred years."[25] Unsurprisingly, von Gottberg's participation in the Hitler assassination attempt is Heimat-inspired. To his mind, Hitler has perverted the "true Germany," an imaginary for which he holds a "deep allegiance," one that is thoroughly "spiritual" (hence his attraction to the Hegelian narrative of spirit).[26] In contrast, Mendel is rootless; he's an immigrant Jew from Riga in Latvia and is utterly without a deep attachment to a homeland or to a heritage. He shares neither von Gottberg's heart-quickening longing for a Heimat nor his aristocratic instincts, his *noblesse oblige*. Unsurprisingly for Mendel, residing in Oxford's All Souls College looms much larger than the fact that it's in England. He identifies with thought worlds rather than grounded territories.

As the foregoing suggests, to heed how the novel thinks requires attention to its mobile literary geography, which is at the service of Cartwright's "narrative form"[27]; it emerges as the plot follows the movements of its characters. As *Song's* nonchronological narrative crisscrosses a global map that includes cities in England, German, Palestine/Israel, the US, Czechoslovakia, Latvia, Switzerland, and the Netherlands, it interweaves history with the novel's plot. Its spatial mapping jumps back and forth between the events associated with the assassination attempt on Hitler, the subsequent trial of the plotters, and a contemporary plot, an attempt by Conrad to recover and come to critical philosophical terms with the mentalities of two characters: the Hegel-inspired von Gottberg and the Nietzsche-inspired Mendel, who locate themselves differently with respect to one's obligations to place and history. The precipitating event in which an assassination plot fails is a minor geopolitical drama when compared with the events involved in "thought's territories,"[28] delivered through the investigatory efforts of *Song's* Conrad.

The temporal structure of the novel, which has Conrad recovering the significance of past events and dispositions, is radically entangled with its literary geography. As Franco Moretti points out (noted in Chapter 3), to recover how a historical novel works is to appreciate the way the novelist is able to "read time in space."[29] However, because *Song* is also a concatenation of road stories – Mendel exiling himself from Riga to England, von Gottberg nation-hopping as he tries to muster support for opposing Hitler's Third Reich, and Conrad on the road years later collecting information to assemble the significance of their lives – M. M. Bakhtin perspective on road stories also helps to situate the novel's literary structure. Bakhtin's most relevant genre analysis for *Song* refers to "chronotopes of the road," which render the road as

> both a point of new departures and a place for events to find their denouement. Time, as it were, fuses together with space and flows in it (forming the road)…the road is especially (but not exclusively) for portraying events governed by chance…[thus] the important narrative role of the road in the history of the novel.[30]

As applied to *Song*, Bakhtin's genre perspective suggests a tension between the novel's chance-governed form and von Gottberg's Hegelian view of history in which he privileges destiny over chance. To pursue that issue is to recover the novel's normative mentality.

Song's Metahistorical Message

> Death…is so definitive and irreversible that it barely leaves any time for other fears.
>
> *Leonardo Padura, The Man Who Loved Dogs*

> All plots tend to move deathward.
>
> *Don DeLillo, White Noise*

DeLillo's remark contains a productive ambiguously because it refers simultaneously to the plots hatched by persons/characters, to the plot structure of a novel that foregrounds death, and to "life," a plot that that ends in death. It applies well to *Song* because the assassination plot ends in the death of one of the plotters, von Gottberg's and the novel's plot ends with a commemoration of the significance of that death. To approach the way Cartwrights novel-as-form delivers its metaphysical framing, or more specifically its metahistorical ontology, I want first to rehearse an instructive piece of writing that helps me illustrate the role of a novel's meta-level form. In a discerning reading of the metaphysical force of William Faulkner's novel *The Sound and the Fury*, Jean Paul Sartre's emphasizes the approach to time. "Faulkner," he says, "has broken the time of his story and disarranged the fragments."[31] What holds the fragments together, Sartre suggests, is a "metaphysic of time." For Faulkner, "It is man's misfortune to be confined in time…a man is the sum of his misfortunes."[32]

Given *Song's* literary structure, a series of interconnected narrative fragments that jump back and forth among disparate historical moments, Sartre's suggestion about the metaphysic that oversees Faulkner's "disarranged fragments" is especially apropos. In the case of Cartwright's story, which stages a clash of perspectives between the zealous von Gottberg and the philosophically reflective Mendel, what ultimately holds it together is the progression of what is happening in the head of Conrad as he recovers their contrasting ideational impulses. The narrative thread that follows the intellectually nomadic Conrad is structured as a *Bildungsroman* in which Conrad becomes progressively edified about how to judge lives. The "ontological hypothesis"[33] that emerges is that there is no definitive advice – from nature, from history, or from any transcendent sphere – to validate a way to live one's life. While the novel's drama is based on a failed assassination plot and is embellished with stories of the romantic successes and failures of its three protagonists, it achieves its coherence through the meta-level consciousness toward which Conrad ascends.

A Eulogy

The ideational sensibility that *Song* ultimately delivers emerges at the end of the novel when Conrad fulfills his obligations to both von Gottberg and Mendel by delivering a memorial eulogy in Pleskow on the occasion of the unveiling of a memorial plaque at von Gottberg's family home. Risking an oblique approach to the proceedings, he chooses to begin with remarks about his teacher and Axel's friend E. A. Mendel, making the eulogy one in behalf of von Gottberg's and Mendel's "tragic friendship." Before satisfying those assembled with a focus on how "Axel von Gottberg lived his life according to his principles," he refers to the most important thing he has learned from Mendel:

> Professor Mendel was very fond of a quote from Alexander Herzen, who asked. Where is the song before it is sung? To which Mendel replied, Where

indeed? Nowhere is the answer. One creates a song by singing it, by composing it. So, too, life is created by those who life it, step by step[34]

"it is made day by day, as best you can."[35]

However, the Pleskow assemblage might have been expected to view that summation (the novel implies that their attention was solely on the remarks about Axel living a principled life), the existential, anti-Hegelian tenor of Conrad's eulogy is a rejection of ontological nationalism and the zealotry it inspires. Although the text to which I now turn, Leonardo Padura's *The Man Who Loved Dogs* features another zealous assassin, the object of this one's zealotry is quite different; it's a global ideological movement rather than a Heimat.

Padura's Fresco

Referring to the "great twentieth-century" novels of "Proust, Musil, Thomas Mann, etc.," Milan Kundera, uses the term "fresco," for writing that paints a large-scale view of the life world.[36] It's an apt metaphor for Padura's *The Man Who Loved Dogs*, which is about much more than the dog-loving Trotsky assassin, Ramón Mercader. This passage in the middle of Padura's nearly 600-page representation – of the years of Trotsky's exile, of those involved in the fashioning of his assassin, of those affected by the planning and ultimate act, and of the author's implication in the story that he's telling (after receiving an account from Mercader himself) – suggests the size of the wall that the novel covers:

> [T]hat story…was like an explosion of light illuminating not only Mercader's dismal fate, but also that of millions of men. It was the very chronicle of the debasement of a dream and the testimony of one of the most abject crimes ever committed because it not only concerned the fate of Trotsky, at the end of the day a contender in that game of power and the protagonist in various historical horrors, but also that of the many millions of people dragged - without their asking, many times without any one asking them what they wanted – by the undertow of history and by the fury of their patrons, disguised as benefactors, messiahs, chosen ones, as sons of historical necessity and of the unavoidable dialectic of class struggle…[37]

Padura's three-legged story about the protagonists – Lev Davidovic (Leon Trotsky), Ramón Mercader (who has several aliases), and Iván Cárdenas (Padura's alias as the writer who is telling the story) – has a plot that not only moves toward death (*pace* DeLillo), but also opens with one. One reviewer picks up the fresco metaphor: "The three alternating stories resonate with one another, acquiring deeper meaning as they paint the complete fresco of a political paradigms downfall."[38] However, to appreciate the composition of the fresco, which when completed provides a compelling picture of Stalinism's "debasement of a dream," we need to note the nuances of Padura's writing strategy.

Gravediggers and Dogs

The death with which the novel opens in its first chapter is Ana's, the writer Iván's wife, who has succumbed to a prolonged illness. It's not immediately evident why three details are prominent in the first chapter: the last words of the presiding pastor, the "well-worn formula": "Rest in peace" (the novel's very first words), the mention of "the grave diggers…moving over the stone" and placing "the wreaths of flowers"[39] on the grave, and the fact that Ana's beloved dog, a poodle named Tato ("brother") had died and been replaced by a mangy stray named Truco ("trick") bought to try and "alleviate the situation."[40] The role of Ana's death (and the phrase "rest in peace") is recovered within the first chapter. She is spared what the narrator refers to as the larger, anything but peaceful, beginning of the "death rattle" of the Soviet Union, which produced "lightning bolts of the crisis that would devastate the whole country [Cuba] in the 1990s."

As the chapter ends, Iván refers to his conversations with the "character whom I have always called, from the very day I met him, 'the man who loved dogs,'" the man who had related to him, "the dreadful story of hate betrayal and death." Iván becomes privy to the story as a result of a chance encounter, which has turned contingency into destiny: "God," he says, had put that story "in my path."[41] The path then devolves as the process by which Iván becomes a writer with a daunting task. He has to compose a story that captures not only what led up to the assassination, but also discloses the ongoing effects of the collapse of the Stalinist Soviet system that planned it. He suggests that to cover a story so central to "the history of the twentieth century," he has to heed "that whole series of global, national, and personal decisions" involved: the national level, involving Cuba's "hunger blackouts the devaluation of our salaries, and a transportation standstill,"[42] situated within a global level of upheavals associated with the cold war. In addition, as a novel writer (standing in for Padura), he has to treat how all those dynamics are experienced by specific people: those making and affected by the decisions that recruited the individuals involved in the events into their roles. Covering all those levels renders Padura's novel as an exemplary work of historiographic metafiction in which micro level (i.e., personal) lives are explored to illuminate macro level national and global historical dynamics. There are no simple *trucos* for all of that.

As Iván begins to tell that multilevel story in Chapter 2, we learn one of the novel's compositional "tricks," repetition. Like O'Brien's *The Little Red Chairs* and Pynchon's *Mason & Dixon,* Padura's *Dogs* is composed with re-inflected repetitions. They are a major aspect of "the immanent structure [of] the work."[43] It becomes apparent, for example, why Chapter 1 featured dogs and gravediggers. As Chapter 2 opens, we find Lev Davidovic in one of the first stops of his exile. He's in Alma-Alta, Siberia in 1928 near the Chinese border and at the end of the line of the Russian railway.[44] As was the case for Iván's Ana, he derives comfort from a beloved dog Maya, a Russian wolfhound from whom he has found "warmth and a comforting sense of reality,"[45] but from whom he might become estranged because Stalin's official insists he must abandon the dog while moving on to his exile out of the country. As for his forced departure that brought him to Siberia, "it had taken four men to drag him to the train station as he continued to scream and curse the faces of the *Grave Diggers* [my emphasis] of the Revolution."[46] Later, as Padura begins to make history an active subject of his sentences, it takes over the scream. At a moment in which Lev Davidovic has received news of the deaths of his fellow revolutionaries, "History came to yell his ear."[47]

However, Padura's main literary trick is the use of repetition in the sense in which Gilles Deleuze famously construes its contribution to critical thinking. It involves variations that do not simply repeat the same thing but rather expose, "the differential mechanisms which belong to the essence and origin of that which is repeated."[48] Lev Davidovic's (hereafter Trotsky's) exile from Moscow is thus a re-inflected repetition of Ana's exile from life, which is preceded by a loss of the comforting intimacy of her dog and followed, after her death, with her body in the hands of gravediggers. Importantly, both dog experiences are repetitions that anticipate the primary one, the assassin-as-dog lover from whom Iván learns the story he writes, not only a tale about an event in Mexico, the assassination, but also about the series of global events that comprise the way Stalin and his subordinates performed as "grave diggers of the revolution." Those repetitions – differences that cohere by thematizing intimacy (symbolized with dog-loving repetitions) and death in both in smaller and larger contexts – are embedded within Padura's macro level compositional strategy. The novel interweaves narrative threads that follow Trotsky from his initial exile to his death in Mexico, Mercader from his recruitment, through the assassination and incarceration for the crime, to his later years walking his dogs (also Russian wolfhounds) on a beach in Cuba, and Iván as he struggles to tell the story that brought Mercader and Trotsky together in the room in Mexico where a feigned intimacy allowed for their proximity during the fatal encounter.

The Road Stories

The novel's literary geography in both territorial and ontological senses is launched in Chapter 2 with the expression about Trotsky's difficulty orienting himself on his county's "turbulent map." Thereafter a series of chapters covering Trotsky's exile itinerary alternate with those covering Mercader's and Iván's. They are all road stories not only in Bakhtin's sense (already noted – "Point[s] of departures [where] events find their denouement…[while] 'governed by chance'" – but also in Deleuze's sense that they are shaped as subjects by the existence of what he calls, "*a prior* Others," virtual subjects that precede the identity events in which persons are actualized to fill the preexisting subject positions. The Deleuzian "*a priori* Other is the absolute structure....of the possible"; it is what "establishes the relativity of others as the terms actualizing the structure within each [subjecting-making] field."[49] Padura reproduces that insight about identity relationships at a moment in which he has Trotsky realize why "Stalin still hadn't broken his neck" (having already eliminated many other rivals with his show trials):

> Lev Davidovic understood that the Great Leader's macabre game still demanded his presence because his back had to serve as a springboard in Stalin's race to the most inaccessible summit [until such time as]...his usefulness as the perfect enemy was exhausted.

Trotsky was thus groomed as Stalin's essential *a priori* Other, a temporarily needed "counterrevolutionary."[50] Padura also has Trotsky figure out, while sitting in exile in Siberia, that once "all the requisite mutilations had been carried out...Stalin would fix the moment of a death that would then arrive with the same certainty with which snow falls in the Siberia winter."[51]

Accordingly, the work that Stalin's agents do on Mercader, once he has been selected as the instrument for Trotsky's "moment of death," requires first constructing the "*a prior* Other," the counter-revolutionary or "enemy of the revolution," one located in an ideology-saturated perceptual field to be filled with an actualized or particular other. In short, they had to tutor Mercader on the structure of that field and then convince him that Trotsky occupied the subject position that had preexisted him. As a result, the chapters reviewing Mercader's preparation for the assassination describe his ideological tutelage as well as instruction in hiding his identity by adopting a series of aliases. That preparation in stealth is another of Padura's re-inflected repetitions; Ana had named her stray dog Truco because of "his ability to hide."[52] However, hiding is but one aspect of the preparation. During his training Ramón takes "theoretical classes" in the Soviet Union and is turned into "soldier 13," "a man of marble, convinced of the need to carry out whatever mission was asked of him."[53] Ultimately, Stalin's agents succeed in creating a weapon without human sentiments, a man able to exploit relationships without succumbing to empathic feelings; he has learned to live "feeling like his insides had been emptied."[54]

The Itineraries

Two kinds of road are involved in the protagonists' itineraries. One kind is territorial: While the narrator/writer Iván's travels are restricted to a small urban zone (back and forth from central Havana to the beach where he meets Mercader) the travels of Trotsky during his exile and Mercader during his tutelage (up to the period in which they meet in Mexico) has them stopping in many states and capitals. The other is an ontological road. It's life's journey toward death. As Hélène Cixous puts it,

> The country from which we come is always the one to which we are returning. You are on the return road, which passes through the country of children in the maternal body. You have already passed through here: you recognize the landscape. You have always been on a return road [with]…a face toward death.[55]

That remark resonates with DeLillo's epigraph above, "All plots tend to move deathward."

Iván with Ramón

Although the itineraries of the three protagonists are covered in separate chapters, they are not separated thematically. One of the significant parallels between Iván and Ramón consists in the similar influences they face while being fashioned as becoming subjects. Composed with Padura's use of repetition, a strong woman influencing Iván's writing projects is repeated with strong women influencing what is to become Mercader's assassination project. At the close of Chapter 1, we find Iván referring to his conversation with Ana after having revealed the story he has learned from "the man who loved dogs." As he refers to his "delayed, repressed, and often forgotten desire to write the story," he mentions being able to feed off Ana's extraordinarily demanding vitality. Once she has read Iván's notes, which had lain fallow for 14 years, she admonishes him:

> She had barely finished reading them when Ana stared at me with the weight of her black eyes – those eyes that would always look like the most living thing of her body – began to berate me and she finally said, with appalling conviction, that she didn't understand how it was possible that I, especially I had not written a book about that story…[56]

Fast forward to Chapters 3 and 6 in which Mercader falls under the influence of two women who also have extraordinary vitality. Both are dedicated to "the revolution." His mother, Caridad, who is in the midst of the republican struggle against Franco's forces during the Spanish Civil, is pushing him toward a commitment: 'What would you be willing to do to defeat fascism, and for socialism', she demands, … 'We need to hear you says it'."[57] And his occasional lover, África inspires him with her revolutionary zeal:

> Her parents named her África, like the patron saint of Ceuta, where she had been born, and rarely had a name fit someone so well: because she

was vigorous, unfathomable, and wild. Like the continent to whom she owed her name. Ever since the day he met her, at a meeting of the Young Communists of Cataluña, Ramón felt absorbed by the young woman's beauty, but above all, it was her rock-solid ideas and her telluric drive that ensnared him: África de las Heras was like an erupting volcano who roared a permanent clamor for revolution.[58]

In contrast with the zealous Ramón, radicalized initially by Caridad and África and subsequently by Stalin's agents, Iván, appears in the chapters devoted to his project as a man with (in his words) "meager ambitions,"[59] and a level of "(shitty) apathy" in the words of his second wife, Raquelita, who asks for a divorce.[60] However, as is the case with the contrast between Cartwright's von Gottberg and Mendel in *Song*, there are territorial experiences that contribute to their very different dispositions. Mercader's racialism was gestated during the Spanish Civil war and the heady early days of the spread of communist ideology. It was a period in which those associated with the movement sensed a world historical change underway, a situation unlikely to breed apathy. Iván's situation vis a vis communism is radically different. He lives in a country with severe restrictions, shut down by his island's dual fundamentalism. A bureaucratic, censorship-imposing communism shares the space with a church-structured Catholicism, both contributing to (among other things) institutionalized homophobia (which afflicts Iván's gay brother) and more generally to control over the way people are allowed to live. What had once "constituted vitality and vivacity" inherent in acts of religious and political faith had become the "self-serving management" of his Cuban world.[61] Having lived with the restrictions for a decade, Iván's apathy is unsurprising. To the extent that he has a reprieve from his apathy and a threshold for ultimately being able to write, it's owed to the stimulation of his imagination; it is "thanks," he says, "to the real literature I was reading" (he mentions Kafka, Hemingway, Garcia Marquez, Cortazar, Faulkner, Rulfo, and Carpentier).[62]

By the time Iván and Ramón have met often enough to have developed a friendly intimacy, both have undergone significance changes. Iván, having learned the remarkable story of the "man who loved dogs" – initially hidden with Mercader's last alias (Ramón is using the pseudonym Jaime López) – has shaken off his malaise and is prepared to write. And Ramón is no longer "the man of marble." Telling Iván that one of his two Russian wolfhounds, Dax has a brain tumor, he wants to spare the dog the inevitable period in which he would suffer; he wants him to be able soon (as was the case for Iván's Ana suffering from bone cancer) to rest in peace and asks Iván to do the killing. Ironically, the man who had once been able to drive an ice ax into the skull of Trotsky says, "I'm incapable of killing a dog, I swear."[63]

The Exile and His Assassin

Although their encounter is ultimately fatal for one and a source of life-long anguish for the other – Iván says at one point, "I read in a newspaper that Ramón heard Trotsky's cries for the rest of his life."[64] – Padura creates a homology between the two, first with the figure of stones. At the beginning of his exile (early in the novel), "Lev Davidovic had seen how they rested away from him the last few stones that still allowed him to orient himself."[65] Roughly 150 pages later the stone imagery is repeated with a different valence; Ramón's Russian handler, Kotov, disparaging the Spanish revolutionary mentality, says to him, "Where I come from people are like stones. You are all flowers."[66] Thereafter, Trotsky and Mercader are distinguished with reference to their identity struggles while circumstances are estranging them from their past lives. In Trotsky's case he has been given identities, both territorial and political, which he doesn't welcome. As for the former, throughout the chapters that cover him, his most frequent subject position Padura lends him is as "the Exile." It's an identity that interferes with his work, his self-fashioning as an architect of the revolution, e.g., "Barely settled, the Exile began to prepare his counteroffensive and decided that the first necessity was to unite the opposition outside the Soviet Union …"[67] Adding to the instability he is coping with to do his work as writer and revolutionary while in exile is his constant need to be asylum-seeking. He has to land somewhere, and with each stop, the political identity Stalin and his agents have lent him – *the* counterrevolutionary – makes him a destabilizing media personality and terrorist target and thus eventually persona non grata at every stop. His fraught asylum-seeking, which lands him temporarily in Turkey, France, and Norway, exhaust him, making him a weary holder of the identities he does welcome: the "cosmopolitan man, the protagonist of the struggle, the leader of the multitude, [while] had begun to grow old at fifty-two."[68]

By the time he is finally granted asylum in Mexico, it has become clear that his entry into history will be based at best on his writing. That had picked up temporarily during his first foreign stop, Turkey where "the Exile regained his work rhythm and dedicated ten and even twelve hours a day to writing the *History* and to the preparation of two articles for the *Bulletin*."[69] Thereafter, his writing persona had to compete with his role as unwelcome guest, as at each foreign stop his hosts curtailed his attempts at a public life and the dissemination of his ideological struggle with "the grave diggers of the revolution." In contrast with Iván, for whom deadening apathy owed to a territorial/moral lockdown (what Padura renders as Cuba's fundamentalisms) inhibited the ability to write, Trotsky's writing was compromised by his territorial instability. Until he was welcomed to Mexico he had to struggle for his and his family's survival. And even in Mexico a significant inhibition compromised his writing, his affair with Frida Kahlo. As Padura figures it, "Wrapped in the dense spiderweb of desire, Lev Davidovic had to rely on all of his discipline to concentrate on his work."[70] Ultimately, even while having to look over his shoulder as a target for Stalinist-allied terrorists, he manages to put his Mexico house in sufficient order "to make a final push to compete his Stalin biography."[71]

Mercader's identity problem is in stark contrast to Trotsky's. While Trotsky is struggling to hold on to his past as a main protagonist in the Revolution and maintain his influence on the future of communism, Mercader is struggling to cooperate with a plan that requires him bury his past while looking toward an uncertain future. At one point he laments, "I've spent my two years preparing myself for something I might never do. I left my comrades in Spain, I don't have a single fiend, I've turned into someone else, and it could all be in vain."[72] For better or worse, throughout the narrative, Trotsky remains the Trotsky he recognizes, while trying to stay on track as a historical agent. After Mercader starts as an apprentice and begins a tutorial, the aim of which is to prepare him to be the one who will leap into history with a single act, he becomes increasingly unrecognizable to himself. He's first welcomed into his Soviet training period as "Comrade Roman Pavlovich." Very soon afterwards, he's told, "Until we decide your new identity, you'll be 'soldier 13'."[73] Once he is ideologically programmed and estranged from empathic sensibilities – "he had become an obedient and ruthless machine"[74] – a series of new identities are imposed so that he gradually leaves Ramón Mercader behind. By the time he has absorbed himself into the main cover he is given to use for most of his post-Soviet preparation for the act, a Belgian business man named Jacques Mornard, his Ramón self has almost disappeared. Nevertheless, it remains perilously close to the surface. At one point while he's speaking Catalan with his mother, Caridad, the use of his original language threatens the façade he's been cultivating. It "had him visit a closed-off region of himself."[75] It is one of the "days," he confesses to one of his trainers, "on which I can't stop being Ramón Mercader."[76]

How then does desire function for a man lost to himself and shielded with an emotionless carapace? As noted, while Trotsky is having an affair with Frida Kahlo, it takes extra effort to concentrate on his work because he is "wrapped in the dense spiderweb of desire," Mercader has to feign desire as part of his assassination plan. On the one hand, the suggestion is that it's because of his estrangement from human contact that he selects an ice axe rather than a knife as the murder weapon. Discussing the method with one of his handlers, "Tom," he says, "A knife would force me to cover his mouth, to grab him by the hair...I prefer the ice axe. Just one blow and I leave...You don't want to touch him?' Tom smiled."[77] On the other hand, to get close to Trotsky as a familiar visitor to his home, the man who has been dependent on "the impalpable paths of history,"[78] on an itinerary in which "he cannot *feel* his way forward," palpability becomes something he has to cultivate. He has to initiate and manage a physically romantic relationship with a woman who holds no appeal for him, Sylvia Ageloff, a Trotsky confidante who has access to his Mexico household. Ramón is able to summon convincing erotic feelings for her during the planning for the assassination and show absolutely no regrets about the betrayal thereafter.

Inasmuch as *Dogs* is a novel, structured as a result to show how what happens is experienced by those making it happen and those to whom it happens, the somatic narrative becomes a necessary part of the story for all the characters. And crucially, the temporal rhythms of the character's embodied experiences (the aesthetics of their stories), are important parts of the construction of the events: the making of revolutionaries, of conspirators, of assassins, of victims, and the consequences for the outcome of what we understand as history.

Padura/Iván

By the time Iván meets the man who loved dogs, Ramón (living as his last pseudonym Jaime López) has served a 20-year term in prison for the assassination, has been released and welcomed in the Soviet Union as a hero of the revolution, and has left Russia with his two beloved wolfhounds to spend his last years in Cuba (where he dies in 1978). Writing his story is Ramón's his way of recovering his nomadic, identity-dispersed self. Iván's (re)writing of the story constitutes his own self-making. While Ramón's story produces the historical coherence of his multiple personae, Iván's provides a lesson in writing history. What then constitutes the metahistorical coherence of Padura's story? For that we have to recover the novel's metahistorical, essayistic moments. At one point, for example, Iván offers an insight that links the personal with the historical:

> I now saw the true dimension of my solitude [an experience of self that Iván has shared with Ramón throughout the story] and how the decisions of history can come in through the windows of some lives and destroy them from the inside.[79]

As Padura renders the contingencies that brought them together, they are associated grammatically. Ramón and Iván are objects as much as subjects. Recalling the many places in which Padura has "history" as a subject/actor, we can observe how the novel's form answers the question about its metahistorical coherence. The assassination plot needed someone to carry it out; history chose Ramón as its agent. Similarly, it needed someone to tell the story. As Padura's agent, Iván puts it in sentences that merge Padura and Iván as objects of historical forces (much like Ramón):

> Where had I gotten the idea that I, Ivan Cardena Maturall, wanted to write it and perhaps publish it? Where, at some point in a far-off life, had I pretended and thought I was a writer? And the only answer within my reach was that the story had pursued me because *it* needed someone to write it. And the bitch had picked me.[80]

"Cuba"

Dramatically different Cuba imaginaries provide a bridge from Padura's *Dogs* to DeLillo's *Libra*. While for Padura's Iván, Cuba is experienced as a place of institutionalized fundamentalism and demoralizing restrictions (hence the lassitude he feels), for *Libra's* conspirators it's an ideologically fueled abstraction, a bastion of subversive, region-endangering communism. The difference becomes especially evident in a telling conversation that DeLillo invents between his main protagonist, Lee Harvey Oswald and David Ferrie, one of the operatives involved in the infamous Bay of Pigs invasion, then subsequently involved in a new conspiracy. The beginning of their encounter recalls the two fundamentalisms dominating Cuba, communism and Christianity. Ferrie, a devout Christian (as well as anti-communist) asks Oswald if he practices religion and if he goes to church. Oswald replies, "I'm an atheist" and supplies a Marxist justification: "Religion just holds us back. It's the arm of the state."[81]

Those fundamentalisms, nurtured outside of Cuba, accompany conflicting images of Cuba's size. As they discuss the logistical issues that impeded the Bay of Pigs invasion, Ferrie complains that the strike force was inadequate: "You can't invade an island that size with fifteen hundred men." Oswald responds, "Cuba is little"; Ferrie rejoins, "Cuba is big"; Oswald says again, "Cuba is little."[82] What distinguishes the Cuba imaginaries of DeLillo's two characters from Padura's Iván are the different loci of enunciation. While Iván sees it from the inside, Ferrie and Oswald see it from the outside, the former constructing it as an invasion-challenging space and the latter as simply a small splash of color on a global map.

Had the actual planners seen it from the inside, the ill-fated mission might have never been attempted. As Harold Wilensky points out in his analysis of "organizational intelligence," secrecy prevented the invasion planners – from President Kennedy on down – from looking at Cuban from the inside:

> the operations branch of the CIA kept its plans to itself; the intelligence branch was never officially apprised of the Cuban expedition…[and crucially] The men on the Cuban desk [in the State Department], who received the daily flow of information from the island, were not asked to comment on the feasibility of the venture.[83]

Secrecy's pervasive impediment to "organizational intelligence," also prevented the planners from looking at relevant evidence from a Roper Center survey which, contrary to their assumption that the Cuban population yearned to be free from Castro's communist government, indicated that the Cuban government enjoyed popular support.[84] In *Libra*, as in much of his subsequent fiction, DeLillo addresses the consequences of a security agency's cult of secrecy (which Wilensky's inquiry discloses), the withholding of information, the codes used to mask identities (as conspirators develop their plans):

Knowledge was a danger, ignorance a cherished asset. In many cases the DCI, the Director of Central Intelligence, was not to know important things. The less he knew, the more decisively he could function. It would impair his ability to tell the truth at an inquiry or a hearing, or in an Oval Office chat with the President, if he knew what they were doing in Leader 4, or even what they were talking about or muttering in their sleep. The Joint Chiefs were not to know.[85]

However, DeLillo's focus is more on individual mentalities than on organizational practices and more on various media influences on what will-have-been than on the immediate actions that inaugurate plans. Accordingly, in addition to the Cuba link with Padura's *Dogs* is a cinematic link with Cartwright's *Song*. The famous "Zapruder film [of the assassination], the 8mm home movie made by a dress manufacturer who stood on a concrete abutment above Elm Street as the shots were fired"[86] occupies as important a place in DeLillo's novel as does the film of von Gottberg's execution in Cartwright's. Moreover, as Norman Wacker points out, the novel as a whole is cinematic in style: "DeLillo's *Libra* imitates television docu-dramas, treating history, politics and social movements of the period through the biography of a key participant."[87] And just as Padura, constructs a period of history by showing "how the decisions of history can come in through the windows of some lives," DeLillo "details the historic and cultural construction of the [assassination] melodrama voiced in Oswald's consciousness [as well as in the consciousnesses other characters]."[88] Although there are many in DeLillo's cast of characters, most of my emphasis in this reading is on two, Oswald and Win Everett, the retired CIA operative organizing the novel's version of a conspiracy.

Oswald is "Libra" for DeLillo not simply because his horoscope is Libra but because of what the scales in the Libra horoscope imply. When Ferrie takes Oswald to what amounts to a job interview with one of the conspirators, Clay Shaw, a conversation ensues about Oswald being a Libran (owed to his October 18th birthday). After Shaw refers to "The Balance," the text proceeds, "It seemed to tell them everything they had to know." Shaw distinguishes "the positive Libran who has achieved self-mastery" from "the negative Libran who is…somewhat unsteady and impulsive. Easily, easily, easily influenced. Poised to make the dangerous leap. Either way, balance is the key."[89] It's clear as to which one they think they have. As I've put it elsewhere, "Oswald is ultimately 'turned' by [the conspirators] because he is a susceptible character."[90]

Early in the novel, to address history's contingencies, DeLillo creates an encounter that anticipates Oswald's precarious ideational balance.

A woman on the street, completely ordinary, maybe fifty years old, wearing glasses and a dark dress, handed him a leaflet at the foot of the El steps. Save the Rosenbergs, it said. He tried to give it back, thinking he would have to pay for it, but she'd already turned away. He walked home, hearing a lazy radio voice doing a ballgame. Plenty of room, folks. Come on out for the rest of this game and all of the second. It was a Sunday, Mother's Day, and he folded the leaflet neatly and put it in his pocket to save for later. There is a world inside the world.[91]

Precarious balance and contingency. To follow the implications of that encounter, we can imagine another possible one. What if the woman had been an agent of the sales organization, scientology (the "psychosis-machine as religion"[92])? The "world inside the world" to which her leaflet would have referred is an aspect of the inner self that has been heretofore unreachable because of mental blockages (scientology's perversion of what neuropsychologists refer to as engrams, cognitive memory units). Had such a leaflet liberated Oswald from the disappointing world that had been his lot, instead of a would-be assassin he would have been turned into a client, scrambling to pay for the scientology courses alleged to instruct on clearing the engrams.

The other mentality that the novel explores, also at length, is the "semi-retired" Win Everett's. His character is shaped by DeLillo's tendency to make his characters after effects of thoughts; "The thought seems to be thinking the characters."[93] Secrecy is the thought that shapes the characters of three of DeLillo's main protagonists, Oswald, Everett and "Branch" (in charge of assassination-relevant data collection). For example, Oswald, "kept Marxist books in his room…but he didn't show the books to bis mother. The books were private, like something you find and hide, some lucky piece that contains the secret of who you are."[94] For Everett, secrecy is intrinsic to his beliefs and associations:

> He believed it was a natural law that men with secrets tend to be drawn to each other, not because they want to share what they know but because they need the like-minded, the fellow afflicted – a respite from the other life, from the eerie realness of living with people who do not keep secrets as a profession or duty, or a business fixed to one's existence.

And finally, there is Nicholas Branch, who "sits in the book-filled room, the room of documents…in the fifteenth year of his task," wondering "if he is becoming bodiless" because his very being is absorbed in his "contract to write the secret history of the assassination of President Kennedy."[95]

While Branch is a more or less disembodied character whose task resembles DeLillo's, making sense of an event that he sees as "an aberration in the heart-land of the real" (DeLillo never lets him out of that book and documented-filled room),[96] Win Everett's life world is explored right down to the details of his gestures. One in particular has strong resonances for me. Because it's instructive, I take a brief detour to a personal relationship. As is with case with Everett, who is forced into early retirement from the CIA, my father was forced into early retirement from his ownership and management of a construction equipment dealership. Deprived of what for him was his favorite work activity, driving around (at excessive speed) to see potential customers, his domestic world became the space of an increasing obsessive compulsiveness. Among other things, he spent at least five minutes buttering his morning toast, taking care to ensure a perfectly even spread. Having watched that ritual (with lamentably little tolerance as I saw a man whom I'd admired descending into what looked like mental deterioration), I was taken aback and chastened reading this passage about Everett:

> Mary Frances [Everett's wife] watched him butter the toast. He held the edges of the slice in his left hand, moved the knife in systematic strokes, over and over. Was he trying to distribute the butter evenly? Or were there other; deeper requirements? It was sad to see him lost in small business, eternally buttering, turning routine into empty compulsion, without meaning or need.[97]

As DeLillo's narrative shows, there *were* "deeper requirements." Everett is constructed as a foreign policy zealot, a zealotry deployed as much on the outside world as it is on his morning toast. Unlike my father, for whom domestic routines were all that remained, Everett had a line of flight from the compulsions with which he carried out domestic policy. Officially, he is in "semi-retirement."

> A semantic kindness. They set him up in a teaching post here and paid him a retainer to recruit likely students as junior officer trainees. In a college for women, this was a broad comic thrust even Win could appreciate in a bitter and self-punishing way, as if he were still on their side, watching himself from a distance. This is what we end up doing, he thought. Spying on ourselves. We are at the mercy of our own detachment. A thought for breakfast. He folded the lightly toasted slice, ready at last to eat.[98]

While away from such routines, he is involved in running a conspiratorial foreign policy annex, meeting with his former CIA colleagues with whom he's plotting to stage an attempted assassination, arrange to have it blamed it on Cuban operatives, and thereby resuscitate the Kennedy administration's attention to Cuba as a communist threat to the hemisphere. The compulsions of Everett's domestic sphere manifested at the breakfast table are mirrored in the way he goes about the details of the plot

> in his basement ... hunched over the worktable ... putting together a man with scissors and tape [reminiscent with the way Mercader is invented] ... His gunman would emerge and vanish in a maze of false names. Investigators would find an application for a post-office box, a certificate of service, U. S. Marine Corps; a social security card; a passport application; a driver's license, a stolen credit card and half a dozen other documents ...[99]

As was the case of those who selected and shaped the Trotsky assassin, Ramón Mercader, Everett is constructing (what Deleuze *supra* calls) an "*a prior* Other," a virtual subject that Oswald will actualize once he passes the audition.

Meanwhile, the *world* has been auditioning Oswald. It too – the spaces, agencies and persons he encounters (and plots) – affects how he imagines being part of a world that exceeds what he has experienced in the claustrophobic apartments he shared with his mother and ultimately how he will decide to enter history. His nomadic existence, which takes him from New York, to an army base (and army brig) to Russia, to New Orleans, and to the fateful moment in Dealey Plaza, ends in the Dallas Police Headquarters, shot by Jack Ruby (whose mentality and affiliation with the plot the novel also explores). That outcome is part of the script that Win Everett believed in. DeLillo has his character deliver his oft expressed suggestion about the relationship between plots and death: "There is a tendency of plots to move toward death. He [Everett] believed that the idea of death is woven into the nature of every plot." As that thought continues, it is still ascribed to Everett but is clearly DeLillo speaking: "A Narrative plot no less than a conspiracy of armed men."[100] The statement succinctly locates *Libra*, with the other assassin novels as historiographic metafiction. Emphasizing what Hutcheon identifies as the genre's parodic impetus in which (to repeat her characterization) "the intertexts of history and fiction take on parallel (though not equal) status in the parodic reworking of the textual past of both the 'world' and literature," *Libra's* narrative subverts any attempt to anchor history while also challenging traditional realist fiction, which is "the theoretical foundation of the naturalistic novel."[101]

All the key characters posit alternative metahistorical positions. In contrast to Win Everett's desire to participate in the deathward movement of events is Oswald's realization that he is always fighting restrictions while confined in small spaces – in addition to the claustrophobic apartment shared with his mother is one in the military brig, where he's serving time for a self-inflicted wound and is controlled by movement-constricting white line protocols. "Maybe," we're told from Oswald's point of view, "what has to happened is that the individual must allow himself to be swept along, must find himself in the stream of no choice" and then "use the restrictions and penalties they invent to make yourself stronger .... the purpose of history is to climb out of your own skin."[102]

David Ferrie has the most paranoid metahistorical perspective. "History" for him is "the sum total of all the things they aren't telling is,"[103] while for Oswald's mother Marguerite, history is a story of deprivation, of, for example, their not even having a right to "decent heat" in her apartment,[104] and her son's character going off the rails because he was deprived of a father. Doubtless, it is Nicholas Branch who is closest to the metahistorical view that the DeLillo embraces. After 15 years of research, he sees that the "secrets," which shape characters and "build their own networks," defy clear trajectories of intentional cause or agency. Ultimately, despite the many variations in the way his characters view their relationships to events, DeLillo's implicit suggestion is that the driving force of a plot (rendered as an intersection of contingencies) is the most appropriate trope for approaching history.

Although it's evident that DeLillo's *Libra* thinks with its proliferation of the diverse metahistorical imaginaries of his characters, that approach doesn't exhaust what it thinks and how it thinks what it thinks. The intertextual dimension of DeLillo's event parody references popular culture rather than canonical literary works. Since his debut novel *White Noise*, he has scripted a model of mentality that is colonized by media voices, film and television especially. Early in the narrative DeLillo has Oswald and his mother sitting in front of the TV screen "where blue heads spoke to them,"[105] and as he did in *White Noise* he has the TV voice staging interruptions "'Natures spelled backwards' the TV said."[106] And perhaps most tellingly, at the point in which Oswald is sitting on his footlocker after having shot himself and is telling "Radar Man" Bushnell about it, Bushnell makes sense of the scene by turning to popular media: "He thought Ozzie's remark sounded historical and charming, right out of a movie or TV play."[107] Later in the narrative, DeLillo has Oswald deliver his suggestion that popular media constructs the meaning of events. While watching reading newspapers and watching television coverage of the capture of U 2 spy plane pilot Francis Gary Powers after being shot down in Soviet territory,

> It occurred to Oswald that everyone called the prisoner by his full name. The Soviet press, local TV, the BBC, the Voice of America, the interrogators, etc. Once you did something notorious, they tagged you with an extra name, a middle name that was ordinarily never used. You were officially marked, a chapter in the imagination of the state. Francis Gary Powers. In just these few days the name had taken on a resonance, a sense of fateful event. It already sounded historic.[108]

Although many misread DeLillo's *Libra* as yet another support for a conspiracy version of the assassination of President Kennedy – the journalist George Will even went so far as to call the book irresponsible and label DeLillo as a "bad citizen"[109] – it's better seen as a metafictional speculation about what contributes to the emergence of the "historic." As is the case with Padura's *Dogs*, DeLillo's characters are windows on history. However, in the case of *Libra*, those windows are filtered through other windows, the cultural media – "books, films, communiques, part of a free-floating third person which structures contemporary American subjectivity"[110] – which are responsible for the event-readiness that prepares what turns out to be "historic." Moreover, as DeLillo suggests, years after his metafictional venture into the history of the Kennedy assassination, the "plot" is not completed.

> Some stories never end. Even in our time, in the sightlines of history, in the retrieved instancy of film and videotape, there are stories waiting to be finished, opened to the thrust of reasoned analysis and haunted speculation.

These storied, some of them, undergo a kind of condensation, seeping into the texture of everyday life, barely separable from the ten thousand little excitations that define a routine day of visual and aural static processed by the case-hardened consumer brain.[111]

Notes

1 The quotation, which appeared in a fuller version in Don DeLillo, "American Blood: A Journey Through the Labyrinth of Dallas and JFK," *Rolling Stone* December 8th, 1983, is from my reading of his novel *Libra:* Michael J. Shapiro, "American Fictions and Popular Culture," in *Reading the Postmodern Polity: Political Theory as Textual Practice* (Minneapolis: University of Minnesota Press, 1992), 69.

2 Jane Shilling, "New Depth to a Profound Story," *The Telegraph* 18 February 2007, at: www. telegraph.co.uk/culture/books/3663076/New-depth-to-a-profound-story.html.

3 I am referring to what is for Bergson a third type of memory, which is less prominent in his texts than his more well-known two types, "habitual and pure" memory. The quotations are from a commentary on that third type: David Gross, "Bergson, Proust, and the Reevaluation of Memory," *International Philosophical Quarterly* 25(1985), 375.

4 Justin Cartwright, *The Song Before It Is Sung* (London: Bloomsbury, 2007), 1

5 The expression is in quotations because it's from Deleuze's analysis of sensuous signs affecting memory in Proust: Gilles Deleuze, *Proust and Signs* trans. Richard Howard (Minneapolis: University of Minnesota Press, 2000), 65.

6 *Ibid.*, 2.

7 *Ibid.*, 260.

8 *Ibid.*, 2–3.

9 *Ibid.*, 3.

10 *Ibid.*, 163.

11 *Ibid.*, 56.

12 Don DeLillo, *Running Dog* (New York: Vintage, 1986), 236.

13 Cartwright, *The Song Before It Is Sung*, 225.

14 *Ibid.*, 107.

15 *Ibid.*, 106–107.

16 Cartwright, *The Song Before It Is Sung*, 1.

17 *Ibid.*, 5.

18 *Ibid.*, 13.

19 *Ibid.*

20 *Ibid.*, 14.

21 *Ibid.*, 16.

22 *Ibid.*, 18.

23 *Ibid.*, 60.

24 *Ibid.*, 78.

25 *Ibid.*, 71.

26 *Ibid.*, 100.

27 The quotations indicate my borrowing from Franco Moretti's analysis of the geographies of European novels, Sir Walter Scott's in this instance; Franco Moretti, *Atlas of the European Novel* (London: Verso, 1998), 38.

28 The expression belongs to Gilles Deleuze and Felix Guattari, *What is Philosophy?* trans. Hugh Tomlinson and Graham Burchell (New York: Columbia University Press, 1994), 69.

29 Moretti, *Atlas of the European Novel*, 38.

30 M. M. Bakhtin "Forms of Time and the Chronotope in the Novel: Notes toward a Historical Poetics," in *The Dialogic Imagination* trans. Caryl Emerson and Michael Holquist (Austin: University of Texas Press, 1981). 84.

31 Jean Paul Sartre, "Time in Faulkner's *The Sound and the Fury*," in Frederick J. Hoffman and Olga W, Vickery eds. *William Faulkner: Three Decades of Criticism* (East Lansing: Michigan State University Press, 1960), 225.

32 *Ibid.*, 226 and see *The Sound and the Fury* (New York: Modern Library, 1946), 123.

33 The expression belongs to Kundera, *The Art of the Novel*, 49.

34 Cartwright, *The Song Before it is Sung*, 267.

35 *Ibid.*, 268.

36 Milan Kundera, *The Art of the Novel* trans. Linda Asher (New York: Harper, 2000), 47.

37 Leonardo Padura, *The Man Who Loved Dogs* trans. Anna Kushner (London: Bitter Lemon Press, 2014). 317.

38 Alvaro Enrique, "Trotsky's Pursuer Finds a Pursuer to Call His Own," *New York Times*, January 22, 2014, on the web at: www.nytimes.com/2014/01/22/books/the-man-who-loved-dogs-centers-on-trotsky.html.

39 Padura, *The Man Who Loved Dogs*, 3.

40 *Ibid.*, 10.

41 *Ibid.*, 10–11.

42 *Ibid.*, 8–9.

43 I am quoting Walter Benjamin, "The Concept of Criticism," in *Selected Writings: V olume 1, 1913–1926* ed. Marcus Bullock, Howard Eiland, and Gary Smith (Cambridge, MA: Harvard University Press, 1996), 155.

44 *Ibid.*, 13.

45 *Ibid.*, 14.

46 *Ibid.*, 18.

47 *Ibid.*, 103.

48 Gilles Deleuze, *Difference and Repetition* trans. Paul Patton (New York: Columbia University Press, 1994). 17.

49 Gilles Deleuze, *The Logic of Sense* trans. Mark Lester with Charles Stivale (New York: Colombia University Press, 1990), 307.

50 Padura, *The Man Who Loved Dogs*, 185.

51 *Ibid.*

52 *Ibid.*, 3.

53 *Ibid.*, 209.

54 *Ibid.*, 373.

55 Hélène Cixous, "Fiction and its Phantoms: A Reading of Freud's Das Unheimliche ('The Uncanny')," trans. Robert Dennome *New Literary History* 7:3 (spring, 1976), 544.

56 Padura, *The Man Who Loved Dogs*, 10–11.

57 *Ibid.*, 28.

58 *Ibid.*, 75.

59 *Ibid.*, 61.

60 *Ibid.*, 314.

61 I am borrowing expressions from Jean Luc Nancy: *Dis-Enclosure: The Deconstruction of Christianity* trans. Michael Smith (New York: Fordham University Press, 2008), 2.

62 Padura, *The Man Who Loved Dogs*, 69–70.

63 *Ibid.*, 181.

64 *Ibid.*, 244

65 *Ibid.*, 13.

66 *Ibid.*, 162.

67 *Ibid.*, 48.

68 *Ibid.*, 85.

69 *Ibid.*, 99.

70 *Ibid.*, 259.

71 *Ibid.*, 384.

72 *Ibid.*, 333.

73 *Ibid.*, 201.

74 *Ibid.*, 210.

75 *Ibid.*, 282.

76 *Ibid.*, 321.

77 *Ibid.*, 423.

78 *Ibid.*, 271.

79 *Ibid.*, 311.

80 *Ibid.*, 497.

81 Don DeLillo, *Libra* (New York: Viking, 1988), 320.

82 *Ibid.*, 321.

83 Harold Wilensky, *Organizational Intelligence* (New Orleans, LA: Quid Pro Quo Books, 2015), ebook loc. 1526–1543.

84 In addition to Wilensky's account, see the obituary for Lloyd A. Free, one of the designers of the survey, "Lloyd A, Free, 88, is dead; Revealed Political Paradox", *New York Times* November 14, 1996, B 15.

85 *Ibid.*, 20.

86 DeLillo, *Libra*, 441.

87 Norman Wacker, Mass Culture /Mass Novel: The Representational Politics of Don DeLillo's *Libra*," *Works and Days* 8 (1990), 69.

88 *Ibid.*

89 DeLillo, *Libra*, 314.

90 Shapiro, "American Fictions and Popular Culture," 76.

91 DeLillo, *Libra* 12.

92 The expression is from Anthony Curtis Adler, *Celebricities* (New York: Fordham University Press, 2016), 143.

93 I am borrowing the expression from James Wood who ascribes that tendency in Chekhov: *Serious Noticing: Selected Essays, 1997–2019* (New York: Farrar, Straus and Giroux, 2019), 42.

94 DeLillo, *Libra*, 41.

95 *Ibid.*, 14–15.

96 *Ibid.*, 15.

97 *Ibid.*, 16.

98 *Ibid.*, 17.

99 *Ibid.*, 145–146.

100 *Ibid.*, 221.
101 Paul Civello, "Undoing the Naturalistic Novel: Don DeLillo's *Libra*," *Arizona Quarterly* 48 (Summer, 1992). 33.
102 DeLillo, *Libra*, 101.
103 *Ibid.*, 312.
104 *Ibid.*, 4.
105 *Ibid.*
106 *Ibid.*, 5.
107 *Ibid.*, 90.
108 *Ibid.*, 197.
109 See George Will, "Shallow Look at the Mind of An Assassin," *The Washington Post*, September 22, 1988, on the web at: www.washingtonpost.com/archive/opinions/ 1988/09/22/shallow-look-at-the-mind-of-an-assassin/f8a4c3c6-8355-43c3-8a04- 03d6588688e6/.
110 That apt summation belongs to Wacker, "Mass Culture / Mass Novel," 71.
111 Don DeLillo, "Introduction: Assassination Aura," in the 2006 ebook version of *Libra*, loc. 52.

Bibliography

Bakhtin, M. M. 'Forms of Time and the Chronotope in the Novel: Notes toward a Historical Poetics,' in *The Dialogic Imagination*, trans. Caryl Emerson and Michael Holquist, Austin: University of Texas Press, pp. 84–258.
Benjamin, Walter (1996) 'The Concept of Criticism,' in *Selected Writings: Volume 1, 1913– 1926* ed. Marcus Bullock, Howard Eiland, and Gary Smith, Cambridge, MA: Harvard University Press, pp. 116–200.
Cartwright, Justin (2007) *The Song Before It Is Sung*, London: Bloomsbury.
Civello, Paul (1992) 'Undoing the Naturalistic Novel: Don DeLillo's *Libra*,' *Arizona Quarterly* No. 48, pp. 33–56.
Cixous, Hélène (1976) 'Fiction and its Phantoms: A Reading of Freud's Das Unheimliche ('The Uncanny'),' trans. Robert Dennome, *New Literary History* Vol 7 (3), pp. 525–645.
Deleuze, Gilles (1990) *The Logic of Sense*, trans. Mark Lester with Charles Stivale, New York: Colombia University Press, 307.
Deleuze, Gilles (1994) *Difference and Repetition*, trans. Paul Patton, New York: Columbia University Press.
Deleuze, Gilles (2000) *Proust and Signs*, trans. Richard Howard, Minneapolis: University of Minnesota Press.
Deleuze, Gilles and Guattari, Felix (1994) *What is Philosophy?* trans. Hugh Tomlinson and Graham Burchell, New York: Columbia University Press.
DeLillo, Don (1983) 'American Blood: A Journey Through the Labyrinth of Dallas and JFK,' *Rolling Stone* December 8 issue.
DeLillo, Don (1986) *Running Dog*, New York: Vintage.
DeLillo, Don (1988) *Libra*, New York: Viking.
Enrique, Alvaro (2014) 'Trotsky's Pursuer Finds a Pursuer to Call His Own,' *The New York Times*, on the web at: www.nytimes.com/2014/01/22/books/the-man-who-loved-dogs-centers-on-trotsky.html.
Gross, David (1985) 'Bergson, Proust, and the reevaluation of Memory,' *International Philosophical Quarterly* No. 25, pp. 369–380.

Kundera, Milan (2000) *The Art of the Novel*, trans. Linda Asher, New York: Harper.

Moretti, Franco (1998) *Atlas of the European* Novel, London: Verso.

Nancy, Jean Luc (2008) *Dis-Enclosure: The Deconstruction of Christianity*, trans. Michael Smith, New York: Fordham University Press.

Padura, Leonardo (2014) *The Man Who Loved Dogs*, trans. Anna Kushner, London: Bitter Lemon Press.

Sartre, Jean Paul (1960) 'Time in Faulkner's *The Sound and the Fury*', in Frederick J. Hoffman and Olga W, Vickery eds. *William Faulkner: Three Decades of Criticism* (East Lansing: Michigan State University Press).

Shapiro, Michael J. (1992) 'American Fictions and Popular Culture,' in *Reading the Postmodern Polity: Political Theory as Textual* Practice, Minneapolis: University of Minnesota Press, pp. 68–85.

Shilling, Jane (2007) 'New Depth to a Profound Story,' *The Telegraph*, on the web at: www.telegraph.co.uk/culture/books/3663076/New-depth-to-a-profound-story.html.

Wacker, Norman (1990) 'Mass Culture /Mass Novel: The Representational Politics of Don DeLillo's *Libra*,' *Works and Days* No. 8, pp. 67–87.

Wilensky, Harold (2015) *Organizational Intelligence*, New Orleans, LA: Quid Pro Quo Books.

Will, George (1988) 'Shallow Look at the Mind of An Assassin,' *The Washington Post*, on the web at: www.washingtonpost.com/archive/opinions/1988/09/22/shallow-look-at-the- mind-of-an-assassin/f8a4c3c6-8355-43c3-8a04-03d6588688e6/.

EPILOGUE

Aesthetic Methods

There is no single totalizing methodological frame that can serve to unite the diverse analyses in the preceding chapters. The aim of this epilogue is to distil a methods pedagogy from the diverse investigations in the chapters. Operating throughout the book is an aesthetic methodology that draws on aspects of the contentious field that identifies as literary criticism and on philopoetic interventions, – what Cesare Casarino calls (after Deleuze) "interferences" – compositional encounters between concepts drawn from philosophical perspectives and experiential moments in literary texts. The methods I use are rooted in the "romantic concept of art criticism," which as Walter Benjamin notes, "stands completely upon epistemological considerations."[1] However, the essayistic feature of the novels central to my analyses – those belonging to the genre historiographic metafiction – are epistemologically distinctive in that the protagonists themselves engage in conceptual interventions. Philopoesis-as-method is thus immanent in the texts as well as outside of them. Such is the case, for example, in Thomas Pynchon's *Mason & Dixon*, the main text in Chapter 3, in which as I suggested his protagonists, Charles Mason and Jeremiah Dixon are conceptual personae as well as aesthetic subjects. The novel is punctuated by their conceptual interventions – for example when they refer to themselves as "philosophical frigates" and explicitly acknowledge that their survey has them trespassing in the domain of another "civic entity."

The expression "aesthetic methods" I am attributing to my investigations carries a complication beyond the observation that the method resides within the texts as well as in my approach to them because there are two difference senses in which "aesthetics" had been historically understood. As derived from the Greek *aisthetikos,* it refers to one's embodied experience, while in its more familiar usage aesthetics refers to art appreciation. The two senses can be reconciled if we recognize that, on the one hand, an artistic text (novel, story, painting, film, piece of music, architectural monument, etc.) is crafted. For example, in the case of literature, to see *how* a work thinks one has to heed the way its composition – narrative structures, syntax, grammatical choices, and figuration – constructs its thinking. On the other hand, there is the question of what it can *do,* which implies among other things how the reader as a complex biological and historical subject (a person with a body and an experiential duration) receives the text, is affected, and is potentially activated. Moreover, in the case of influential, innovative styles, what an artistic text or work does is to reshape the terrain of the genre within which it locates itself, e.g., the way Stéphane Mallarmé restructured "the syntactic hierarchy of the poetic line"[2] and Claude Debussy radically intervened in the structure of musical composition with melodic structures that were no longer "contingent on a rigid tonal scheme."[3]

Those examples turn me back to the Rancière epigraph at the beginning of my Introduction, which equates literary form with political expression. My presumption is that literary texts are political not because they refer to extant political issues but because of what they do. For example, as I have noted elsewhere, what Toni Morrison's novel, *Paradise* does is contest both "the puritan reading of American exceptionalism and the African American attempt to simulate that exceptionalism" (in the all Black community featured in the novel).[4] Her writing challenges what she calls the "oppressive language" that is "designed for the estrangement of minorities, hiding its racist plunder in its literary cheek ..."[5] More generally, the political is engendered in the way a text is composed, i.e., the way its form allows for the possibility of "revolutionary action," occasioned as Blanchot suggests by "set[ting] down a few words side by side," to create the thoughts necessary "to change the world."[6] "To write," according to Blanchot's approach to writing-as-politics, "is to act as the vector by which the new might enter the world."[7]

Crucially, as I've noted within the chapters, something new also happens experientially to the artist/producer/writer. The author (as the literary critic M. M. Bakhtin observes) is "unconsummated" and is always becoming a revised subject. While addressing the phenomenology of writing, Michel Foucault offers a similar yet more radical suggestion. Juxtaposing a self-changing approach to writing with the conventional phenomenological approach to subjectivity, which "tries to grasp the significance of daily experience in order to reaffirm the fundamental character of the subject,"[8] he identifies himself with a phenomenology of writing he ascribes to "Nietzsche, Blanchot, and Bataille," for whom the purpose of the writing "task" is one of "'tearing' the subject from itself in such a way that it is no longer the subject as such, or that it is completely 'other' than itself ... a 'desubjectifying'."[9]

Heidegger, who also theorized a durational subjectivity, figured an authorial becoming similarly but on the plane of the author-reader engagement, referring to their "co-becomings." In his analyses of the apostle Paul's epistles, for example, he emphasizes a temporality of co-emergence. Treating the epistle to the Thessalonians, he writes, "Paul experiences the Thessalonians in two determination: 1. He experiences their having become. 2. He experiences that they have knowledge of their having-become. That means that their having-become is also Paul's having become."[10] Ultimately then, when we ask what the artistic work does, we are inquiring about the author/producer as well as the reader/viewer. And insofar as we are concerned with a work's effects as well as (or at times apart from) how it can mean, we are on are way toward connecting the two senses of aesthetics.

In order to illustrate that connection, I take a detour here to a different artistic genre and consider the effects of the canvasses of the English painter J. M. W. Turner (1775–1851). Looking at his *Rough Sea* (1840), one's first impression is that it's blurry (Epilogue Figure 1: Turner's *Rough Sea*). Compositionally, to achieve that impression the painter made the boundaries of each element in the painting indistinct. Turner's "visible world," as Julie Watkins, puts it, "was dissolved by dazzle, mist and light."[11] She goes on to refer to "what Turner sought to achieve." He composed a painting designed to share his experience of the seascape: Not satisfied with slavish reproduction, Turner sought to bring the viewer into his paintings, into his sensation of the light. In *Rough Sea ...* he creates a viewpoint with no shoreline – the viewer does not have the safety of being on land [and] Turner compounds the effect by not defining the horizon – leaving the viewer off balance, moving with the sea and light.[12]

As Watkin's commentary on Turner's painting implies, rather than mere aesthetic appreciation, an artistic work can open itself to a *politics* of aesthetics, which refers not to politics as it is traditionally understood – politics based on authoritative decision-making institutions – but to a political apprehension that emerges when an event or encounter is unsettling rather than reassuring. Within such a conception of the political – as eventual rather than institutional[13] – politics takes place when forms of consensus are disturbed. A voice in a Herman Broch novel provides a way of figuring the issue. Submitting to a consensus, it implies is like wearing "a generic uniform" whose "true function" is "to manifest and ordain order in the world, to arrest confusion and flux of life."[14] That submission gets tested by an encounter with something that makes one think. It can lead – if it arouses our social conscience – to becoming politically activated or attuned. Political apprehension is the effect of the passivity-disturbing forms of the literary texts I've engaged throughout my investigation. To think politically one has to be "shaken not [merely] stirred"[15] by an encounter with something that cannot easily be stored within the archive of one's learned, habitual expectations. As Gilles Deleuze puts it in his reading of Proust, "It is the accident of encounter that guarantees the necessity of what is thought."[16]

To illustrate the implications of such an accident for a politics of literature, I recur to an event I've addressed elsewhere. The late Mexican writer, Carlos Fuentes, reports an encounter that took place on a driving trip in the Morelos region of Mexico. Operating under the assumption that maps have a unitary and stable set of addresses, he asked a local *campesino* the name of the village where he had stopped. The *campesino's* reply disrupted that assumption: "That depends," he said, "we call the village Santa Maria in times of peace. We call it Zapata in times of war." The response stunned Fuentes, who then reflected on the multiplicity of temporal presences in the contemporary world. "The old *campesino*" possesses a knowledge that "most people in the West have assiduously ignored since the seventeenth century: that there is more than one time in the world, that there is another time existing alongside, above, underneath the linear calendars of the West."[17] The encounter affected Fuentes; it led him to ponder his vocation as a novelist and suggest that literature, the novel in particular, is the genre best suited to convey that multiplicity: "The novel is the literary form that, with most complexity, permits us to reappropriate time."[18] The after effect of that encounter registers itself in Fuentes last novel, *Destiny and Desire*, where he composes a narrative in which different social classes have experienced Mexico's history differently and as a result have had – from their varying perspectives and experiences as differing durational subjects – to make sense of the new century's country-wide precarity, which Fuentes succinctly characterizes: "Today, the great drama of Mexico is that crime has replaced the state."[19]

The edifying effect of an encounter that made Fuentes think was thus subsequently registered in his compositional style. In his final literary act Fuentes reappropriated time to challenge Mexico's dominant national mythology (That was his mode of political activation). He located Mexico in a narrative that contests the progressive democratizing story that its elites had been promoting along with the conceit that the state contains a unitary political culture. In his literary intervention into Mexico's Governing-enabled narco-politics, Fuentes addresses Mexico's historic political moment, which he characterizes as a form of governance aimed at ensuring popular submission to structures of class privilege while at the same time perpetuating the illusion that it governs a "democracy." Form-wise, to do so he contrasts the lived, experiential times of diverse types, as his protagonists/aesthetic subjects embody the biographical and social times of those with different heredities and different class backgrounds, and locates the contrasts within Mexico's national time. The diverse situations of his characters have recruited them into different vocations, all affecting the alternative ways they attempt to manage their relationships with Mexico's political realities.

My illustration from Fuentes's encounter and its subsequent effect on his novel *Destiny and Desire* is enabled by an adjustment to the lexicon that shaped my Introduction. Along with Barthes's semiotic privileging of writerly texts, which encourage a productive reader that extends (and often re-inflects) the text's implications, I am adding Deleuze's language of encounter in which the emphasis is on disruption when worldly signs – read or otherwise experienced – provoke an "act of thinking" because they "implicate something that does violence to thought."[20] To articulate Deleuzian criticism with Barthes's semiotics is therefore to conceive the productive effect of a text as a "shock to thought."[21] At a minimum, the methodological implications of heeding the Deleuzian language of encounter can be realized as an instructive narrative of inquiry, which I want briefly to sketch.

The narrative begins at the level of proto inquiry with the injunction, be prepared to be "afflicted"[22] by the text because the affects derived from encounters are (in Deleuze's terms) the "dark precursors" of our conceptual capabilities.[23] Then to proceed with the inquiry, the focus moves to an analysis of how the text works compositionally. I discovered, for example, that it took several rereadings to appreciate the role of repetition in Edna O'Brien's *The Little Red Chairs*, Robert Musil's *The Man Without Qualities*, Thomas Pynchon's *Mason & Dixon* and Leonardo Padura's *The Man Who Loved Dogs*, crucial to what those novels were saying and doing. Thereafter, with the help of conceptual elaboration – the next step in the methods narrative – a text can be extended to show how much more it implies than it explicitly says. However, "elaboration" doesn't quite capture a critical approach to concepts. A politically perspicuous conceptual practice seeks to reestablish the multiplicity that preexisting systems of consensual concepts obscure.

However, I want to interject a caution. There is also the important issue of resisting an impulse toward ultimate conceptual mastery. While all the novels that I've designated as historiographic metafiction treat specific historical moments, beyond the temporal terrains they canvass is the implication that what we can learn by evoking and re-textualizing historical moments can never be ultimately consummated. Each textual moment always will-have-been different when it accedes to new ones. That lesson in the temporality of textuality emerges clearly in an interview with the Chinese pianist Lang Lang, focused on his innovative approach to Bach's "Goldberg Variations." Because "Bach's set of 30 variations" is the musical equivalent of a writerly text – it "is written with such austerity that it's something of a blank canvass [with] no rule book for ornamentation" – Lang Lang felt free to engage in what for many baroque enthusiasts seemed to be shocking departures. However, for Lang Lang, his productive interpretations of the Variations aim to provide "another level of thinking," implemented by among other things varying the participation of the left hand. That hand performs in his playing as the "roots in Bach's music" in one section, the Aria, but in other Variations as "the middle voice."[24]

I want to add another relevant musical illustration, the African American vocalist Bettye LaVette's reinterpretation of the classic Beatles song "Blackbird." As a commentator describes her innovation,

> LaVette rejiggered the song into the first-person, slowed the tempo to a crawl and added a bed of strings. Her wholesale reinvention of the classic tune became the foundation of an album … [in which] all the songs, save for the Beatles song that inspired it, were originally popularized by Black female singers.

The album, which makes the Beatles' song say more than it was originally designed to say, serves as an *homage* that delivers credit to a group of "Black female singers, including Nina Simone, Billie Holiday and Dinah Washington," artists to whom LaVette refers as "Black Birds."[25]

The illustrations of Lang Lang's and LaVette's innovative compositions, which presume that Bach's "Goldberg Variations and the Beatles' 'Blackbird'" have not been ultimately consummated, provide a prologue for the last part of the pedagogical narrative, a reflection on implications for further inquiry. Their productive interpretations encourage asking oneself what more work, on textualized history, remains possible and how to convey that compositionally. To frame that as a pedagogical responsibility for teacher/scholars, I want to borrow a remark by David Milch (the creative producer of the HBO series *Deadwood*) about how the artistic process should be conceived. It's a "process," he said, "of passing on, for better or worse, as well as one can, what you've learned,"[26] which I take to mean that the work's pedagogy, which affected the author/writer, should be immanent in how it is assembled to be passed on. That implies the question of how compositionally to fulfill that "passing on."

To pose that issue, which presumes writing *as* method, as opposed to writing about something to which a method has been applied (e.g., describing the results of one's inquiry, the typical assumption of social science writing), I want emphasize that drawing on a literary text to extract political thinking involves an encounter of compositions. As I put it in the engagement with William James on mentality (in

Chapter 2), "Ultimately, James *writes* his way toward a view of mentality. He stages an encounter between compositions; his written composition engages the dynamic of cognitive composition he ascribes to mentality." Methodologically therefore, the politics of literary form that my investigations provide are realized as a meeting of literatures; one's writing is a literary accomplishment that encounters other literary accomplishments. What is to be accomplished? To answer that I want to expand on the "purpose of literature" statement I attributed to Blanchot in my analysis of W. G. Sebald's *Austerlitz* in Chapter 4. There I noted that for Blanchot, the purpose of literature is "to interrupt the purposeful steps we are always taking toward a deeper understanding and a surer grasp of things."[27] I went on to quote a commentary on Sebald's writing styles: "[His] interruptions – his many instances of "suspenseful stasis" – work through three stylistic effects: "byzantine structures for his characters to explore as well as mazes … repetition to draw out the moment in which one is 'on the brink' … [and] virtually imperceptible transitions into essayistic digressions."[28]

The writing-as-method with which I engage Sebald's text (as I do with all the other literary texts in this investigation) operates with similar effects. As I have put it elsewhere, the epistemological yield from my inquiries are not signaled by a frequent meta statements about what I am doing. Rather, the epistemic implications emerge from the form of the writing. It's a writing style that *shows* connections and disjunctions among forces and events instead of embedding an accompanying explication narrative. It's a style that Walter Benjamin professed, "literary montage."[29] And it proceeds with what Gilles Deleuze (in his analysis of a writer's style) refers to as the use of "transversals," confrontations of "different signs in different worlds."[30] Describing that style similarly while addressing its effect, Jacques Rancière refers to the staging of a "clash of heterogeneous elements" that "provoke[s] a break in our perception."[31] What all those stylistic idioms suggest is that the literature-effected thinking that makes a contribution to politically attuned knowledge is articulated in attention-alerting compositional practices that comprise what I am calling "writing politics."

Notes

1 See Walter Benjamin, "The Concept of Criticism in German Romanticism," in *Walter Benjamin: Selected Writings Volume 1 1913–1926* trans. David Lachterman, Howard Eiland, ad Ian Balfour (Cambridge, MA: Harvard University Press, 1996), 116.
2 The quotation is from David Michael Hertz, *The Tuning of the Word: The Musico-Literary Poetics of the Symbolist Movement Carbondale* (Southern Illinois University Press, 1987), 17–18.
3 *Ibid.*, 117.
4 Shapiro, *Deforming American Political Thought*, 22.
5 I am quoting from Morison's *Nobel Lecture*, on the web at: www.nobelprize.org/prizes/literature/1993/morrison/lecture/.
6 The quotation belongs to Maurice Blanchot, "Literature and the Right to Death," in *The Work of Fire*, trans. Charlotte Mandel and Lynda Davis (Stanford, CA; Stanford University Press, 1995), 302.

7 The quotations are from Eric Richmyer's Blanchot commentary: "Maurice Blanchot: Saboteur of the Writer's War," *Journal of the Western Society for French History* 35 (2007), 256.

8 Michel Foucault, *Remarks on Marx: Conversations with Duccio Trombadori* trans. R. James Goldstein and James Cascaito (New York: Semiotext(e), 1991), 31.

9 *Ibid.*

10 Martin Heidegger, *The Phenomenology of Religious Life* trans. Matthas Fritsch and Jennifer Anna Gosetti-Ferencei (Bloomington: Indiana University Press, 2010), 64.

11 Julie Watkins, Visual Music and Embodied Visceral Affect," in Andrew Knight-Hilled ed. *Sound & Image* (London: Routledge, 2020), 135

12 *Ibid.*, 135–136.

13 I am drawing on Michel Foucault's approach to critique, where he asserts that for purposes of inquiry, a politically oriented, historically sensitive epistemology should concern itself with an examination of *eventualization* rather than legitimacy, looking for example at how, "at a given point in time and in a specific domain," certain kinds of knowledge are regarded as "acceptable." See his "What is Critique?" in Michel Foucault, *The Politics of Truth*, trans. Lysa Hochroth (New York: Semiotext(e), 1997), 49–51.

14 Herman Broch, *The Sleepwalkers*, trans. Willa and Edwin Muir (New York, Vintage, 1996), 20.

15 As the reader will likely recognize, I am borrowing the language of the legendary James Bond's Martini orders.

16 Gilles Deleuze, *Proust and Signs* trans. Richard Howard (Minneapolis: University of Minnesota Press, 2000), 12.

17 Carlos Fuentes, "Writing in Time," *Democracy* 2 (1962), 61. I am paraphrasing and quoting from a discussion of Fuentes's experience and reactions in Chapter 4, "Borderline Justice," in Michael J. Shapiro, *War Crimes, Atrocity, and Justice* (Cambridge: Polity, 2015), 119–153.

18 Fuentes, "Writing in Time," 72.

19 Carlos Fuentes, *Destiny and Desire* trans. Edith Grossman (New York: Random House, 2011), 382.

20 Deleuze, *Proust and Signs*, 62.

21 Brian Massumi, *A Shock to Thought*, (London, Routledge: 2002).

22 I am using he terms the way it figures in the thinking of Emmanuel Levinas, who uses it to imply openness to alterity. See for example his *Totality and Infinity* trans. Alphonso Lingus (Pittsburgh: Duquesne University Press, 1969).

23 See Gilles Deleuze, "Spinoza and the Three 'Ethics." In *Essays Critical and Clinical*, trans. Daniel W. Smith and Michael A. Greco (Minneapolis: University of Minnesota Press, 1997), 144.

24 Joshua Barone, "Lang Lang, Piano Thunderer, Greets Bach's Auster 'Goldbergs'," *New York Times*, August 21, 2020, on the web at: www.nytimes.com/2020/08/21/arts/music/lang-lang-bach-goldberg.html?searchResultPosition=1.

25 See David Peisner, "Bettye LaVette Didn't Know the Beales' 'Blackbird.' Then it Helped Her Fly," *New York Times*, August 24, 2020, on the web at: www.nytimes.com/2020/08/24/arts/music/bettye-lavette-blackbirds.html?searchResultPosition=1.

26 See Mark Singer, "David Milch's Third Act," *The New Yorker Magazine*, May 27, 2019, on the web at: www.newyorker.com/magazine/2019/05/27/david-milchs-third-act.

27 I am quoting Ann Smocks characterization of Blanchot's position, her "Translator's Introduction" to Maurice Blanchot, *The Space of Literature* (Lincoln: University of Nebraska Press, 1982), 3.
28 See Mark R. McCulloh, "The Stylistics of Stasis: Paradoxical Effects in W. G. Sebald," *Style* 38: 1 (Spring 2004), 42.
29 See Walter Benjamin, *The Arcades Project*, trans. Howard Eiland and Kevin McLaughlin (Cambridge, MA; Harvard University Press, 2002), 460.
30 The quotation is from Andre Pierre Colombat, "Deleuze and Signs," in Ian Buchanan and John Marks eds. *Deleuze and Literature* (Edinburgh: Edinburgh University Press, 2000), 30.
31 Jacques Rancière, "The Politics of Aesthetics," on the web at: www.stroom.nl/media/Ranciere_The%20Distribution%20of%20The%20Sensible_Politics%20of%20Aesthetics.pdf.

Bibliography

Barone, Joshua (2020) 'Lang Lang, Piano Thunderer, Greets Bach's Auster "Goldbergs",' *New York Times*, on the web at: www.nytimes.com/2020/08/21/arts/music/lang-lang-bach-goldberg.html?searchResultPosition=1.

Benjamin, Walter (1996) 'The Concept of Criticism in German Romanticism,' in *Walter Benjamin: Selected Writings Volume 1 1913–1926* trans. David Lachterman, Howard Eiland, ad Ian Balfour (Cambridge, MA: Harvard University Press), pp. 116–200.

Benjamin, Walter (2002) *The Arcades Project*, trans. Howard Eiland and Kevin McLaughlin, Cambridge, MA: Harvard University Press.

Blanchot, Maurice (1982) *The Space of Literature*, trans. Ann Smock, Lincoln: University of Nebraska Press.

Blanchot, Maurice (1995) 'Literature and the Right to Death,' in *The Work of Fire*, trans. Charlotte Mandel and Lynda Davis, Stanford, CA: Stanford University Press, pp. 300–331.

Broch, Herman (1996) *The Sleepwalkers*, trans. Willa and Edwin Muir, New York: Vintage.

Colombat, Andre Pierre (2000) 'Deleuze and Signs,' in Ian Buchanan and John Marks eds. *Deleuze and* Literature, Edinburgh: Edinburgh University Press.

Deleuze, Gilles (1997) Spinoza and the Three 'Ethics.' In *Essays Critical and Clinical*, trans. Daniel W. Smith and Michael A. Greco, Minneapolis: University of Minnesota Press, pp. 138–151.

Deleuze, (2000) *Proust and Signs*, trans. Richard Howard, Minneapolis: University of Minnesota Press.

Foucault, Michel (1991) *Remarks on Marx: Conversations with Duccio Trombadori*, trans. R. James Goldstein and James Cascaito, New York: Semiotext(e).

Foucault, Michel (1997) *The Politics of Truth*, trans. Lysa Hochroth, New York: Semiotext(e).

Fuentes, Carlos (1962) 'Writing in Time', *Democracy* No, 2, pp. 59–73.

Fuentes, Carlos (2011) *Destiny and Desire*, trans. Edith Grossman, New York: Random House.

Heidegger, Martin (2010) *The Phenomenology of Religious Life*, trans. Matthas Fritsch and Jennifer Anna Gosetti-Ferencei, Bloomington: Indiana University Press.

Hertz, David Michael (1987) *The Tuning of the Word: The Musico-Literary Poetics of the Symbolist Movement Carbondale: Southern Illinois University Press*

Levinas, Emmanuel (1969) *Totality and Infinity*, trans. Alphonso Lingus, Pittsburgh: Duquesne University Press.

McCulloh, Mark R. (2004) 'The Stylistics of Stasis: Paradoxical Effects in W. G. Sebald,' *Style* Vol. 38 (1), pp. 38–48.

Morrison, Toni (1993) '*Nobel Lecture*,' on the web at: www.nobelprize.org/prizes/literature/1993/morrison/lecture/.

Peisner, David (2020) 'Bettye LaVette Didn't Know the Beales' "Blackbird." Then it Helped Her Fly,' *The New York Times*, on the web at: www.nytimes.com/2020/08/24/arts/music/bettye-lavette-blackbirds.html?searchResultPosition=1.

Rancière, Jacques, (2004), *The Politics of Aesthetics*, trans. Gabriel Rockhill, London: Continuum.

Richmyer, Eric (2007) 'Maurice Blanchot: Saboteur of the Writer's War,' *Journal of the Western Society for French History* 35 (2007), 247–262.

Shapiro, Michael J. (2016) *Deforming American Political Thought: Challenging the Jeffersonian Legacy* second edition, New York: Routledge.

Shapiro, Michael J. (2015) *War Crimes, Atrocity, and Justice*, Cambridge: Polity.

Singer, Mark (2019) 'David Milch's Third Act,' *The New Yorker Magazine*, on the web at: www.newyorker.com/magazine/2019/05/27/david-milchs-third-act.

Watkins, Julie (2020) 'Visual Music and Embodied Visceral Affect,' in Andrew Knight-Hilled ed. *Sound & Image*, London: Routledge, pp. 135–148.

INDEX

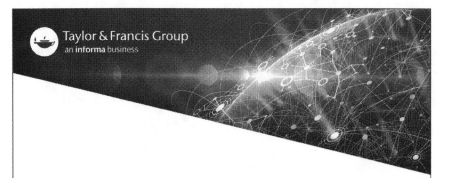